D1738107

WONDROUS IN HIS SAINTS

STUDIES ON THE HISTORY OF SOCIETY AND CULTURE
VICTORIA E. BONNELL AND LYNN HUNT, EDITORS

WONDROUS
IN HIS SAINTS

COUNTER-REFORMATION
PROPAGANDA IN BAVARIA

PHILIP M. SOERGEL

University of California Press
Berkeley · Los Angeles · London

University of California Press
Berkeley and Los Angeles, California

University of California Press, Ltd.
London, England

© 1993 by
The Regents of the University of California

Library of Congress Cataloging-in-Publication Data

Soergel, Philip M.
  Wondrous in his saints : counter-Reformation
propaganda in Bavaria / Philip M. Soergel.
    p. cm. — (Studies on the history of society and
culture ; 17)
  Includes bibliographical references and index.
  ISBN 0-520-08047-5 (alk. paper)
  1. Christian pilgrims and pilgrimages—Germany—
Bavaria—History—16th century. 2. Christian shrines—
Germany—Bavaria—History—16th century. 3. Christian
literature—Germany—Bavaria—History and criticism.
4. German literature—Early modern, 1500–1700—History
and criticism. 5. Counter-Reformation—Germany—
Bavaria. 6. Bavaria (Germany)—Church history.
I. Title. II. Series.
BX2320.5.G3S64   1993
263'.042—dc 20   92-36732
                                    CIP

Printed in the United States of America
9 8 7 6 5 4 3 2 1

A shorter version of Chapter 5 was previously published
as "The Counter-Reformation Impact on Anticlerical
Propaganda," in *Anticlericalism in Late Medieval and Early
Modern Europe*, ed. Heiko A. Oberman and Peter Dykema
(Leiden: E. J. Brill, 1992). Some paragraphs of Chapters 4
and 6 appeared in "The Image of Saints in the Bavarian
Counter Reformation," *The Historian* 53, no. 2 (Winter
1991): 223–240. Some material from Chapter 6 and the
Epilogue also appeared in "Spiritual Medicine for Heretical
Poison: The Propagandistic Uses of Legends in Counter-
Reformation Bavaria," *Historical Reflections* 17, no. 2 (Spring
1991): 125–149. Permission to draw upon these previously
published pieces is gratefully acknowledged.

For Marcia and Elizabeth

Darumb schreibt David nit vergebenlich Gott ist wunderbarlich in seinen heiligen: Wunderlich ist der Herr in den Hochen. Der Gott Israel wil seinem Volck krafft und starck geben.

So it is not without reason that David writes, "God is wondrous in His Saints. Wondrous is the Lord in his mighty ones. The God of Israel will give his people power and strength."

Anonymous seventeenth-century
Bavarian pilgrimage book

Contents

Illustrations

Acknowledgments

This project, originally submitted as a dissertation, would not have been completed without the encouragement and financial support of numerous scholars, family members, foundations, universities, and libraries. Parts of the doctoral research were underwritten by the Department of History and the Rackham Graduate School at the University of Michigan. In addition, stipends from the Friedrich-Ebert-Stiftung in 1983–84 and the Charlotte Newcombe Foundation in 1986–87 provided for a research year in Germany and an uninterrupted year of writing, respectively. More recently, I have also become indebted to the College of Arts and Sciences at Arizona State University for travel and research funding.

Both in the United States and in Germany, the librarians and staffs of the following institutions were invaluable in tracking down my obtuse requests: the university libraries at Michigan, Regensburg, Munich, and Arizona State; the state libraries at Regensburg, Passau, and Eichstätt; the Bavarian Central State Library in Munich; the diocesan library in Regensburg; the Metropolitan Library in Munich; and the Princely Thurn and Taxis Library in Regensburg. In addition, Elisabeth Mayer from the University Library at Regensburg was particularly helpful. An employee in the manuscript reading room, she befriended me during 1983–84, sharing her first-hand knowledge of Bavarian piety and religion. For more than six months Elisabeth gave up her Sunday afternoon walks to drive me to obscure Bavarian pilgrimage shrines. Through her, my knowledge of Bavarian culture and religion was infinitely deepened.

While I was engaged in writing the dissertation, the members of my committee, Diane Owen Hughes, Marvin Becker, and Gerhard Dünnhaupt, offered insight and criticism. And if what appears here now in book form bears little resemblance to the earlier dissertation, it is happily in part because of their gentle prodding.

Numerous scholarly friendships forged along the way have also strengthened the arguments presented here. In Ann Arbor, Joel Harrington was always especially willing to lend an ear. Over the years we have exchanged many a comic anecdote and useful tip from our reading in sixteenth-century documents. In addition, the members of our cohort—Nancy Horn, Ann Moyer, Lee Wandell, Ron Delph, Deborah Mahoney, and Anne McKernan—were an unusually caring and cooperative circle. Each has been forced at one time or another to listen to my renditions of Bavarian lore, sometimes until the small hours. Beyond Ann Arbor, Lionel Rothkrug, who had himself previously ventured into the tempestuous waters of German religion, also took an interest in this research. Our conversations have certainly enriched the coffers of AT&T, but they have also broadened my arguments. Lionel's good humor and the cooperation he has extended to someone so junior have been exemplary.

Once I left graduate school and entered the world of job talks, conferences, and publishing, I found numerous people interested in this research. Many have read and commented on drafts, papers, and articles. Among these, Steven Sargent, Virginia Reinburg, Carlos Eire, Kristin Zapalac, and Barbara Wisch have all offered insight. Lynn Hunt, too, read the dissertation and assured me that here was a story that might be of interest not just to Reformation historians, but to early modern scholars generally. The readers for the University of California Press, Tom Brady and Philip Hoffman, offered incisive suggestions for engaging this broader audience, while my editor, Sheila Levine, fielded my numerous telephone calls and resolved innumerable issues concerning publication.

At Arizona State, my colleagues have provided an ideal atmosphere for work. I am grateful to them all, and especially to several who have also discussed, read, and commented on the work I present here. My fellow sixteenth-century scholar and friend Retha Warnicke in particular has often been forced to endure my ramblings on South German legends. Lynn Stoner, Miguel Tinker Salas, Hans Sebald, and Rachel Fuchs read or listened to portions of this manuscript. In addition, my graduate assistant Lauren Hackett Kuby freed me from numerous mundane tasks so that I could write. As a student in the editing program, she was also able to offer useful advice concerning style and presentation.

My principal debt intellectually remains to Tom Tentler. It was he who originally suggested a topic on lay religion in early modern Germany. As a *Doktorvater*, he was willing to discuss this research with me with what now seems a kind of superhuman endurance. His concern continued long after the dissertation was completed, and his Erasmian wit and wisdom remain an inspiration.

Finally, I would like to thank my family. My parents, Ray and Donna Soergel, have supported my education and this research from the beginning. My mother also helped with the final proofing of the manuscript. Both my parents, and my mother-in-law, Irene Willis, have contributed financially and with a large dose of moral support to what is presented here. Beverly Ogdon, my aunt, also read and commented on this work in manuscript form. As an intelligent literatus unfamiliar with the sixteenth- and seventeenth-century German scene, she provided some of the most insightful criticism. Her sense of style and her wisdom, I hope, are to be found reflected in these pages. And her discussions of the current state of bel canto have been welcome relief from footnoting and bibliographical chores.

It is a convention for authors to offer profuse thanks to spouses and children. It is not duty, however, but happy gratitude that compels me to dedicate this book to my wife, Marcia, and our daughter, Elizabeth. Elizabeth was born when this book was nearly finished, and although her joyful babbling in the throes of its completion provided little in the way of useful commentary, her glowing face did manage to keep her father focused on the task at hand. For her mother, this book has been a project of longer standing. Marcia has undertaken this work with me, first as a thesis and later as a book, with unusual forbearance and grace. It has taken her at various times away from her own profession, forcing her to abandon Ann Arbor's idylls for the sparer charms of a German industrial ghetto and, later, drawing her into the heat and savage beauty of the Sonoran desert. Through this, her own long pilgrimage, her good humor has rarely been strained; consequently there could be no more fitting testimony to her achievement than a work on saintly miracles.

Introduction

This study examines the genesis of a genre, the apologetic pilgrimage books that were printed in early modern Bavaria. In Germany, folklorists refer to this kind of work as a "mixed miracle book," because it combines the testimonies of individual pilgrims to contemporary miracles with fantastic legends about a local shrine and information concerning the development of the site's cult. These books served, in effect, as advertisements for specific local pilgrimages. Anglo-American historians have long commented on the absence of a great secular, literary tradition in early modern Catholic Germany.[1] The intricate and complex legends recounted in the baroque pilgrimage book, however, provided an elite literary entertainment similar to the novels and other fictive forms common in various parts of Europe. Rather than treating the joys and perils of life in society in the manner of a Cervantes or a Rabelais, early modern pilgrimage literature recounted myths about local places that glorified the landscape. Although examples of this pilgrimage literature are numerous, they have never attracted the systematic attention of English-speaking scholars. This book, which treats the origins of this literature in the Reformation and Counter-Reformation, is meant to remedy this oversight.

Those who have traveled in southern Germany and Austria may

1. Gerald Strauss, *Luther's House of Learning: Indoctrination of the Young in the German Reformation* (Baltimore, 1978), esp. p. 128; R. Po-Chia Hsia, *Society and Religion in Münster, 1535–1618* (New Haven, 1984), esp. pp. 1–2; James Melton, "From Image to Word: Cultural Reform and the Rise of Literate Culture in Eighteenth-Century Austria," *Journal of Modern History* 58 (March 1986): 97; Lionel Rothkrug, *Religious Practices and Collective Perceptions: Hidden Homologies in the Renaissance and Reformation*, published as vol. 7 of *Historical Reflections* (1980): 196–198; and Elizabeth Eisenstein, *The Printing Press as an Agent of Change: Communications and Cultural Transformation in Early Modern Europe* (Cambridge, 1979), 1:334, 355, and passim. The position is not without validity, since the creation of a national literature in Germany was overwhelmingly the preserve of Protestant writers. See Albrecht Schöne, *Säkularisation als sprachbildende Kraft. Studien zur Dichtung deutscher Pfarrersöhne* (Göttingen, 1958).

well recall the hundreds of slight church guides available for sale in ecclesiastical monuments throughout the region. Those who have noticed these *Kirchenführer* may not have realized how deeply rooted their origins were in the historical circumstances of the Reformation and Counter-Reformation. In southern Germany, few churches or ecclesiastical buildings have been deemed so insignificant as not to require their own detailed history. These church guides are one of the cultural descendants of the early modern pilgrimage book; in these modest pamphlets, the origins of a church, its most important artistic and religious artifacts, and any miraculous legends connected with the site are documented with remarkable felicity and care. In an increasingly secular society, the *Kirchenführer* allows Germans to satisfy their continuing desire for what the masterful historian Frantisek Graus once called the "living past."[2] They reflect an enduring curiosity to learn about the myths and histories of those sites that populate the countryside at what seems like every turn in the road. While the legends and miracles recounted in the modern church guide are retold within a rationalist framework, it is still possible to find more traditional kinds of religious pilgrimage books for sale at many shrines in Bavaria and Austria. Filled with accounts of miracles and legends, they feed the perennial appetite to learn about cases of divine intervention, even if in an industrialized and rationalistic Germany this literature is being increasingly pushed to the margins of human experience.

The present study traces the initial development of this kind of literature in the Reformation and Counter-Reformation. Rather than providing a demographic or statistical reconstruction of the role and function that pilgrimage played in early modern Bavaria, this book focuses instead on the qualitative dimensions of religious practice. It seeks to determine in what ways perceptions concerning shrines, their place within Catholic tradition, and their function as a component of Counter-Reformation religious practice changed from the late sixteenth through the early eighteenth centuries. While I draw on several decades of demographic and social historical research concerning medieval and early modern pilgrimage, I am primarily interested in cultural, rather than social, phenomena.

2. Graus used the term to describe the persisting force of historicized legend to shape interpretations of the German past; see his *Lebendige Vergangenheit. Überlieferung im Mittelalter und in den Vorstellungen vom Mittelalter* (Cologne, 1975).

During the past decades, the social history of pilgrimage as a field of study has reached a high degree of sophistication. For those who wish to gain more detailed knowledge of the social foundations of pilgrimage in medieval and early modern Europe, a large bibliography now exists. Within this body of work, the studies of Victor and Mary Turner, Lionel Rothkrug, Mary and Sidney Nolan, Peter Brown, William Christian, Patrick Geary, Ronald Finucane, Pierre-André Sigal, Jonathan Sumption, Stephen Wilson, and Steven Sargent were most useful to me.[3] After conducting some initial statistical samplings in the thousands of miracles that Bavarian peasants and burghers reported at early modern shrines, I realized that little change had occurred during these centuries in the popular attitude toward miracles and saintly intercessions. The basic presuppositions about saints' shrines remained largely those that had governed pilgrimage to local holy places throughout medieval Europe. The manuscript collections of miracles read like a catalogue of all the diseases, accidents, and woes suffered by medieval and early modern people alike. Saints' shrines appeared in these records as local marketplaces within a widespread spiritual economy. In seventeenth- and eighteenth-century Bavaria, the laity continued to express their requests to the saints in terms of the relationship of exchange that had been common in medieval Europe. By approaching the celestial figures that resided at specific geographical sites with prayers and promises of gifts and journeys, the faithful hoped to obtain intervention in otherwise hopeless circumstances.

Many of the fundamental assumptions concerning miracles and

3. Victor Turner and Mary Turner, *Image and Pilgrimage in Christian Culture: Anthropological Perspectives* (New York, 1975); Rothkrug, *Religious Practices and Collective Perceptions;* Mary Nolan and Sidney Nolan, *Christian Pilgrimage in Modern Western Europe* (Chapel Hill, N.C., 1989); Peter Brown, *The Cult of the Saints: Its Rise and Function in Latin Christianity* (Chicago, 1981); William A. Christian, Jr., *Local Religion in Sixteenth-Century Spain* (Princeton, 1981); idem, *Apparitions in Late Medieval and Renaissance Spain* (Princeton, 1981); Patrick J. Geary, *Furta Sacra: Thefts of Relics in the Central Middle Ages* (Princeton, 1978); Ronald C. Finucane, *Miracles and Pilgrims: Popular Beliefs in Medieval England* (Totowa, N.J., 1977); Pierre-André Sigal, *L'homme et le miracle dans la France médiévale (XIe–XIIe siècle)* (Paris, 1985); idem, *Les marcheurs de Dieu: pèlerinage et pèlerins au moyen âge* (Paris, 1974); Jonathan Sumption, *Pilgrimage: An Image of Mediaeval Religion* (Totowa, N.J., 1978); Steven D. Sargent, "Religion and Society in Late Medieval Bavaria: The Cult of Saint Leonard, 1258–1500" (Ph.D. diss., University of Pennsylvania, 1982); idem, "Miracle Books and Pilgrimage Shrines in Late Medieval Bavaria," *Historical Reflections* 13 (1986): 455–471; idem, "Saints Cults and Naming Patterns in Bavaria, 1400–1600," *Catholic Historical Review* 76, no. 4 (October 1990): 673–696; and Stephen Wilson, ed., *Saints and Their Cults: Studies in Religious Sociology, Folklore, and History* (Cambridge, 1983).

pilgrimage, then, remained constant between the medieval and early modern periods. At the level of individual dialogue between saint and votant, the manuscript miracle collections maintained at many of Bavaria's shrines echoed patterns of communication whose origins stretched back even until the time of St. Augustine. Yet more generally, it was obvious that the ways in which miracles and pilgrimage were interpreted for the entire body of Catholic faithful did change dramatically during the early modern period. To borrow a phrase used by anthropologists and literary critics, miracles, shrines, and pilgrimage were each granted a new "contextual frame" in this period. Instead of seeking to determine why people made pilgrimages, how they put their requests before the saints, or how they conducted their journeys, I was soon engaged in examining the propagandistic campaigns that Bavarian counter-reformers and state officials waged for local devotions. Simply put, I began to pursue the increasingly extravagant claims the Catholic reformers made for local shrines in the wake of the Protestant Reformation. But the steadily intensifying and expanding discourse on pilgrimage in early modern Bavaria also revealed the dual efforts of the state and the Church to bring order, discipline, and a new rationale to lay religious life. In Bavaria, as later in Hapsburg Austria, popular religious rituals like pilgrimage provided the counter-reformers an important way of reviving enthusiasm for the Church and reestablishing its preeminence after the brief but cataclysmic episode of the Reformation. In turn, early modern pilgrimages and their sister phenomenon, the urban procession, came increasingly to fulfill important roles in the extension of state power and order.

A number of scholars have noted the strongly visual and ritualistic traits of Bavarian and Austrian Catholicism during the Counter-Reformation.[4] My reliance on printed records to study a religious ritual like pilgrimage, which occurred largely in an oral culture, may appear puzzling. This choice, together with its limitations, consequently needs to be explained at the outset. From 1500 to 1700, literacy remained limited in Bavaria and South Germany: at the beginning of that period no more than perhaps 5 to 10 percent of the population could be considered literate. Although the number of readers appears to have increased during the seventeenth century, widespread literacy began to appear in both Bavaria and Austria

4. See Melton's remarks and citations in "From Image to Word," pp. 95–124.

only in the late eighteenth century.[5] Even so, while the duchy of Bavaria was largely a preliterate culture, the press was nonetheless an important conduit through which ideas were placed into circulation. Sermons often digested and circulated the material first recorded in the press, but printed pamphlets and books also extended the audience for miracles beyond those who could hear them only while at the shrine. In towns and villages, reading circles broadened the impact of books as well. Yet as this study will show, both the press and Counter-Reformation rituals moved in similar ways to defend a religious sensibility that retained the primacy of visual experience.

The approach taken here links the ideas set forth in pilgrimage books with other kinds of festive and ritual life encouraged by the Catholic clergy and the Bavarian state. From the book, to the sermon, to praxis may seem to many a natural progression, but in the preliterate context of early modern society the flow of ideas in fact retained a greater fluidity than is often supposed. This is a point that scholars working in the tradition of the *Annales* have brilliantly demonstrated. Printing could just as often expand the audience for ideas that were at their base a part of oral culture.[6]

When I began this study, I was troubled by the too narrow relationship that Elizabeth Eisenstein drew in *The Printing Press as an Agent of Change* (1979) between Protestantism and the rationalizing and standardizing features of the press. From my reading in scholarship on the book trade, I was well aware of the vast output of German Catholic presses.[7] Yet Eisenstein persistently argued that Protestants and Catholics held fundamentally opposing views re-

5. Strauss, *Luther's House of Learning*, pp. 193–202; Gerald Strauss and Richard Gawthrop, "Protestantism and Literacy in Early Modern Germany," *Past and Present*, no. 104 (August 1984): 31–55; James Melton, *Absolutism and the Eighteenth-Century Origins of Compulsory Schooling in Prussia and Austria* (Cambridge, 1988); Rolf Engelsing, *Analphabetetum und Lektüre. Zur Sozialgeschichte des Lesens in Deutschland* (Stuttgart, 1973), chaps. 5–7; and idem, *Der Burger als Leser. Lesergeschichte in Deutschland, 1500–1800* (Stuttgart, 1974).

6. See esp. Roger Chartier, ed., *The Culture of Print: Power and the Uses of Print in Early Modern Europe* (Cambridge, 1989). The history of the press in early modern France is more highly developed than in Germany; Chartier's *The Cultural Uses of Print in Early Modern Europe* (Princeton, 1987) contains references to this extensive bibliography.

7. Lucien Febvre and Henri-Jean Martin, *The Coming of the Book: The Impact of Printing, 1450–1800*, trans. David Gerard (London, 1976); Gerhard Stalla, *Bibliographie der Ingolstädter Buchdrucker des 16. Jahrhunderts* (Baden-Baden, 1977); and idem, *Der Ingolstädter Buchdruck von 1601 bis 1620* (Baden-Baden, 1980).

garding the demands, possibilities, and functions of the new "print culture." A crucial part of her thesis centered on the different positions that each adopted concerning lay Bible reading. Whereas Protestants granted popular demand for the Scriptures free rein in order to create a priesthood of believers, the Tridentine Church attempted continually to keep the vernacular Bible in check: "A deliberate cultivation of mystery, an insistence on withholding pearls of wisdom from the swinish multitude and more emphatic distinctions between educated clergy and uninformed laity characterized the anti-vernacular arguments made at Trent."[8]

Eisenstein agreed that the Tridentine Church had mobilized printers for its counteroffensive, but, she insisted, Catholic policies were designed to keep "print culture" firmly controlled. While it cannot be denied that the counter-reforming clergy and state regulated the book trade to a greater degree than Protestants, their output of vernacular literature was still formidable.[9] To dismiss this corpus because it cannot fit within a modernizing definition of "print culture," in short, has prevented us from assessing the ways in which printing and books functioned within Catholic culture.

Between the Council of Trent and the eighteenth century, hundreds of thousands of books were published in Catholic Europe. Yet the output of a single region like Bavaria, where the Ingolstadt and Munich presses churned out volume after volume during the sixteenth and seventeenth centuries, has been investigated only by linguists, literary critics, and folklorists. Their studies have often focused on the elite theological writings of Catholic preachers like Jacob Gretser or hagiographers like Matthäus Rader or on the great Latin monuments of the Jesuit drama.[10] The present study takes a

8. Eisenstein, *Printing Press as an Agent of Change* 1:344.

9. On censorship in early modern Catholic Germany, see Dieter Breuer, *Geschichte der literarischen Zensur in Deutschland* (Heidelberg, 1982).

10. A few notable studies have been made of popular pious literature in early modern Catholic Germany, including Dieter Breuer, *Oberdeutsche Literatur, 1565–1650* (Munich, 1979); and Dieter Breuer, Wolfgang Brückner, and Peter Blickle, eds., *Literatur und Volk im 17. Jahrhundert. Probleme populärer Kultur in Deutschland* (Wiesbaden, 1985). On the Jesuit drama, see Ruprecht Wimmer, *Jesuitentheater: Didaktik und Fest. Das Exemplum des ägyptischen Joseph auf den deutschen Bühnen der Gesellschaft Jesu* (Frankfurt a. M., 1982); Elida Maria Szrota, ed., *Das Jesuitendrama im deutschen Sprachgebiet* (Munich, 1979); Johannes Müller, *Das Jesuitendrama in den Ländern deutscher Zunge vom Anfang (1555) bis zum Hochbarock (1665)* (Augsburg, 1930). The citations in Nigel Griffin's *Jesuit School Drama: A Checklist of Critical Literature* (London, 1976) are also useful. The various genres of Counter-Reformation pious literature are

different approach. It examines one genre, the pilgrimage book, setting it within its social, political, and cultural milieu and charting its transformations over two centuries.

The pilgrimage book attempted to resolve problems and to satisfy needs among Bavaria's readers that had been made obvious through the Reformation crisis. During the later Middle Ages, pilgrimages of all kinds in Bavaria grew to new heights of popularity, and throughout the territory a number of new cults appeared. In this generally rising tide of devotion, Bavaria's clergy began employing a number of new media to attract the faithful to specific shrines. In the first chapter of this study, I review this late medieval flowering of devotion. Miracles remained in this period the primary testimony to a shrine's power; in the fifteenth century, then, the clergy at shrines used pictures, oral pronouncement, and thin, printed "miracle books" to inform pilgrims about their patron's power to work intercessions. In the thirty years before the Reformation, the use of miracles to publicize local shrines reached its peak, and a number of shrines began keeping detailed manuscript records of their patron's works. At the same time, pamphlets informing readers of a cult's history also found their way into the marketplaces around local shrines. The legends and histories that these accounts related were often terse, remaining firmly rooted in the medieval chronicler tradition. The authors of these histories might relate the miracle of the shrine's foundation or associate their shrine with prominent members of the Bavarian nobility or figures from imperial history. They often failed, however, to draw an explicit connection between the legend of the shrine's foundation and its contemporary miraculous power.

Even as new cults appeared in late medieval Bavaria, local pilgrimages were becoming more controversial, with criticism of shrines and the saints increasing. Throughout Germany, the sudden development of mass pilgrimage sites had inspired attacks from

reviewed in Ludwig Andreas Veit and Ludwig Lenhart, *Kirche und Volksfrömmigkeit im Zeitalter des Barock* (Freiburg i. B., 1956); and Jean Marie Valentin, ed., *Gegenreformation und Literatur. Beiträge zur interdisziplinären Erforschung der katholischen Reformbewegung* (Amsterdam, 1979). There are many general studies of baroque literature in Germany: see esp. Peter Lahnstein, *Das Leben im Barock. Zeugnisse und Berichte, 1640–1740* (Stuttgart, 1974); and Herbert Jaumann, *Die deutsche Barockliteratur: Wertung, Umwertung. Eine wertungsgeschichtliche Studie in systematischer Absicht* (Bonn, 1975).

at least the early fifteenth century; the last of these notorious "instant" pilgrimages appeared at Regensburg in 1519, on the duchy of
Bavaria's northern borders. Although the critique of saintly devotion thus predated the Reformation, the charges brought against the
medieval *cultus divinorum* by Protestant theologians, pamphleteers,
and preachers grew louder and farther-ranging. The early reformers
attacked pilgrimages to saints' shrines for wasting time and money;
for deflecting attention away from the parish church, the "true"
center for religious devotion; for promoting a "false" works righteousness; and for allowing "simple" people the opportunity to
barter with the saints. At an extreme, the propaganda of the early
reformers denounced shrines as part of a false, and even "diabolic,"
religion that Satan was using to destroy and damn mankind. The
disaffection these attacks produced sent Bavaria's local pilgrimages
into decline, though they failed to destroy the appeal of the cult of
the saints completely. In Chapter 2 the Protestant critique of shrines
and its impact on popular devotion is assessed.

Having recently reunited Bavaria into a single state in the early
sixteenth century, the Wittelsbach dynasty was anxious to consolidate its control over its new territory. The Bavarian dukes viewed
the demands for religious reform as a challenge to their authority.
From the earliest years of the Reformation, therefore, they prohibited the circulation of Protestant books and outlawed Reformation
preaching. Yet because the dukes lacked adequate means to enforce
their decrees or to insure uniformity of belief and practice, competing religious positions continued to multiply in Bavaria during the
first fifty years of the Reformation. By the 1560s, consequently, state
officials and the growing vanguard of counter-reforming clergy in
Bavaria faced a disunified and chaotic religious situation. Liberal
Catholics in Bavaria's towns and in the territory's estates agitated
continually for religious reform, while the minority of Protestants
continued to preach the doctrines of the Reformation. Thus in the
years following the conclusion of the Council of Trent, the Bavarian dukes, their growing officialdom, and Catholic reformers were
more than ever resolved to root out Protestant sympathizers from
within their realm.

A host of new prohibitions appeared at the time to fight religious
heterodoxy, but these means were never particularly effective in

achieving religious uniformity. At the same time, Bavaria's state and clerical reformers attempted to revitalize traditional rituals as a way of renewing enthusiasm for the Roman Church. One of their first measures was to expand dramatically the annual celebration of the Feast of Corpus Christi. The enormously elaborated festival that began in the late sixteenth century was emblematic of many of the Bavarian Catholic reformers' efforts. Self-consciously styled in a triumphal manner, the Corpus Christi procession promoted the notion of the biblical and ecclesiastical tradition as a series of crises and resolutions. In the streets of the duchy's towns, it glorified the Church Militant as a unified truth that had marched victoriously through time despite the attacks of heretics, demons, and the "godless." Intended to appeal to the senses—most especially to the eyes—the Bavarian Feast of Corpus Christi failed to muster vernacular language in the way that celebrations of the festival had elsewhere in medieval Europe. It remained a visible testimony to the truths of Catholicism, the immanent majesty of the Eucharistic wafer, and the importance of viewing the body of Christ. The renewed feast juxtaposed the mystery, direct presence, and unity of the Catholic Eucharist against the by then badly disunified Protestant theologies of communion. In Chapter 3 I review these developments and the emerging Counter-Reformation religious sensibilities that underlay the symbolic departure contained in the expansion of the Feast of Corpus Christi.

The counter-reformers, too, sensed that pilgrimage to local shrines could be used to renew a sense of *praesentia,* and by the late sixteenth century many of the Bavarian clergy, state officials, and Wittelsbach dukes had lent their support to the renewal of devotional life at the duchy's shrines. The pronouncement and promotion of miracles at local shrines began to revive at this time, to be duly used as testimony to the numinous power of local holy places. During the late sixteenth and seventeenth centuries, the reforming orders of the Counter-Reformation assumed responsibility for many of the duchy's formerly popular shrines, lending their efforts to restoring the pilgrimage network. This revival was further supported by a renewed confraternal life, firmly located within the structures of the Bavarian state and the Roman Church. Simultaneously, Catholic propagandists pioneered the publication of the pilgrimage book, a genre intended for the emerging cadre of literate, devout laity and clergy who were becoming a recognizable element in the Catholic resurgence.[11]

The first of the many pilgrimage books to appear in Bavaria during the following two centuries was Martin Eisengrein's *Our Lady at Altötting*, which defended the once enormously successful, now sadly declined pilgrimage to Altötting through the skillful retelling of a "legendary myth."[12] Chapter 4 analyzes this largely unnoticed "classic" of Bavarian literature and the career of its author. A member of the Counter-Reformation clerical elite and a key figure in Bavaria's religious politics, Eisengrein was, like many of the territory's first-generation Catholic propagandists, a convert. Together with other leading Counter-Reformation preachers and theologians such as the Wittelsbach's court preacher Johann Rabus and the itinerant field preacher Johann Nass, Eisengrein strove to formulate reasoned defenses for the traditional religious practices and saints' cults of the region. His most widely disseminated work was his defense of the Altötting Madonna, which transformed pilgrimage and that tiny shrine into mute yet visible confirmations of Catholic truth.

Central to Eisengrein's propagandistic achievement was his linking of the contemporary miracles reported at Altötting with the shrine's venerable and often troubled past. The drama that was presently being enacted at the shrine and in the Church, he assured his readers, was emplotted in the same comedic mode as all Christian history. Located in the heart of the duchy, Altötting was, he said, the central site, indeed the protagonist, in the duchy's salvific history. But he also attempted to answer the oft-repeated Protestant charge that pilgrimages and their miracles were a kind of diabolic magic. A large section of the work thus related a dramatic case of ritual exorcism performed by the Jesuit Peter Canisius in the chapel in 1570.

Immediately controversial, *Our Lady at Altötting* initiated a polemical war between Protestants and Catholics that lasted more than four years. In Chapter 5, the charges that Protestant and

11. See Louis Chatellier, *The Europe of the Devout: The Catholic Reformation and the Formation of a New Society* (Cambridge, 1989).

12. Martin Eisengrein, *Unser liebe Fraw zu alten Oetting. Das ist Von der Uralten, heyligen Capellen unser lieben Frawen unnd dem Fuerstlichen Stifft* (Ingolstadt, 1571).

Catholic theologians exchanged in this battle are reviewed and then compared to the popular propaganda circulated by devout Lutherans in the late sixteenth century in their attempt to inoculate coreligionists against the allures of the Catholic resurgence. For Lutheran theologians and propagandists, the revival of pilgrimage was seen as a threat to the fate of the entire Reformation, and they increasingly laid blame for this revival on Satan. Ever since the early Reformation, the circulation of tales involving sorcerous priests, diabolical magic, and scatology had been one component of Protestant propaganda. One detects, however, an increasing urgency in late sixteenth-century attacks on the now-reviving Catholic Church.

The publicity that this polemic and counterpolemic over miracles and shrines inspired lent Eisengrein's pilgrimage book notoriety among the literate laity and clergy of Bavaria. In the decades of the late sixteenth century, the book became a model for a number of Bavarian authors seeking to save their shrines from Reformation-induced decline. At the University of Ingolstadt and in the duchy's capital, Munich, writers began presenting similar defenses of various Bavarian cults. At this time the clergy often began self-consciously to fashion their renewals of devotions as "triumphs" for Catholic truth. The creation of "myth" came to dominate in this resurgence, as through extravagant and often atavistic tales about local holy places the Catholic reformers placed their shrines at the very center of churchly tradition. Legends also served to explain and provide a rationale for the continuing accounts of miracles that were again beginning to be reported and promoted. In Chapter 6 I discuss the pilgrimage books and propagandistic campaigns conducted for these sites during the early decades of the Counter-Reformation. In particular, typological analysis of the mythic histories reveals that propagandists created their stories using only a limited number of emplotments.

The conclusion to this study, "*Bavaria Sancta* and the Living Past," traces into the early eighteenth century the implications of the Counter-Reformation propagandistic campaign. Pilgrimage books continued throughout this period to provide explanations for the origins and miracles of local shrines. More significantly, the enthusiastic promotion of pilgrimages aided the Bavarian state and Church's efforts to sanctify the territory. The polemical legends that early Counter-Reformation authors had pioneered were elevated throughout the seventeenth century into principles of Bavarian piety. By means of popular rituals enacted at local shrines, both peasants and burghers recreated the story lines of legends that had first been codified and promoted by the pilgrimage book. The popular religious life of the duchy, in short, came increasingly to imitate both the art of the pilgrimage book and the state-sanctioned rituals that had dominated the Counter-Reformation program since its inception.

Since the publication in 1978 of Gerald Strauss's *Luther's House of Learning*, Reformation and early modern scholars have often debated the successes and failures of the sixteenth-century Protestant and Catholic reformations. As scholars we are now aware of the often limited, even ephemeral transformations that both Protestant and Catholic elites were able to effect within their societies. In searching for quantifiable differences between late medieval and early modern popular pilgrimage, scholars have likewise been unable to discover evidence of significant alterations in popular perceptions. Certainly pilgrimage grew to new heights of popularity in seventeenth- and eighteenth-century Bavaria, surpassing even the late medieval flowering of devotion. Yet the basic presuppositions and mental perceptions that people had about the saints and their intercession remained those common to the Middle Ages. Indeed, almost any approach that looks to find evidence of massive changes in people's fundamental mental and religious perceptions will, I believe, likely return empty-handed. By the late seventeenth and eighteenth centuries, pilgrimage had become more firmly fixed within the structures of the early modern state. Yet clerical and lay officials labored as they had for more than a century, to limit the potential dangers they sensed in the mobility of their populations. That they were often unable to achieve their ends reveals the relative indifference of popular culture to their ambitions. Although the Counter-Reformation failed to extinguish a vigorous popular culture and to install in its place a dogmatic and doctrinal religion, it was certainly effective in renewing an otherwise attenuated notion of the duchy's spiritual uniqueness and religious mission. As a consequence of the Catholic Reformation's propagandistic campaign, early modern Bavarians inhabited a landscape sacralized by several generations of clerical- and state-supported myth making, and looked to the crises and trials of the present and the future as reflections and recreations of those of the past. For most, the holy had become once again something that could be viewed close at hand in the countryside. In the area of qualitative cultural and religious perceptions, a mental topography that remains admittedly difficult to quantify, the Counter-Reformation program continues to reveal itself a success.

1

Bavaria and Its Pilgrimages in the Later Middle Ages

Around 1500, Bavaria possessed both reserves of an enduring, conservative stability and swift sources of change. A region dominated by a traditional agrarian order, the territory was undergoing a revolution in government that would eventually place it within the vanguard of German states. During the Middle Ages, the duchy's ruling dynasty, the Wittelsbachs, had frequently partitioned its lands. Through consolidation in the fourteenth and fifteenth centuries, the number of independent territories had been reduced to just two: Upper Bavaria, with its capital at Munich, and Lower Bavaria, ruled from Landshut. Following the brief War of the Landshut Succession (1503–1505), most of Lower Bavaria was brought under the control of the Munich Wittelsbachs. One year later, in 1506, the Upper Bavarian duke secured the passage of a primogeniture ordinance forbidding future partitioning of the duchy.[1]

The newly reunified Bavaria comprised a large, mostly geographically consolidated territory within the southeastern Holy Roman Empire (see map). Its topography sloped gradually downward from the Alps in the south into a region of hills and high plateaus, before reaching the fertile farmland of the Lower Bavarian plains. The Upper Palatine highlands and the Bohemian Forest formed natural frontiers along most of the territory's northern reaches. Within this considerable expanse of land, the Wittelsbach dukes exercised a greater degree of authority and control than many German princes. Already in the late 1400s, the Upper Bavarian dynasty had begun introducing the bureaucratic innovations and revenue and judicial systems typical of early modern states. They had divided their territory into four administrative districts, each with its

---

1. Max Spindler, ed., *Handbuch der bayerischen Geschichte* (Munich, 1967–1975), 2:258–294, 565–585. The War of the Landshut Succession and its consequences are also discussed in Thomas A. Brady, Jr., *Turning Swiss: Cities and Empire, 1450–1550* (Cambridge, 1985), pp. 72–73.

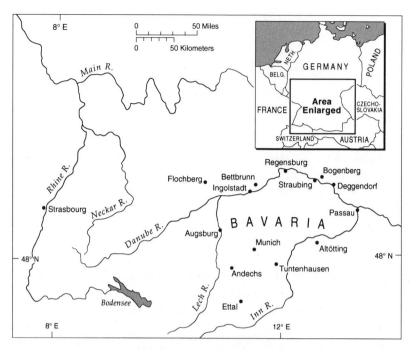

Southern Germany, with pilgrimage sites and other places frequently mentioned in the text. Courtesy of Barbara L. Trapido

own master official, a *Rentmeister,* who controlled a growing army of local officials; he was also granted broad powers to police the countryside and to supervise the machineries of ducal justice, administration, finance, and security.[2] With the reunification of Bavaria in the early sixteenth century, the Upper Bavarian dukes moved to establish this efficient bureaucratic system in the formerly autonomous regions of their realm.

Such developments placed Bavaria well along the path to becoming a centralized, semiautonomous state. Even with reunification, however, the Wittelsbachs continued to face considerable resistance to their state-building ambitions. Most of the Lower Bavarian nobility had supported their own duke in the civil war and were distrustful of the new regime centered in Munich. The Wittelsbachs' growing bureaucracy, moreover, often assaulted and subverted the

2. Gerald Strauss, *Law, Resistance, and the State* (Princeton, 1987), p. 259.

ancient privileges, customs, and rights of the duchy's various estates in favor of establishing measures and institutions that favored
the ruling dynasty's authority. As a consequence, numerous disputes erupted in the meeting of the duchy's parliament, the *Landtag*, comprising members of the three estates: the nobility; the
higher, aristocratic clergy; and the burghers. Jealous of the rights
they had built up during the centuries of territorial partition, the
three estates resisted the Wittelsbach state's efforts at centralization,
frequently attempting to stem the growth of ducal power by refusing to approve decrees and taxes. Even when granted assurances
that their ancient privileges would be respected, the Bavarian diet
retained a suspicion of ducal authority. In 1514, for example, the
estates sided with the mother of the then-ruling Duke Wilhelm IV in
a family inheritance dispute. Rescinding the primogeniture ordinance, the *Landtag* awarded one-third of the duchy to Wilhelm's
brother. Such tactics, however, could produce unexpected results.
Although the diet intended their maneuver to stem the growth of
Wittelsbach power, Wilhelm and his brother coordinated their policies, combining their efforts to weaken the privileges of the clergy,
nobility, and burghers.[3]

Rivalries like these were far removed from the more than four-
fifths of the territory's population that were peasants. Yet governmental squabbling nevertheless affected rural society, since controversies often revolved around the Wittelsbach state's rights to tax
the peasantry. Although this class bore a disproportionate burden
in financing the state, the estates' resistance to taxes and the Wittelsbach's economy in administering their state kept this burden
from becoming too great during the first half of the sixteenth century.[4]

Throughout the period treated in this study—that is, roughly
1450–1700—Bavaria remained more profoundly rural than many
other parts of the German empire. Unlike the Rhineland or the
imperial Southwest, the Wittelsbach duchy (indeed, the German
Southeast generally) contained few great cities. On the duchy's
western and northern borders, Augsburg and Regensburg were in

---

3. Spindler (ed.), *Handbuch der bayerischen Geschichte* 2:301–310.
4. Ibid., pp. 574ff. See also Felix Ammer, "Ein wirtschaftgeschichtlicher Beitrag
zur Sonderstellung Bayerns im deutschen Bauernkrieg" (Ph.D. diss., Munich, 1943),
pp. 24–25, 70–74.

1500 the two largest autonomous or imperial cities; yet while Augsburg consistently enjoyed wealth and prestige in the empire during the fifteenth and sixteenth centuries, Regensburg had entered into difficult financial times. A shift in trade routes had left it impoverished, and by the late 1400s the town had been forced to declare bankruptcy and to surrender its imperial freedom to a Bavarian duke. It eventually regained its imperial status, but its population of about eleven thousand at the outset of the sixteenth century placed it far behind in the ranks of the empire's most powerful and commercially dynamic centers. Within their own duchy, the Wittelsbachs had also granted urban charters to more than 120 towns and markets. Even by the modest standards of the time, most of these territorial "urban centers" remained in the sixteenth century little more than overgrown villages. Until the end of the Old Reich, Munich and Straubing were the only two Bavarian cities with populations in excess of four thousand.[5]

More agrarian than other parts of the empire, Bavaria could also boast a less turbulent history during the fifteenth and sixteenth centuries. Beginning around 1470, the commercial revolution and the "long century" of population expansion began inexorably to alter the character of German society and economy. The change from an older feudal agrarian order to one based on wage, price, and market structures produced increasing stratification in rural society and a tradition of peasant revolt that affected most South German regions. In Swabia, Franconia, and the imperial Southwest particularly, territorial fragmentation, increasingly restrictive tenancies, and the proliferation of forms of unfree serfdom inspired numerous rural rebellions and peasant disturbances in the decades after 1470. Bavaria, however, remained largely free of the tide of agrarian unrest that culminated in the great Peasants' War of 1525.

Although conditions in the duchy were far from idyllic, the issue of land tenure—a clear cause of rural revolt in other parts of the empire—had been resolved there in ways generally favorable to the peasantry. During the later Middle Ages, the Bavarian nobility and

5. Milo Kearney, "A Study of the Regensburg *Rat* in Connection with the Declination of the Town Political Movement in 1389" (Ph.D. diss., University of California, Berkeley, 1970); Guido Hable and Raimund Sterl, *Geschichte Regensburgs. Eine Übersicht nach Sachgebieten* (Regensburg, 1970); and Spindler (ed.), *Handbuch der bayerischen Geschichte* 2:569ff.

the Wittelsbach dukes had begun granting their peasants heritable leases to prevent their flight from the land. These measures helped to preserve a more conservative agrarian order within the territory.[6] From the sixteenth to the eighteenth centuries, moreover, most Bavarians continued to live in small farming villages where populations numbered only several hundred. Thus, while markets were available for agricultural surpluses, the subsistence economy remained more important than the commercial. This enduring conservativism meant that in Bavaria's villages both the agricultural and liturgical year remained the principal ways of demarcating time, and religious modes of explaining and protecting existence prevailed.[7]

Those seeking to understand the complex patterns of thought and perception of this very different world must first divorce themselves from some fundamental modern assumptions. In the modern rationalist framework, the interpretation of religion presumes a dichotomy between sacred and profane, and experiences judged to be "religious" are often relegated to a separate sphere of analysis. This kind of dichotomized approach, however, is not effective for examining the religion that prevailed in the late medieval or early modern German countryside. There, what was considered sacred was, as Robert Scribner has observed, "always experienced from within the profane."[8] Religion formed an "economy of the sacred" that expressed itself in practices aimed at sanctifying and protecting human beings, their actions, property, agriculture, and communities.

Since the publication of Keith Thomas's 1971 investigation of faith in premodern England, *Religion and the Decline of Magic*, historians have become more aware of the complementary roles that "magic" and "religion" played in medieval popular culture. Neither category can be separated from the other with any degree of ac-

6. See Peter Blickle's remarks in *The Revolution of 1525: The German Peasants' War from a New Perspective*, trans. Thomas A. Brady, Jr., and H. C. Erik Midelfort (Baltimore, 1981), pp. 52, 58.
7. The arguments that follow are indebted to Robert Scribner's "Ritual and Popular Religion in Catholic Germany at the Time of the Reformation," *Journal of Ecclesiastical History* 35 (1984): 47–77; and his "Cosmic Order and Daily Life: Sacred and Secular in Pre-industrial German Society," in *Popular Culture and Popular Movements in Reformation Germany* (London, 1988), pp. 1–16.
8. Scribner, "Cosmic Order and Daily Life," p. 2.

curacy, for each sought primarily to enlist power—wherever it resided—and to make it usable for both personal and communal needs. This religion was not "pre-Christian," as some have argued, though it sometimes kept alive ideas and practices that may have been pre-Christian in origin. In Bavaria, the sources reveal a Christianity based in ritual and habituated to a situation that was profoundly rural, agrarian, and local.

The religious perceptions of late medieval and early modern Bavarians often expressed themselves in a chorus of customs and rites performed both within and beyond the parish church. Ecclesiastical and extrasacramental rituals marked the passing of the year, and objects such as the Eucharist, holy water, blessed amulets, and saints' relics were conduits for the transfer of both protection and salvific grace. Rites of passage like baptism and the funeral delineated age groups, marking off the relationships of various cohorts to the community writ large. Prayers, invocations, and conjurations sought protection—sometimes divine, sometimes demonic—and a kind of inoculation from the harsh and malevolent forces people perceived around them. By the late fifteenth century, pilgrimage, too, had become deeply rooted in this sacred economy.

Approaching this period with the benefit of post-Reformation hindsight, scholars have identified in the general popularity of saints and pilgrimage a deep spiritual incertitude and anxiety about salvation in late medieval Germany. Yet, I would argue, the prominence of these dimensions of late medieval religion did not in fact arise from a pervasive fear about redemption. Both the saints and their special places were routinized sources for the salvific benefits of indulgences and of physical cures, effects procurable by the faithful in exchange for devotion. Pilgrimage was at this point less a matter of propitiation and expiation than it would become in a later, post-Tridentine age. In Bavaria, shrines were in large part centers of "faith healing," revered and prized because the saints resolved certain otherwise insoluble human dilemmas in ways more effective than those of other institutions. In the absence of effective medication, for example, the onslaught of an illness was often perceived as life-threatening, and its cessation a case of supernatural intervention. While indulgences, too, attracted people to these sites, pilgrims were not necessarily uncertain about their salvation. For most, ultimate redemption was rarely doubted; indulgences merely lessened inevitable purgatorial suffering. Thus, while the popularity of the cult of the saints in this period may suggest a pessimism and anxiety with regard to the human condition, it does not necessarily reveal a populace prepared for the radical departure of Protestant justification by faith.

In the course of the Middle Ages, Bavarians had both imported and created their own panoply of sanctities that resided at specific, observable sites in the landscape. The history of these places differs significantly from that observed in other parts of Europe. Generally speaking, the course of European pilgrimage displayed a gradual progression away from objective kinds of relic and grave cults to ones, like the Marian image cults, that granted the pilgrim's subjectivity greater play. Western Europe's first pilgrimages were to the graves of local martyred and ascetic saints. In late antiquity and the early Middle Ages, the faithful actually journeyed to these sites to pray for healing or aid in the very presence of the saint. In subsequent centuries, however, devotion departed from direct attachment to the saints' tombs. This trend is observable already in late antiquity, when Christians began dismembering and redistributing martyred saints' relics. To satisfy an immense appetite for sanctity, an active commerce and even thievery developed in the remains of the saints, and pilgrimages ensued to churches throughout Western Europe that possessed relics of saints embraced by Roman Christianity. These new international cults gradually displaced the appeal of the early, local saintly tumuli.

After the twelfth century, the popularity of these relic cults waned again in favor of new devotions in which miraculous images, statues, and the Eucharist were revered. The reason for this gradual waning of relic popularity was a new piety that venerated Mary, and later worshipped Christ, as the two most important persons in the celestial hierarchy. Because neither figure had left behind an extensive collection of relics beyond bits of hair, blood, or milk, the image often assumed a greater importance as a central cultic object. At each stage in this progression—from graves to relics to images—the importance of the saint's physical presence at the shrine decreased, while the pilgrim's subjective, imagined experience of the patron increased. One telling result of this change was that the patrons of later medieval shrines did not usually heal people within their church, but at the place where they were invoked.

Early medieval customs like incubation—the sleeping or taking up of residence within the shrine to effect cures in the saint's presence—thus became increasingly rare. As a result of these complex and centuries-long transformations, Europeans gradually transferred their loyalties from local thaumaturgists to universally revered members of a celestial hierarchy that included the apostles, early Church martyrs, the Virgin, and Christ.[9] At least one scholar has seen in this displacement a grass-roots source for the late medieval political integration of Western European states.[10] Yet pilgrimage and shrines continued to be marked by profound local variations, despite the external similarities of shared celestial patrons; interpretation of these developments, therefore, should be undertaken with caution.

The specific implications of pilgrimage for our understanding of political and cultural patterns will likely remain controversial for some time. Nevertheless, it is clear that the general course of cultic development sketched here for Western Europe as a whole does not hold true for Bavaria, or for Germany generally. As in other European regions, Bavaria's first pilgrimages had as their destination saintly graves, the figures most often revered in the early Middle Ages usually being the missionaries and first bishops of the territory. In Germany, however, the tumulus cult remained rare, and in Bavaria in particular no pilgrimages to local saints' graves arose in the early Middle Ages, besides those to cathedrals and monastic churches.[11]

---

9. On the late antique and medieval cult of the saints, see E. D. Hunt, *Holy Land Pilgrimages in the Later Roman Empire, A.D. 312–460* (Oxford, 1982); J. Wilkinson, ed. and trans., *Jerusalem Pilgrims Before the Crusades* (Warminster, 1977); B. J. Kötting, *Peregrinatio Religiosa*, 2 vols. (Giessen, 1912); Brown, *Cult of the Saints*; Lionel Rothkrug, "The 'Odour of Sanctity' and the Hebrew Origins of Christian Relic Veneration," *Historical Reflections* 8 (1981): 95–142; Georg Schreiber, ed., *Wallfahrt und Volkstum* (Düsseldorf, 1934); Geary, *Furta Sacra*; Sigal, *Marcheurs de Dieu*; idem, *L'homme et le miracle*; Martin Heinzelmann, *Translationsberichte und andere Quellen des Reliquienkultes* (Paris, 1979); C. Bremond, J. Le Goff, and J.-C. Schmitt, *L'exemplum* (Turnhout, 1982); Finucane, *Miracles and Pilgrims*; and Helmut Sperber, *Unsere Liebe Frau* (Regensburg, 1980).

10. Rothkrug, *Religious Practices and Collective Perceptions*.

11. The cults of native Bavarian saints are treated in Georg Schwaiger, ed., *Bavaria Sancta. Zeugen christlichen Glauben in Bayern*, 3 vols. (Regensburg, 1970–1972). See also J. B. Lehner, "Wallfahrten im Bistum Regensburg," in *1200 Jahre Bistum Regensburg*, ed. Michael Buchberger (Regensburg, 1939), pp. 216–222; and Stephen Beissel, *Die Verehrung der Heiligen und ihrer Reliquien in Deutschland bis zum Beginn des 13. Jahrhunderts* (Freiburg i. B., 1890), 1:101–120, 2:40–55.

During the later Middle Ages, new kinds of cults competed with these older tumulus devotions. Perhaps the first to emerge to challenge the grave cult, in the thirteenth and fourteenth centuries, was the eucharistic cult, occupying an intermediary position between the physicality of the older types of devotion and the subsequent forms of visual and imagistic piety. At the shrines of these cults, the Eucharist was revered much like a relic; but it was the sensual act of viewing the hosts that transferred onto the faithful a kind of salvific grace. The legends associated with these sites vividly evoke the steady rise of eucharistic devotion in the later Middle Ages and the diffusion of the belief in the Real Presence. Miraculously preserved from mistreatment at the hands of women, magicians, heretics, and Jews, the host was celebrated at Bavaria's shrines as a divine locus that possessed the power to protect and avenge itself. The consecrated wafer performed its miracles in various ways. When dropped by the careless, it refused to be moved from its resting place. For those who desired to use it for magic, the wafer bled as a warning. For those who doubted the divine presence, apparitions appeared to convince them. And when tortured, the host revealed its agonies to Christians who avenged the crime.[12]

In Bavaria, this last, most frequently retold legend about the Eucharist was often associated with the Jews. During two successive waves of pilgrimage foundations in the mid fourteenth and late fifteenth centuries, a number of shrines dedicated to "Bleeding Hosts" appeared in the territory. The legends retold about these sites often explained and justified Jewish pogroms. Drawing details from the New Testament Passion narratives, these stories of "crimes against the host" (*Hostienfrevel* or *Hostienschändung*) alleged an ongoing tradition of Jewish torture waged against the Christian God. Because of their hatred of Christ, the narrative intoned, Jews would purchase hosts from a Christian betrayer and torture them in ways

---

12. On host shrines and their legends, see Johann Heuser, " 'Heilig-Blut' in Kult und Brauchtum des deutschen Kultraumes: ein Beitrag zur religiösen Volkskunde" (Ph.D. diss., Bonn, 1958), pp. 10–13; Sargent, "Miracle Books and Pilgrimage Shrines," p. 468; Peter Browe, *Die eucharistischen Wunder des Mittelalters* (Breslau, 1938); and Caroline Bynum, *Holy Feast and Holy Fast: The Religious Significance of Food to Medieval Women* (Berkeley, 1987), esp. pp. 63–66. The essential starting point for investigating the history of medieval traditions of salvific display is still Anton Mayer, "Die heilbringende Schau in Sitte und Kult," in *Heilige Überlieferung: Ausschnitte aus der Geschichte des Mönchtums und des heiligen Kultes. Festschrift für Ildefons Herwegen* (Münster, 1938), pp. 234–262.

that recalled the Passion and Crucifixion, scratching them with thorns, driving nails through them, or pounding them on an anvil. When the hosts would begin to bleed as a warning, the Jews, to hide their crime, would throw the wafers into a fiery furnace, but they would not be consumed. In the legends of some shrines, a vision of the Christ child also appeared. In desperation, the myth related, the Jews would cast the wafers into wells or into a river that would immediately turn blood-red. The Virgin or angels would appear to announce the crime to Christians, who would avenge the deed by executing the offending Jews and the "Judas" who had betrayed Christian society by supplying the wafers to the Jews.[13]

Within the boundaries of Bavaria, shrines with legends like these were especially common in the *Donauraum*, the region of northern Lower Bavaria straddling the Danube River, a fact that reveals the presence of a deeply rooted tradition of Jewish hatred in the region.[14] In addition, however, legends about host crimes helped to sustain the widespread perception that holy objects like the Eucharist were vulnerable to attack. They could be tortured and defiled, and yet could triumph over their oppressors. Legends of the Bleeding Host celebrated the Eucharist as a locus for overcoming evil.

Even while cults like these proliferated in Bavaria in the later Middle Ages, a number of others also appeared. Late medieval Bavarians journeyed to holy places associated with a saint, to wonder-working images of the Virgin, and to the graves of long-deceased thaumaturgists. The first of these types of cults, that of the *locus sanctus*, was particularly widespread in Bavaria in the later Middle Ages. In contrast to sites with relics or saintly graves, a "holy place" shrine possessed no physical remains of the saint. Its appeal resided primarily in the perception that it was a locale particularly blessed with the saint's patronage. In the absence of the tangible presence of the patron by way of objects like relics or artistic images, legends served to link the saint to specific places, and the subsequent tradition of thaumaturgy and intercession—often assidu-

13. Peter Browe, "Die Hostienschändung der Juden im Mittelalter," *Römische Quartalschrift* 34 (1926): 167–197; and idem, *Die eucharistischen Wunder*, pp. 140–141.
14. Heuser, " 'Heilig Blut,' " pp. 35–36; Lionel Rothkrug, "Holy Shrines, Religious Dissonance, and Satan in the Origins of the German Reformation," *Historical Reflections* 14 (1987): 161ff.; and Peter Browe, "Die Hostienschändung der Juden," pp. 178ff.

ously publicized by medieval clerics—affirmed the saint's continued patronage over the shrine.

At the *locus sanctus* of St. Leonhard at Inchenhofen, for example, the church possessed not even an image of this French noble saint until centuries after the pilgrimage had commenced. The church was in fact home to but a tiny and insignificant devotion for quite a while; then as one medieval cleric tells us, Leonhard performed a stunning miracle of retribution. One day, three knights and forty horsemen visited Inchenhofen looking for a place to set up camp. Seeing signs of devotion at the church, though, and recognizing it as a holy place, the warriors searched elsewhere. Immediately after they left Leonhard's presence, one of the knights was struck dead, and his companions discovered two stolen chickens in his saddle bags. Knowledge of this judicious punishment soon circulated in the region; Inchenhofen's pilgrimage grew dramatically, and Leonhard's presence continued to be confirmed through an ongoing tradition of thaumaturgy and intercession. The case of Inchenhofen was typical.[15]

At the same time as numinous "holy places" like these were growing in popularity, Bavaria's older grave cults also experienced a renaissance. In much of Europe, these shrines survived only as a kind of archaic remnant; yet in Bavaria, the clergy at a number of ancient abbeys, monasteries, and cathedrals moved to revive these devotions in the years around 1450. Long-forgotten saints like St. Simpert at Augsburg or St. Rasso at Grafrath were rediscovered and their bodies ceremonially exhumed and transferred to newer, grander tombs that became the destination for large numbers of pilgrims.[16]

In much of Western Europe, widespread Marian devotion had first begun to appear in the twelfth and thirteenth centuries. Such worship was a fundamental departure from preexisting cults, since

15. On Inchenhofen's precipitant legend, see Sargent, "Religion and Society," pp. 100–101. On the importance of *locus sanctus* devotions in late medieval Bavaria, see Josef Staber, *Volksfrömmigkeit und Wallfahrtswesen des Spätmittelalters im Bistum Freising*, published as vol. 20, no. 1, of *Beiträge zur altbayerischen Kirchengeschichte* (1955): 59; and Sargent, "Miracle Books and Pilgrimage Shrines," pp. 468ff.

16. Heinrich Gläser, "Die kirchlichreligiöse Entwicklung bis 1500," in Spindler (ed.), *Handbuch der bayerischen Geschichte* 2:611ff.; Romuald Bauerreiß, *Kirchengeschichte Bayerns* (St. Ottilien, 1949–1970), 5:192ff.; and Sargent, "Miracle Books and Pilgrimage Shrines," pp. 462ff.

Marian pilgrimages were tied to images and statues rather than to sacred places, relics, or hosts. According to legend, Mary's body had been assumed into heaven with few relics left behind; as a consequence, images became the central object for the faithful's devotion at the Virgin's shrines.

In a study of the Marian images of Bavaria, however, Torsten Gebhard proved unable to verify the presence of a single statue or image of the Virgin within the territory before the early fourteenth century. The oldest Marian images from this period employ the iconography of the *sedes sapientiae,* or "throne of wisdom," an early medieval type of depiction that had already fallen into disuse in most of Western Europe by the time it appeared in Bavaria. These images portray Mary as the *theotokos,* or "God-bearer"; she sits in a rigid forward direction and presents the Christ child to onlookers as the embodied Word of God.[17] After 1340 a new depiction of the Virgin, the *pietà* or *Vesperbild,* is detectable in Bavaria, but these images did not inspire independent Marian pilgrimages. Because the *pietà* concentrates attention on the role of Mary as the suffering mother of Christ, it was employed first as an adjunct to the eucharistic devotion at Bleeding Host shrines, appearing alongside the *imago pietatis* or *Schmerzenmannsbild,* a bleeding depiction of the tortured Christ that was often displayed at sites of host desecration.[18]

This iconographic evidence suggests that a widespread, autonomous Marian devotion did not exist in Bavaria during much of the fourteenth and fifteenth centuries. Although several Marian shrines appeared in Bavaria in the mid–fifteenth century, devotions at these places remained localized. They were in any case soon eclipsed by the development in the 1490s of Altötting, a site destined to be celebrated variously as a symbol of imperial unity and a sign of the imminent Apocalypse. In 1489, miracles began to be reported at a small chapel in this town believed to date to Carolingian times. Within several years thousands of pilgrims from

17. Torsten Gebhard, "Die Marianische Gnadenbilder in Bayern: Beobachtungen zur Chronologie und Typologie," in *Kultur und Volk. Festschrift für Gustav Gugitz* (Vienna, 1954), pp. 100–102. On the iconography of the *sedes sapientiae,* see Ilene Forsyth, *The Throne of Wisdom: Wood Sculptures of the Madonna in Romanesque France* (Princeton, 1972).

18. Gebhard, "Marianische Gnadenbilder," p. 99; and Romuald Bauerreiß, *Pie Jesu. Das Schmerzenmannsbild und sein Einfluß auf die mittelalterliche Frömmigkeit* (Munich, 1931), pp. 108ff.

Bavaria and the southern empire had transformed the formerly insignificant church into one of the most popular destinations in Germany. Members of the imperial nobility, the Lower and Upper Bavarian dukes, and even the Holy Roman emperor processed there, showering the site with ostentatious gifts. In 1492 alone, the shrine's revenue totaled 12,375 *pfund pfennig*, a sum equivalent to the contemporary value of roughly 4,000 horses or 6,600 cows.[19] By the early sixteenth century, the church's treasury was rich enough to serve as a war chest for the Lower Bavarian duke in waging the so-called War of the Landshut Succession against his Munich cousins. And despite the pilgrimage's decline from 1503 to 1505 as a result of that conflict, it soon revived and continued to be a popular destination until 1520. Throughout the period 1490–1520, the Wittelsbach dynasty had continually supported the site, bestowing it with attentions otherwise reserved for only a few of the most important places of pilgrimage in the territory. As the premier Bavarian edifice dedicated to the Virgin, Altötting was to continue influencing Marian devotion in the region throughout the early modern period.

Although the Marian cult was the last major type of pilgrimage to develop in Bavaria, it quickly enjoyed a widespread appeal. Rather than supplanting the other already-established host and saints' cults, however, Marian devotion continued in the late fifteenth and early sixteenth centuries to flourish alongside older pilgrimages. Indeed, the late medieval flowering of lay piety in Bavaria was expressed largely through the simultaneous popularity of these various cults. Describing his fellow countrymen in the early sixteenth century, the humanist Johannes Aventinus included the observation that Bavarians were "pious, . . . going happily on pilgrimages," and that they had "many shrines."[20] Modern historical research has confirmed the truth of his assessment. By 1500, an explosion of devotion in the region had forged a sacral landscape characterized by an almost bewildering variety of sacred sites and the frequent processions of villages and individual pilgrims.

19. A pfund pfennig was made up of 240 silver pennies. In the late fifteenth century, 3 pfund 30 pfennig would buy a horse, 1 pfund 210 pfennig a cow. See Maria Angela König, *Weihegaben an U.L. Frau von Altötting* (Munich, 1939–1940), 2:5.

20. From the author's *Baierischer Chronik*; reprinted in Johannes Aventinus, *Sämmtliche Werke* (Munich, 1881–1908), 4:42.

Bavaria's shrines were marketplaces in a sacred economy, exchanging healing, intercession, and indulgences in return for a pilgrim's visits, prayers, and gifts. Although visited by all types of people, including burghers, artisans, and nobles, these were primarily sites of peasant pilgrimage.[21] At the sacred destinations, religious life featured the same longing after protection evidenced in other dimensions of the rural mentality. Seeking cures or aid in some otherwise hopeless circumstance, the faithful approached their saintly patrons with prayers and vows, promising journeys if they received aid. To make their entreaties more attractive, however, the prospective pilgrim offered a gift along with the appeal. Most often, votants cautiously stipulated that they would present the gift only if they were helped. In the later Middle Ages much gift-giving was a fairly simple affair: it involved specific quantities of wax (an important medium of exchange throughout Europe and a source of lighting for the church), grain, cloth, and other raw commodities. The giving of basic materials like these was usually deemed sufficient to entice the saints to use their powers of intercession. These items, moreover, were an important source of revenue for the clergy who resided at the pilgrimage church, and markets sometimes developed to resell the gifts to other pilgrims.[22]

The relationship established by a votant's invocation of the saints was a contractual one and an essential first step on the path to receiving aid. For those who were incapacitated and incapable of making the vow, others would promise for the afflicted. The recipients of saintly help, however, were bound to fulfill the promise of pilgrimage and gift presentation. Shirking this responsibility invalidated the original vow and resulted in punishment by the saint—a sort of spur to make good on the contract. Medieval miracle records include numerous stories warning pilgrims not to neglect the timely completion of their promise lest they begin to suffer their diseases or hardship again. In surviving records from late medieval Bavaria, this perception of miracles as the product of an unequal yet contractual exchange is common. Would-be pilgrims prayed to the saints,

21. See Staber, *Volksfrömmigkeit und Wallfahrtswesen;* Irmgard Gierl, *Bauernleben und Bauernwallfahrt in Altbayern,* published as vol. 21, no. 2 of *Beiträge zur altbayerischen Kirchengeschichte* (1960); Sargent, "Religion and Society."

22. Gerlinde Stahl, "Die Wallfahrt zur Schönen Maria," *Beiträge zur Geschichte des Bistums Regensburg* 2 (1968): 79. The patterns of gift-giving at the Altötting shrine are reviewed in König, *Weihegaben an U.L. Frau in Altötting.*

promising a pilgrimage and gift, but then cautiously waited before completing their vow to see if their request had in fact been granted.[23]

Shrines may have functioned thus as important components in a sacred economy, yet they were not completely free, unregulated markets. The clergy labored to control, nurture, and expand them, turning to a variety of media for purposes of promotion. Since late antiquity, the recording and pronouncement of a saint's miracles had served numerous polemical, apologetic, and propagandistic purposes. In his *City of God*, for example, the fourth-century bishop Augustine, having overcome early doubts about the reality of contemporary saintly intercession, used numerous miracles worked by the orthodox saints Stephen, Gervasius, and Protasius to polemicize against the Arians and Donatists.[24] In the Middle Ages, the recording of intercessory testimonies—now increasingly routinized and formulaic—continued to lend supernatural confirmation to cults and to expand devotion. In an increasingly orthodox Europe, however, the clergy who ministered at various cultic centers often considered it helpful to collect pilgrims' testimonies that proved the efficacy of their own patron and allowed their cult to compete in the increasingly diverse and crowded arena of devotion. In twelfth- and thirteenth-century France and England, scribal records of miracles began to be made at numerous places. In Bavaria, the practice of setting down these testimonies was known as early as the eleventh century, but only in the later Middle Ages did it become truly widespread. Prompted by a rising desire to learn about cases of supernatural intervention, as well as the general increase in pious devotion, Bavaria's clergy became some of Europe's most diligent recorders of saintly miracles.[25]

23. These conclusions are based on a reading of the surviving printed miracle books from late medieval Bavaria. The exchange relationship has also been noted for France and England; see Sigal, *L'homme et le miracle*, pp. 79–116; and Finucane, *Miracles and Pilgrims*.

24. St. Augustine, *De Civitate Dei: The City of God*, trans. John O'Meara (Harmondsworth, Middlesex, 1972), bk. 22, chap. 8, pp. 1033–1047. Augustine's attitude toward miracles is discussed in Brown, *Cult of the Saints*, pp. 27–28, 38, 77–78; Finucane, *Miracles and Pilgrims*, pp. 17–20; and Benedicta Ward, *Miracles and the Medieval Mind: Theory, Record, and Event, 1000–1215* (Philadelphia, 1982), pp. 1–5, 7–11.

25. On the tradition of miracle recording in medieval France and England, see Finucane, *Miracles and Pilgrims*; Ward, *Miracles and the Medieval Mind*; and Sigal, *L'homme et le miracle*. More than twelve thousand miracles survive from the later

This cataloguing of a saint's contemporary miracles served several functions. First, because the shrines at which the cures and interventions occurred were generally small, drawing their clientele largely from the immediate vicinity, publicity helped the clerics to assure devotees of the saint's continued effectiveness in the region. Recorded miracles were thus proclaimed to pilgrims on the church's annual feast days, when traffic at the shrine was heaviest. Included in the records were the votant's name and place of residence, the nature of his or her problem, and, usually, the year in which the miracle occurred. Second, the details of these wonders concretized a patron's intercession, thus bolstering the shrine's viability; through use of this information, clerical promoters labored to increase the size and scope of their cult. Third, miracles supported a cult's claim to indulgences—the official Church's sanction for a pilgrimage and an important currency in the late medieval spiritual economy.

Oral proclamation was well suited to a society in which only a small fraction of the entire population was literate. Yet a growing desire to hear and learn about cases of supernatural intervention—a desire evident from the rising attention in the fifteenth century to the recording of such miracles—also inspired the adoption of new media to expand the advertisement of specific sites. Crystallized into pictures, retold in sermons, lauded in songs and poems, and published in modest broadsides and pamphlets, miracles became the focus of an active trade by Bavaria's clergy and laity in the generations immediately preceding the Reformation.

Around 1500, the pictorial depiction of these testimonies in commissioned altar cycles began to flourish in Bavaria. The first Bavarian "miracle picture cycle" (*Mirakelbildzyklus*) was likely commissioned for the Altötting shrine sometime around 1500; it retold in cartoon fashion the initial miracles that had revealed the site's power and precipitated its pilgrimage. The distilling of wonders into narrative pictorial cycles possessed a unique advantage over oral pronouncement: pictures worked continuously, conveying the shrine's intercessions to pilgrims even when priests were not present in the church. It would be a mistake, though, to view such developments as born solely of clerical calculation. For roughly at

---

Middle Ages in Bavaria, far more than in France or England; see Sargent, "Miracle Books and Pilgrimage Shrines," pp. 455–471.

the same time as the clergy moved to present their patrons' miracles pictorially, the Bavarian laity began bringing illustrated votive tablets as gifts to their saintly intercessors. These representational offerings, painted or carved in wood and wax, described pictorially the aid the pilgrim had received thanks to his or her prayerful vow to the saint. Left at the shrine, they functioned like the altar cycles as an enduring testimony, stronger than mere wax or money, to the saint's aid.[26]

Both the pictorial and oral pronouncement of miracles functioned only within the pilgrimage church proper. In the late fifteenth century, however, the clergy adopted printing as another medium for broadcasting the news of their patron's effectiveness. With the publication of printed pamphlets, illustrated broadsides, and thin chapbooks they moved to extend their promotional campaigns beyond the physical confines of their churches. Procured at the souvenir booths that surrounded the pilgrimage church, the printed work traveled home with its new owner and could spread word of a shrine's miraculous power among those who had not personally made the journey.

In an environment saturated with claims of supernatural intervention, Bavaria's pilgrims appear to have questioned the veracity of these accounts but rarely. For these people, miracles served as the primary confirmation of the sanctity of local holy places. As a result, in the generation before the Reformation, the thin "miracle book" emerged as the single most common kind of printed document used to advertise a shrine. Nevertheless, its adoption remained relatively limited. Printed editions from this period survive from only three sites, all of the Marian cult: Altötting, Tuntenhausen, and Regensburg.[27]

26. Dieter Harmening, "Mirakelbildzyklen—Formen und Tendenzen von Kultpropaganda," *Bayerisches Jahrbuch für Volkskunde*, 1978, pp. 53–56. Harmening notes the relationship between these two developments—that is, miracle picture cycles commissioned by shrines and representational votives given by pilgrims: "Etwa zur gleichen Zeit als um 1500 Votivbilder brauchmäßig im Wallfahrtskult auftauchen, entstehen an mitteleuropäischen Wallfahrtsorten große Mirakelbildzyklen." Two of the earliest of these miracle picture cycles appeared at Mariazell in Austria (ca. 1519) and Altötting in Lower Bavaria (ca. 1500). On Mariazell, see Peter Krenn, "Der große Mariazeller Wunderaltar von 1519 und sein Meister," *Jahrbuch des Kunsthistorischen Instituts der Universität Graz*, 1966–1967, pp. 31–51; on Altötting, see Philipp Maria Halm, "Die Mirakelbilder zu Altötting," *Bayerischer Heimatschutz* 21 (1925): 1–27.

27. The extant works from before 1570 are as follows: for Altötting: *Vermerckt dye Grossen wunder zaichen so dye Junckfraw Maria hye zu alten Oettingen wuercken ist an vil*

A common style characterizes most of the printed miracle books published between 1490 and the onset of the Catholic Reformation around 1570. Usually thin, about eight to ten pages long, having a title page decorated with a print of the Virgin, these books presented a series of miracle reports taken from the shrine's manuscript collections. The accounts were usually retold in simple succession, with miracles tumbling one after another. To keep costs low, the literary style remained simple, even terse, with conjunctions and sentence subjects frequently omitted. Only occasionally did the author attempt to corroborate or fortify these accounts with the names of witnesses or an explanation of all the circumstances surrounding the event.[28]

Even more rarely was any effort made to place these testimonies into an interpretive framework. Most often, the pamphlet's title page announced simply that these "wonders" had been reported at the shrine and were now being published so they could be more widely known. Although briefer than most, the first surviving Alt-

---

Cristen menschen (Augsburg, 1494); Jackob Isseckemer, *Das Buchlein der Zuflucht zu Maria der Mutter Gottes in alten Oding* (Nuremberg, 1497); *Hye heben sich an Dye grosse wunderzaychen Unser lyeben frawen dye do sen geschehen zu alten Ottingen* (Munich, after 1512). For Regensburg: H. Harder, *Die wunderbarliche zaichen beschehen zu der schönen Maria zu Regenspurg im xix. Jahr* (Nuremberg, 1519); *In dysem buchlein seind begriffen die wunderbarliche zaychen beschehen zu Regenspurg zu der schoenen Maria der mutter gottes* (Nuremberg, 1519); *In dysem Buchlein seind begriffen die wunderbarlichen zaychen beschehen zu Regenspurg zu der schoenen Maria der mutter gottes* (Nuremberg, 1520); *Wunderbarlichen czychen vergangen Jars beschehen jn Regenspurg tzw der schoenen Maria der mueter gottes hye jn begriffen* (Regensburg, 1522). For Tuntenhausen: *Hierinn vermerckt ettliche zaichen in unnser lieben frauwen gotzhaus Tuntenhau[sen] angesagt auff ains jeglichen begern verkuendt* (Augsburg, 1506); and *Thuntenhausen unnser lieben frawen Gotzhauß in . . . Bayrnn zc. Landt Freysinger Bistumbs gelegen. Etliche Mercklich furpit Marie seiner werden Mueter* (Munich, 1527). Under this last title the Tuntenhausen clerics published updated miracle books in the following years: 1530, 1531, 1532, 1533, 1534 (2 different books), 1535, 1536 (2 different books), 1537, 1538, 1539, 1544, 1547, 1551, 1561, 1564, 1567, 1569. Facsimile editions of the Altötting miracle books appear in Robert Bauer, "Das älteste gedruckte Mirakelbüchlein von Altötting," *Ostbairische Grenzmarken* 5 (1961): 144–151; idem, "Das Büchlein der Zuflucht zu Maria," *Ostbairische Grenzmarken* 7 (1964–1965): 206–236; and idem, "Das Altöttinger Mirakelbuch von 1540," *Ostbairische Grenzmarken* 6 (1962–1963): 241–248. Bauer dates this last miracle book 1540; Steven Sargent argues ("Miracle Books and Pilgrimage Shrines," p. 458) that its true date is closer to 1512.
28. A more complete examination of these themes is included in my "Wondrous in His Saints: Popular Pilgrimage and Catholic Propaganda in Bavaria, 1470–1620" (Ph.D. diss., University of Michigan, 1988), pp. 108–189; and in Hermann Bach, "Mirakelbücher bayerischer Wallfahrtsorte: Untersuchung ihrer literarischen Form und ihrer Stellung innerhalb der Literatur der Zeit" (Ph.D. diss., Munich, 1963), pp. 34ff., 67–72.

ötting miracle book from 1494 is typical of many of those published in Bavaria during the late fifteenth and sixteenth centuries. It recounted a mere twenty-five miracles, a small selection from the scores that were likely on the books at the shrine at this time. Its title page, emblazoned with a print of the Virgin and child, noted that these miracles had only recently been recorded in the Marian chapel at Altötting, centuries after its construction by the Emperor Charlemagne. This book, like many published in Bavaria before the Reformation, was not organized in strict chronological fashion: miracles reported in 1494 appeared before those that occurred in 1492. Nor was any classification scheme used. Cases of people revived from death or near death appeared alongside the stories of those who received relief from rheumatism or a difficult childbirth. Each miracle was piled one on top of another in simple succession in a kind of ongoing narrative testimony to the multiplicity and diversity of the Virgin's intercession.

One exception to this general pattern was a book published for Altötting in 1497, entitled *The Little Book of Mary, God's Mother's Refuge at Altötting*. Its author, Jakob Isseckemer, was the administrator of Altötting's collegiate church. Longer at fifty-four pages than most of the early miracle books, it exhibits a greater degree of technical and literary finesse than the others as well.[29] Its title page (fig. 1) is decorated with a print of the Madonna and child standing in a half moon and surrounded by a flaming halo—iconographical references to the doctrine of the Immaculate Conception. Wax votive images of arms, legs, and children hang all around the Virgin, and pilgrims flank her on the right and left. Two pilgrims kneel in prayer before Our Lady's altar; another approaches on a wooden leg, offering a wax foot as a votive gift. To the left of the Virgin, a man is depicted impaled on a torturing wheel; blood flowing from his body is being lapped up by a dog. This section of the print refers to the last miracle narrated in the book, the story of an unjust imprisonment and torture rectified by the Virgin.[30]

There are considerable differences between the style of the 1494 book and that of Isseckemer's 1497 edition. A lengthy dedication and preface precedes the miracle narratives in the latter work, in

29. Jakob Isseckemer, *Das Buchlein der Zuflucht zu Maria*.
30. Ibid., fol. Eiiij.

which Isseckemer outlines a radical apocalyptic Mariology. He begins by tracing the history of the Virgin's veneration at Altötting back to Charlemagne's time, when the great emperor captured the site from heathens and built a chapel dedicated to Mary there. Yet the shrine became prominent only around 1490, he reports, when the Virgin began to reveal miracles there. Since that time, all who have called on her "in good will and with their entire trust" have been answered.[31]

In Isseckemer's dedication, though, the tiny chapel at Altötting assumes far more than a thaumaturgic role in the divine historical plan. Mary, he writes, has only lately begun to perform miracles at Altötting to prepare the world to resist the Antichrist. The miracles the Virgin is working at the shrine are consequently transformed in this account into signs intended to draw the righteous away from evil. Here "in the heart of the Holy Roman Empire," the grace of God and the intercession of Mary have been made visible to encourage the faithful to seek out the Altötting Madonna's refuge and be readied for the judgment soon to be levied on the world:

> For God has held to one rule since the beginning of the world: more than once when he wanted to alter the course of the world he has sent someone who has proclaimed this with miracles, or miracles have begun to occur. Thus when he wanted to change the entire world he sent Noah who proclaimed this with many miracles. . . . When he wished to alter the promised land and to keep the unfaithful out of it he sent the people of Israel forty years filled with miracles. . . . And now God will change the course of history once again and will punish the entire world. Following the rules that he has followed in the past, he has now sent us the Virgin Mary with her goodness, which is so overflowing to those who flee to her and truly call upon her; this has been confirmed by the countless men from many lands and birth who have come to Altötting to pronounce the graces of Mary that have occurred to them.[32]

The preface that follows these remarks is written in the form of a sermon, with text from John 19: "Behold your Mother." Isseckemer transforms Christ's statement to John the Beloved from the cross into a metaphor for the Church's relationship to Mary. He then

31. Ibid., fol. Aii.
32. Ibid., fol. Aiii.

proceeds to narrate his selection of miracle stories from the "many thousands" reported at Altötting.

Isseckemer's *Little Book of Mary* is unusual among the early printed miracle books in many respects. The style, vocabulary, and syntax of the work show immediately that Isseckemer was writing for an elite audience. In contrast to the 1494 edition, this later book contains longer, more involved sentences and more descriptive information. Its length would have made it costlier than the typical thin printed miracle pamphlet as well. With regard to content, Isseckemer's explanation of Our Lady of Altötting's miracles in terms of an apocalyptic Mariology is singular among Bavarian miracle books printed before the onset of the Counter-Reformation. Unusual, too, is his grouping of similar miracles together under subdivisions, based on Bernard of Clairvaux's sevenfold mission of Mary: from her, the imprisoned receive release; the sick, health; the sad, comfort; the sinner, indulgence; and so forth.[33] Although this style of presentation was later adopted by many early modern miracle books, Isseckemer's 1497 book is one of only two extant works from before the Catholic Reformation to employ an organizing schema.[34]

Most important is the fact that Isseckemer invested the miracles of the Altötting Virgin with broad historical, religious, and geographical significance. Here in the center of the Holy Roman Empire, he argued extravagantly, God was performing miracles through the Virgin's intercession to call the world away from sin and to repentance. This attempt to enhance the meaning of the shrine's wonders was not imitated in other, more modest miracle books; most often, the mere printing of miracles was considered sufficient to prove the power of shrine patrons. In this respect, then, Isseckemer's *Little Book of Mary* remained a solitary phenomenon.

In the period before the Counter-Reformation, the printed miracle book remained closely tied to the oral and pictorial pronounce-

---

33. Ibid., fols. Aiiij–Aviii.
34. The other, for Tuntenhausen, is titled *Thuntenhausen unnser lieben frawen Gotzhauß in . . . Bayrnn* (Munich, 1527). It uses a less sophisticated schema than Isseckemer's. The clerical overseer of this church, Pantaleon Weidringer, divides Mary's miracles into five categories: revivals from death, cases of people in danger of dying, illnesses of the eyes, difficult births, and serious illnesses.

ment of wonders within the pilgrimage church. Indeed, one scholar has characterized these books as a kind of "extended arm" of the pilgrimage preacher who pronounced the shrine's miracles regularly.[35] This broadly addressed literature, in short, served primarily to augment patterns of promulgation, promotion, and advertisement that were fundamentally oral in conception. Still, the use of printing to circulate miracle stories had revolutionary potential in that it offered the clergy an opportunity to promote their cults to wider audiences removed from aural and visual immediacy.

Although most Bavarians were apparently concerned chiefly with learning about the continuing proofs of a shrine's saintly guardianship, the legendary associations of that power were also a matter of some interest. As we have seen, the legitimacy of Bleeding Host and *locus sanctus* cults in particular were often initially validated through legends about the Eucharist or the saint.[36] In the later Middle Ages, Bavarians celebrated the tales, histories, and myths of other sites within their territory as well. And again, multiple media played a role. Exploited and retold in broadsides and printed chronicles, depicted in art, and lauded in poetic ballads, legends focused attention on the precipitating incidents that had revealed the shrine's numinous power.

Depictions of these narratives in song may have been common in Bavaria in the generations before the Reformation; yet, unlike the thousands of miraculous testimonies that survive, only a few such songs still exist. In late medieval Germany, itinerant balladeers and bards plied their trade in town and countryside, sometimes performing at pilgrimage shrines in exchange for donations. Often they sang before banners or panels that told the story of a shrine's foundation visually. These early multimedia shows allowed audiences to visualize the events that had transpired to produce the cult. The texts that accompanied such performances have endured only when wandering minstrels or poets prized their creations enough to have them written down.

One such poetic legend treats the origins of the Bleeding Host shrine at Deggendorf, a Lower Bavarian village just north of the

35. Bach, "Mirakelbücher bayerischer Wallfahrtsorte," p. 29.
36. Hanns Bächtold-Stäubli, ed., *Handwörterbuch des deutschen Aberglaubens* (Berlin and Leipzig, 1927–1937), s.v. "Ort."

Danube River.[37] In it, the poet tells of the purchase by Jews of consecrated hosts from a local Christian woman and subsequent tortures inflicted on the objects. As the wafers began to bleed, angels appeared to warn the sentinel, who rushed to tell the town fathers of the crime in progress. The resulting vindication of the host and the punishment of the crime, the poet alleges, gave rise to a tradition of thaumaturgy in Deggendorf. The specter of the Real Presence—tortured, made to bleed, and yet triumphing over its oppressors—had subsequently produced a plethora of miracles at Deggendorf. Thus, as in other legends about the Bleeding Host, the poet establishes a convergence between the actions and events recorded in the New Testament and the specific incident at Deggendorf. What happened in the Lower Bavarian village was essentially a recurrence of the Passion narrative in the gospels. And following the crime against the Eucharist, the Savior's miracles had shown forth at Deggendorf: the blind had been made to see, the deaf to hear, and the lame to walk. It is interesting, and important from the standpoint of our investigation, that no contemporary records by clerics of miracles survive from the Bleeding Host shrine at Deggendorf. Nor do miracle records exist from other sites of alleged Jewish eucharistic desecration. The bard of the Deggendorf legend may have linked the Eucharist to an ongoing tradition of thaumaturgy, but Bavaria's clergy do not appear to have associated miracles with the Bleeding Host.[38]

In addition to poems and songs, the illustrated broadside served to advertise and communicate the lore of late medieval shrines. And again, very few examplars survive. Since illustrated single-page prints were often used as household wall decorations, their scarcity might be explained by their expendability. One extant print for the Bleeding Host shrine at Passau (fig. 2), printed sometime around 1478, may be typical of a genre that was common in the late fifteenth century, though it is impossible to know for certain.

37. *Vom Tegkendorff das geschicht wie die Juden das hailig sacrament haben zugericht* (Augsburg, 1520); discussed in R. Po-Chia Hsia, *The Myth of Ritual Murder* (New Haven, 1988), pp. 50–56. Another version of the Deggendorf legend is reprinted in Rochus von Lilliencron, *Die historische Volkslieder der Deutschen vom 13. bis 16. Jahrhundert* (Leipzig, 1805), 1:45–48.
38. After years of investigation, neither Steven Sargent nor I have found any evidence that miracle records were ever kept at Bleeding Host sites.

Through a series of cartoonlike images relating the Jewish purchase and torture of the Eucharist, the discovery and execution of the perpetrators, and the expulsion of the Jewish community from Passau, the print retells the events that produced the new pilgrimage. Such images would likely have been bought by literate and illiterate alike, since the simple visual presentation of the Bleeding Host miracle was readily understood and the print's modest cost made it an affordable souvenir of the journey to Passau.

More complex is a broadside (fig. 3) recounting a miracle that occurred in the Upper Bavarian village of Schöffau and was attributed to a Marian statue in the nearby Benedictine abbey of Ettal. Printed in 1517, the anonymous broadside, the text of which was likely created by a brother at the powerful monastery, recounts the story of a child who was lost in the wilds near his village for several days. To aid the search, the child's father prayed to the Virgin, who preserved the boy until he could be rescued. An illustration depicts this rescue and shows the Ettal Virgin and Christ child floating above the Upper Bavarian landscape in which the miracle occurred. Surrounding the image of the Virgin are the names of five Marian pilgrimage sites: Loreto in Italy; Einsiedeln in Switzerland; and Aachen, Altötting, and Ettal in Germany. The accompanying rhymed text tells of the child's preservation and tersely relates the legends of these five sites. By connecting the Ettal abbey with the Virgin's house at Loreto, the angelic shrine at Einsiedeln, and the churches allegedly built by Charlemagne at Aachen and Altötting, this advertisement attempted to lend luster to the less well known Ettal—whose location at the crossroads between these four major Christian sites, notably, marked a crucifix in the earth. At Ettal, too, visitors could see a Marian image revered by the German emperor Louis the Bavarian. To heal the ruler's famous breach with the papacy, a monk had presented Louis with this special Marian image and instructed him to build a monastery to house it. From that date until the present, the publication claimed, the Virgin's presence had served to confer blessing and protection on the region's inhabitants.[39] Thus the terse Schöffau miracle broadside ultimately connected the miracle of the

39. *Von aim grossen wunderzaychen das unser fraw gethan hat vor dem birg in aim dörflin Scheffaw genant nacz bey Etal. Darnach von den vier walfarten wie sy creutzweyß ligen im mittel Etal* (1517); reprinted in *Bayerisches Jahrbuch für Volkskunde*, 1957, p. 157.

child's preservation with a famous event in Bavarian and imperial history: the papal deposition of the flamboyant Wittelsbach emperor Louis. These links, however, remained subtextual; although they would have been obvious to those who read the broadside, they were not made explicit in the work.

In addition to miracle pamphlets, songs, and broadsides, interested parties could turn for a shrine's history to written chronicles, which were also to be found for sale at some late medieval places of pilgrimage. In Bavaria, they survive only from Altötting and Andechs. Both these chronicles tell about the history of the shrine and connect these cults with prominent imperial, noble, and clerical officials. Including information about the church's major relics, indulgences, and endowments, or about the pilgrimage church itself, these works use the tradition of the site—its historical vicissitudes and continued survival—to prove divine blessing.

The oldest of these pilgrimage histories, the *Chronicle of Mt. Andechs,* was first printed around 1473 and had apparently gained a wide readership before the end of the fifteenth century. By 1500, five separate editions of the book had been published.[40] An Upper Bavarian shrine, Andechs had become popular in the late fourteenth century, when a mouse "miraculously" discovered a large cache of relics and three hosts. The author of the Andechs chronicle focused on the dramatic discovery of these sacred objects, but he also delved into the "prehistory" of the shrine, delineating the church's development before it became a widely revered pilgrimage destination.

Created in Carolingian times, the county of Andechs had been blessed with a saintly, noble line of custodians. Avid relic collectors, these counts had endowed ten monasteries in their territory and given them notable relics, each of which the author of the *Chronicle of Mt. Andechs* carefully catalogued. One of the most important

---

40. *Von dem Ursprung und loblichen heyltum auff dem heyligen perg Andechs genant in Obern Bayrn* (Augsburg, 1473). My statements here employ the revised and slightly expanded version published (in two printings) in 1495 under the title *Kronick von dem Hochwirdigen und loblichen heyltum auff dem heyligen perg Andechs genant in Obern Bayrn* (Wessobrunn, 1495). Ludwig Hain also lists another edition printed at Wessobrunn; *Repertorium Bibliographicum* (Leipzig, 1891), no. 970. A. Brackmann provides a full listing of these editions and all the surviving sources for the history of Andechs in "Die Entstehung der Andechserwallfahrt," *Abhandlungen der preussischen Akademie der Wissenschaften* 5 (1929): 3–39.

pious members of this lineage was St. Rasso, who brought back various impressive relics from the Holy Land in the tenth century, installing them in a monastery he endowed on the Amper.

In subsequent centuries, the relic collection of the counts of Andechs continued to grow. Another lineage member, Bishop Otto of Bamberg, acquired an assortment of holy hosts from the saintly Emperor Henry, who in turn had been given the wafers by Pope Leo IX (r. 1049–1054) in hopes of ridding the emperor's lands of plague and warfare. Upon receiving these precious items, Otto, Henry's bishop, had forwarded them to his father for safekeeping in the family's mountaintop fortress. Two of these hosts, significantly, had been consecrated by the early medieval pope Gregory I (r. 590–604), and the third by Pope Leo himself. The Andechs chronicle connected the shrine's hosts to two dramatic eucharistic miracles that had occurred at pontifical masses. At the first, Gregory had performed the sacrament before the Spanish queen Elvira, who doubted the Real Presence of the body of Christ in the Eucharist. During the celebration, a divine light bathed Gregory, and the instruments of Christ's torture, including the crown of thorns, appeared before the mass celebrants; the queen was apparently convinced. Similarly, in the second of these eucharistic miracles, this time at the mass performed by the eleventh-century Pope Leo, the name *Jesus* was made visible in blood on the host, assuring those present of the reality of Christ's presence.

These hosts, together with the counts' relic cache, were sealed in the walls of the family's castle for protection in 1229, during yet another period of imperial warfare. In the subsequent fighting, the mountaintop fortress was largely destroyed; the holy relics, however, remained safe in their hiding place. Later, a church was built on the spot, and the former fortress walls were incorporated into this structure. The relics remained forgotten and neglected until one day in 1388, when a mouse came during mass to the high altar of the church and deposited a parchment scrap identifying some of what lay hidden nearby.

The chronicle then discusses the development of popular devotion at Andechs. A year after the relics were discovered the Wittelsbachs transferred the collection to their capital at Munich, but when "terrifying" signs in and around the city were witnessed, they returned the items to their proper place of devotion on Bavaria's "Holy Mountain." On the night they were reinstalled, an earthquake occurred—clearly a sign. Realizing the power of these items and their place of veneration, the Wittelsbachs anxiously supported the pilgrimage site, securing numerous indulgences for the powerful collection and, in 1451, endowing a monastery there to minister to the faithful. In its conclusion, the Andechs chronicle carefully catalogues the numerous noble and ducal benefactions and indulgences that had been given the cult and lists all the relics housed in the church.[41]

Although the style of the chronicle is terse, lacking extensive commentary or exposition, Andechs emerges in this work as a place to be revered for more than the miracle of the relics' discovery or the ongoing testimony of intercession. Andechs's sanctity, the work made clear, rested on a centuries-long tradition of pious benefaction on the part of Bavaria's nobility and clergy. From time immemorial, the aristocracy and ecclesiastical hierarchy had showered this site with attention, using it to house numerous impressive relics, including the miraculous Eucharists, remains of the Holy Apostles, and even part of the crown of thorns.

Just as the Andechs chronicler made his shrine into an embodiment of imperial history and aristocratic pretensions, so too did the Wittelsbachs' humanist court tutor Johannes Aventinus in his *History of Altötting*. Unlike the Andechs work, however, Aventinus's short book does not treat the later development of this famous pilgrimage site, but is confined to tracing the shrine's early medieval history. Aventinus begins with a long prologue on the history of Bavaria from its settlement after the biblical Flood to the Roman conquest and the barbarian invasions. He then focuses on the conversion of the heathen "Bajuwaren" to Christianity during the sixth-century missions of St. Rupert. After their baptism in the new religion, he reports, two Bavarian dukes, Otto and Dieth, hastily constructed chapels at Regensburg and Oting. From this point, Aventinus restricts his history to the latter locale. It became the burial site for Duke Otto, and in following centuries the German emperors showered the place with numerous benefactions. Destroyed by the Magyars in the tenth century, it was rebuilt and lavished with even more gifts and attentions. It is here, however, that the Bavarian court tutor ends his chronicle, declining to treat

<hr/>

41. *Kronick von dem Hochwirdigen und loblichen heyltum,* p. 23. See also Brackmann, "Entstehung der Andechserwallfahrt," p. 11.

the fifteenth-century development of the pilgrimage except to note in a hasty, one-paragraph conclusion that the site had been subsequently blessed "with special graces and miracles."[42]

Both Aventinus's reluctance to detail the course of the pilgrimage to Altötting in the fifteenth and sixteenth centuries and his concern to mold the chapel into a symbol of ancient German culture and imperial unity were common traits of late medieval humanists. In their hagiographies, the humanists often expunged the traditional testimony of saintly miracles and instead molded the saint's life into an example for pious emulation. Aventinus's account, to be sure, did not deal with the person of a saint but rather with the history of a shrine; nevertheless, he remained reticent to discuss the Virgin's miracles at the site. To rectify a pervasive sense of cultural inferiority, moreover, the German humanists had turned to the ancient tribal past to celebrate the pure virtues of the Germanic tribes vis-à-vis the corruption and decadence of late-imperial Rome. This they did in large part by means of geographical and topographical studies.[43] Aventinus's location of the Virgin of Altötting's cult in the time of the early medieval Bajuwaren, then, was of a piece with his humanist training. Yet whereas the elite circle that likely read his chronicle may have accepted the dark and mysterious tribal origins of the shrine, his historiography likely exercised little force beyond that small group. For the thousands of pilgrims who flocked to the site in the late fifteenth and early sixteenth centuries, the story of Altötting's origins was probably far simpler: although the chapel there was an ancient structure, constructed by Charlemagne, its true significance had been made known only in the late 1400s, when the Virgin began to work miracles there.

Similarly, the narratives outlining the origins of most Bavarian holy places appear to have been far less embellished than either Aventinus's history or the Andechs chronicle. The pretensions of the latter two accounts—their attempts to "prehistoricize" the pilgrimage by linking it to events in ancient and imperial history—

---

42. Johannes Aventinus, *Historia Otingae* (Munich, 1518) and *Der hochwirdigen und weit berumten Stifft Alten Oting loeblich herkommen* (Ingolstadt, 1519); both reprinted in *Sämmtliche Werke* 1:30–59.

43. See Gerald Strauss, *Sixteenth-Century Germany: Its Topography and Topographers* (Madison, Wis., 1959); and James Michael Weiss, "Hagiography by German Humanists, 1483–1516," *Journal of Medieval and Renaissance Studies* 15 (1985): 299–316.

were not shared by the primarily oral tales that justified most devotions. Admittedly, our knowledge of this storytelling culture remains incomplete, but here and there we do garner pieces of evidence that reveal its configurations. The stories told about most pilgrimage sites were more spontaneous and unpredictable than the more imposing chronicle-styled creations. Usually a shrine's legend alleged that at some point in the past the site itself, its saintly image, or its relics had simply begun to work miracles. In late medieval Bavaria, it was the devotion of pilgrims that created places of religious reverence. Thus legends that linked sites to the clerical hierarchy, the nobility, or great events in German and Bavarian history were not necessary to elicit the faithful's piety.

A typical case is that of Tuntenhausen in Upper Bavaria, about which a miracle book published in 1506 relates artlessly that a statue of the Virgin had begun to work miracles one day in the 1440s.[44] In a vision Mary appeared to a suffering woman, looking like she did in a statue that stood on the altar of the Tuntenhausen church. The Virgin's message was that the woman could cure herself by making a series of pilgrimages to that church. From that point a cult developed that was confirmed by subsequent miracles.

When compared to Altötting and Andechs, with their more elaborate histories, Tuntenhausen and similar sites were very much creations ex nihilo, for their spontaneous wonder-working was in itself cultic legitimation. In Bavaria, such places continued to multiply until the Reformation. Thereafter, and largely under the impact of Protestant criticism, Bavaria's clerical promoters would only increase the drama and scope of many of the territory's pilgrimage legends. Like Aventinus and the Andechs chronicler, these men attempted to create a prehistory for religious devotion that explained why one site was revered above others. In addition, they labored persistently to anchor the power to work miracles within the tradition of an "official" Church. In this process of legendary and mythic revision, history, understood as an ongoing narrative that continued to shape the present, was to become the explicit justification for the shrine's miraculous numen.

44. *Hierinn vermerckt ettliche zaichen in unnser lieben frauwen gotzhaus Tuntenhau[sen] angesagt auff aine jeglichen begern verkuendt,* reprinted in Anton Bauer, "Mirakelbuch Tuntenhausen," *Erdkreis* 4 (1954): 345–346.

2

The Reformation Decline of
Pilgrimage

In constructing a history of Germany in the decades immediately preceding the Reformation, scholars have often cited a number of incidents of sudden, mass pilgrimage—to Wilsnack, Niklashausen, Sternberg, Grimmental, Aachen, Trier, and Regensburg—to demonstrate the extent of late medieval piety as well as a pervasive anxiety about salvation in that era.[1] For our portrait of these events we are forced to rely primarily on the accounts of contemporary chroniclers, who as observers can scarcely be considered dispassionate. Their reports, filled with stock topoi, frequently betray their own prejudices toward the pilgrims, rather than providing us with a true picture of the behavior and motivations of the participants. "Common people," they write pejoratively, were suddenly seized with an uncontrollable desire, even compulsion, to see some miraculous new shrine. Forgetting everything, peasants would vacate their fields. Servants shirked their duties, children ran away from their parents, and mothers and fathers abandoned their responsibilities. Underlying the criticisms in these accounts was a profound distrust of both religious enthusiasm and mobility, and the disorders each created.

The Reformation and Counter-Reformation attempted to address these issues by bringing order and a new rationale to lay religious life. For the Protestant reformers who launched their war against idolatry, the "excesses" of popular devotion needed to be expunged. Through persistent denigration and ritualized and sym-

1. Gertrud Rüchlin Teuscher, *Religiöse Volksleben des ausgehenden Mittelalters in den Reichstädten Hall und Heilbronn* (Berlin, 1933), esp. p. 67; Bernd Moeller, "Piety in Germany Around 1500," trans. Joyce Irwin, in *The Reformation in Medieval Perspective,* ed. Steven Ozment (Chicago, 1971), p. 54; Willy Andreas, *Deutschland vor der Reformation. Eine Zeitenwende* (Stuttgart, 1959), pp. 180ff.; J. Lortz, *The Reformation in Germany,* trans. Ronald Walls, vol. 1 (London, 1968), p. 114; and Steven Ozment, *The Reformation in the Cities: The Appeal of Protestantism to Sixteenth-Century Germany and Switzerland* (New Haven, 1975), pp. 38, 67, 77, 83.

bolic inversion, Reformation theologians, preachers, and artists transformed the saints into perverse embodiments of a "false" and even demonic religion. From the perspective of many within the institutional Church as well, the rapid development of sacred sites into immensely popular shrines had long been viewed as problematic. Even when we apply a healthy dose of skepticism to accounts concerning the behavior of pilgrims at late medieval shrines, it still must be allowed that the explosion of cults produced enormous disruptions.

Perhaps the most persistently controversial of Germany's late medieval pilgrimage sites was the Holy Blood shrine at Wilsnack. In 1383 after a marauding knight had attacked and burned this Saxon village, the local priest had discovered in the still-smoldering ashes of the church three unconsumed, blood-flecked hosts. Word spread in the surrounding region, and soon a pilgrimage developed, with several German bishops awarding the nascent cult indulgences. One year later, the pope, too, conferred an indulgence on the devotion to support the building of a larger pilgrimage church. A little more than a decade later, in 1395, the shrine's presiding bishop at Havelberg, recognizing its potential income, incorporated the church into his episcopal household. As a consequence, two-thirds of that income flowed directly into his coffers. This practice was not unusual, but Luther and others attacked it early in the Reformation as an incentive for ecclesiastical officials to encourage "false" pilgrimages.[2]

While reports of dubious miracles and hundreds of hysterical pilgrims visiting the site had circulated as early as 1387, no official investigation of Wilsnack was undertaken until 1405, when the archbishop of Prague dispatched a team of examiners.[3] This com-

---

2. F. A. Riedel, *Codex diplomaticus Brandenburgensis*, vol. 4, pt. 1 (Berlin, 1862), pp. 140–143; Ludwig Meier, "Wilsnack als Spiegel deutscher Vorreformation," in *Zeitschrift für Religions- und Geistegeschichte* 3 (1941): 53–60, esp. p. 54. The oldest recorded version of the Wilsnack legend is from the fifteenth century; it appears in P. Heitz and W. L. Schreiber, *Das Wunderblut zu Wilsnack* (Strasbourg, 1904), pp. 8–9. Luther was among the first reformers to denounce the higher clergy's base financial motives for promoting contemporary pilgrimages; see his *Address to the Christian Nobility of the German Nation* of 1520, in *Luther's Works*, ed. Harold Grimm (Philadelphia, 1955–), 44:185.

3. The earliest reports of strange behavior at the shrine appear in the chronicle of the Riddaghausen monastery, *Chronica*, printed in *Scriptores rerum Brunswicensium*, vol. 2 (Hannover, 1710), p. 81; quoted in Sumption, *Pilgrimage*, p. 350n.282.

mittee, which included the later heretic John Huss, concluded that the miracles publicized at the shrine were fraudulent; the archbishop of Prague responded by forbidding the pilgrimage to those who lived within his archdiocese and commanding his clergy to preach against the shrine at least once a month.[4] One year after his visit to Wilsnack, Huss wrote a treatise, *On the Blood of Christ*, that denounced both that cult and a number of other European eucharistic shrines. Relying on an orthodox Thomistic theology, Huss argued that the existence of blood relics of the Savior was physically impossible because Christ's earthly and divine natures had been hypostatically fused following the Resurrection. Blood relics like those at Wilsnack he denounced as sacrilegious, and their miracles as frauds.[5] Yet although Huss's attack may have resonated well within the Prague archdiocese, it had no impact on the shrine's popularity; Wilsnack continued to draw faithful from throughout Central Europe and as far afield as Scandinavia and England.[6]

The general tolerance accorded the cult outside the archdiocese of Prague began to change in 1412, when the archbishop of Magdeburg, metropolitan of the province in which Wilsnack was located, ordered his own investigation. His team, like the Prague visitors before them, reported that the majority of the pilgrims at Wilsnack were poor and that they frequently displayed hysterical behavior at the shrine. Many fell into ecstatic fits, shouting, "Help me, Holy Blood" or "Free me, Blood of Christ." Further, the archbishop's investigators charged that because the pilgrims were unaware of the theological complexities involved, Wilsnack led them into error. The shrine gave them the opportunity to venerate the corporeal blood on the hosts, a heresy again because of the hypostatic union of Christ's earthly and divine natures. An archdiocesan synod discussed the investigators' report and, although it considered suppressing the pilgrimage, settled on the less controversial option of merely condemning it. Despite other unsuccessful attempts to prohibit the pilgrimage, Wilsnack survived, growing even more popular in the second half of the fifteenth century.[7]

4. *Concilia Pragensia, 1353–1413*, ed. C. Höfler (Prague, 1862), p. 47.
5. The tract is reprinted in Jan Huss, *Opera Omnia*, ed. Wenzel Flajhans (Osnabrück, 1966), vol. 1, sec. 3.
6. Sumption, *Pilgrimage*, p. 283.
7. Ibid. The dispute over Wilsnack subsided until 1446, when the clergy at the shrine applied to Rome for an additional indulgence. Irritated by this move, the

This upswing in popularity climaxed in the wake of a series of children's pilgrimages to the site in 1475. Reminiscent of similar events, especially the notorious juvenile processions to Mont-Saint-Michel that had commenced from South Germany in 1456, these journeys to Wilsnack were criticized for their disruptiveness.[8] Groups of youths making their way along the route to the shrine were greeted alternately with horror and enthusiasm. Even as town authorities tried to force the children to disband and return home, others interpreted the processions as a sign of divine grace and aided the participants. By the summer of 1475, the traffic to the shrine was thick as hundreds of peasants, vagabonds, and day workers joined the youthful bands. At towns along the way, late medieval chroniclers tell us, the processions were often greeted as a kind of plague. At Erfurt, for example, the town locked its gates to the approaching pilgrims, refusing to fulfill the traditional Christian duty of providing the travelers with food and lodging. Yet even though the town council prohibited its own youth from joining the processions, one chronicler recorded that 310 children left the city.[9]

Despite the hyperbole that marked the written accounts, it must be admitted that events like these would be bound to result in a degree of chaos. As the ranks of faithful making their way to a shrine suddenly swelled, they passed through towns and villages ill prepared to provide food and accommodation. Yet an increase in poverty and the landless was also beginning to afflict Germany in

archbishop of Magdeburg decided to act decisively against the shrine and sent another commission to Wilsnack to investigate. This team reported much the same findings as the commission of 1412: through skillful preaching and crowd handling, thousands were being manipulated into believing in the power of the fraudulent relics. These findings were taken to a provincial synod presided over by Nicholas of Cusa, who looked with general disfavor on eucharistic pilgrimages. Cusa's synod forbade the devotion. One year later the bishop of Havelberg and the Brandenburg elector Friedrich II were excommunicated for not enforcing the decree; they appealed their case to Nicholas V. The pope permitted the pilgrimage to be revived, but with the stipulation that a fresh consecrated host be placed alongside the blood-flecked ones. See Ernst Breest, "Das Wunderblut zu Wilsnack (1388–1552): quellenmässige Darstellung seiner Geschichte," *Märkische Forschungen* 16 (1881): 242–301; and Meier, "Wilsnack als Spiegel deutscher Vorreformation."

8. Ulrich Gäbler, "Die Kinderwallfahrten aus Deutschland und der Schweiz zum Mont-Saint-Michel, 1456–1459," *Zeitschrift für schweizerische Kirchengeschichte* 63 (1969): 221–223.

9. *Konrad Stolles Thüringisch-Erfurtische Chronik*, ed. L. F. Hesse, published as vol. 32 of *Bibliothek des Literarischen Vereins in Stuttgart*, 1854, pp. 128ff.; and Matthias Döring, *Chronica*, reprinted in Riedel, *Codex diplomaticus Brandenburgensis*, pp. 248ff.

the late fifteenth century. In discussing Wilsnack and other mass pilgrimages, commentators sometimes linked the surge in these cults' popularity with the generally hard economic times. Referring to the pilgrims as "common people" or "the poor," chroniclers drew explicit connections among bad harvests, dearth, and the episodic outbreak of "pilgrimage fever." In an anonymous tract about the Wilsnack pilgrimage of 1475, one writer charged that this journey provided those suffering the effects of the recent famine the generally more attractive possibility of begging for food among strangers:

> For the days are very long and empty of things to do, and many are driven to pilgrimage for lack of bread to eat . . . having no bread, and being too poor to stay with friends or neighbors, they were ashamed to go begging near their own homes. And so they decided to go on this pilgrimage and beg in each town along the route, reckoning that it was better to beg in a strange district than from people they knew.[10]

This writer then associated the onset of famine directly with the rise of the shrine's popularity: Wilsnack provided for many a way of earning a living through begging on the pious journey. We will never know for certain how widespread such a practice was, yet begging remained a widely respected act of ascetic devotion in late medieval Germany. Certainly, not all who begged along the route to Wilsnack did so because of need. As a sign of apostolic poverty, the begging of alms remained a sacrificial act that many believed made their journeys more pleasing in the eyes of God.[11]

Those who commented on phenomena like Wilsnack certainly feared the pilgrims' dispossession and poverty. Given the proper catalyst, they likely reasoned, such events might easily erupt into rebellions in demand of social reform. In the late fifteenth century—even as the ranks of pilgrims making their way to shrines like Wilsnack swelled dramatically—rural revolts were on the rise in

10. Translated and reprinted by Jonathan Sumption in *Pilgrimage*, p. 284; quoted from W. Wattenbach, "Beiträge zur Geschichte der Mark Brandenburg aus Handschriften der Königlichen Bibliothek," *Sitzungsberichte der Königlich Preussischen Akademie der Wissenschaften*, 1882, pp. 605–607.

11. Richard Andree, *Votive und Weihegaben des katholischen Volks in Süddeutschland. Ein Beitrag zur Volkskunde* (Braunschweig, 1904), p. 33; Georg Schreiber, "Strukturwandel der Wallfahrt," in *Wallfahrt und Volkstum* (Düsseldorf, 1934), p. 88; Stahl, "Die Wallfahrt zur Schönen Maria," pp. 153ff.; and Dieter Harmening, "Fränkische Mirakelbücher: Quellen und Untersuchungen zur historischen Volkskunde und Geschichte," *Würzburger Diözesangeschichtsblätter* 28 (1966): 102.

many parts of Germany. Protesting the imposition of new feudal duties and generally unattractive kinds of tenure, peasant rebels sometimes looked to Mary and the saints as their patrons.

The fear that an underlying kinship could exist between mass pilgrimages and rural revolts was bolstered by the processions to Niklashausen that began in 1476. Since the mid–fourteenth century, this tiny village in the Tauber Valley of Franconia had been home to a small Marian cult.[12] An indulgence awarded the church at that time had granted those who visited the site the same rewards as the Roman pilgrimage. During Lent of 1476, an itinerant shepherd, Hans Behem, arrived at Niklashausen and began to preach a world-renouncing and anticlerical message. On the surface, the shepherd's sermons initially resembled those of John of Capistrano, who had conducted preaching missions in Franconia during the 1450s. Into the asceticism typical of many fifteenth-century preachers, however, Behem soon wove strands of apocalypticism, anticlericalism, and social rebellion. Attacking the corruption of Rome, the pope and his officials, and to a lesser degree the emperor and the German princes, the shepherd of Niklashausen voiced the demands of rural revolts both past and future. He called for the woods, streams, and pastures to be made free for all and for the tithe to be abolished—a message that was, he said, confirmed by a steady stream of Marian apparitions. The Virgin, he alleged, had told him that more grace was to be found in the tiny Tauber Valley than in all the churches of Rome. Warning that the Apocalypse was close at hand, she was calling on the faithful to journey to Niklashausen to prevent the wrath of God from being unleashed on the world.[13]

By the summer of 1476, all reports reckoned the number visiting Niklashausen in the thousands.[14] Even if these figures are exaggerated, they do indicate that Behem's message had a widespread appeal in the surrounding region. First drawing its participants from the rural hamlets of the Tauber Valley proper, the new pilgrimage quickly reached areas more distant, and within a short time the

---

12. Klaus Arnold, *Niklashausen, 1476. Quellen und Untersuchungen zur sozial-religiösen Bewegung des Hans Behem und zur Agrarstruktur eines spätmittelalterlichen Dorfes* (Baden-Baden, 1980).

13. Ibid., pp. 93–113.

14. Ibid., p. 61.

agrarian population was augmented by city dwellers from Würzburg, Nuremberg, and other towns. That summer, territorial, ecclesiastical, and urban leaders throughout South Germany repeatedly—and ineffectively—prohibited their subjects from visiting the site.[15] As the pilgrimage continued gathering strength, the bishop of Würzburg reacted decisively by having Behem captured, imprisoned, and burned at the stake, and his ashes scattered in the Main. To clinch the matter, the small Marian church at Niklashausen was torn down to insure that no residual devotion persisted.[16]

A popular preacher like Behem was enough of a catalyst to develop a small, preexisting cult into a phenomenon bordering on full-scale revolt. A steady stream of visions and miracles, moreover, had validated this preacher's social revolutionary message. Frequently, those who reported about mass pilgrimages such as Niklashausen recognized the role that miracles played in creating and sustaining these events, and their accounts resound with attacks on people's credulity. People, they state, were impressionable, gullible, and able to believe in any and all kinds of wonders. The Thuringian chronicler Konrad Stolle, for instance, wrote that when pilgrims on the way to Wilsnack were asked why they were journeying to the shrine they responded that they had to go "there where there was a great miracle." But when asked what the Holy Blood of Wilsnack was, they did not know, except that it was miraculous. Chroniclers and contemporary critics reported that when people heard of miracles a sudden, uncontrollable desire to visit the wondrous place would simply seize them.[17]

In Bavaria, although the cult of the saints was increasing to new heights of popularity in the fifteenth and early sixteenth centuries, pilgrimage was at the same time a source of controversy for ecclesiastical officials. Sanctity could multiply in ways unacceptable to the "official" Church, and spontaneous wonder-working could develop previously insignificant places into popular destinations. In

---

15. Ibid., pp. 68ff.
16. Ibid., pp. 11ff.
17. " . . . Unnd die frawen trugen sie mete unnd wusten ouch nicht, was das heilige blud was, unnd wusten ouch nicht, was sie taten. Unnd das sie sust nirgen anders hin lieffen, danne da hin, das was eyn gross wunder" (*Stolles Thüringisch-Erfurtische Chronik*, p. 130). The charge was legion. See Arnold, *Niklashausen*, pp. 188–289; Stahl, "Die Wallfahrt zur Schönen Maria," pp. 59–80; "Wilhelm Rems Chronica neuer Geschichten," in *Die Chroniken der deutschen Städte* (Leipzig, 1862–1931), 25:131.

1417, for example, a healing spring issued from the earth outside a Marian chapel in the Lower Bavarian village of Laberberg. When its waters were discovered to possess curative powers, local peasants, artisans, nobles, and even a Lower Bavarian duke visited the site to bathe in its flow. Assessing the revered spring a "superstition and an idolatry," the bishop of Regensburg soon investigated. He prohibited the cult, and when his decrees went disregarded, he threatened those who continued to journey there with excommunication. Finally, his emissaries filled in the spring and boarded up the adjacent chapel.[18] In their continuing efforts to prohibit such unsanctioned cults, Regensburg's bishops also forbade the construction of churches, chapels, and altars that had not been approved, their cornerstones laid by the bishop, and their space ritually consecrated. Yet the frequent repetition of these ordinances leads us to conclude that the diocese's officials were never particularly effective in curbing the proliferation of unsanctioned shrines.

In the first quarter of the sixteenth century, the problem persisted. During the 1510s and 1520s, for example, the suffragan of Regensburg, Peter Krafft, collected new revenues for the diocese by touring town and countryside and consecrating the altars, chapels, and churches that had been constructed in previous generations. In months spent on the road in Bavaria and in neighboring Bohemia, Kraft journeyed with no other purpose than to perform the official Church's rite of consecration. The detailed records that he left behind in his diaries testify to the virtual powerlessness of the clerical hierarchy to define the development of cult. The Church could do little more than add its stamp of approval—the consecration—as an after-the-fact legitimation to devotions and churches already in existence.[19]

Such a conclusion is true for all of Bavaria's dioceses. Clearly, from the perspective of the Church hierarchy, the multiplication of unsanctioned shrines and cults was a problem.[20] Yet even when a

18. The incident is described in Johannes Aventinus's *Baierischer Chronik*, in *Sämmtliche Werke* 4:591.
19. Karl Schottenloher (ed.), *Die Tagebuchaufzeichnungen des Regensburger Weihbischofs Dr. Peter Krafft* (Münster, 1920). Concerning the Regensburg bishops' attempts to define cult in the later Middle Ages, see also Josef Staber, *Kirchengeschichte des Bistums Regensburgs* (Regensburg, 1966).
20. See Charles Zika's remarks in "Hosts, Processions, and Pilgrimages: Controlling the Sacred in Fifteenth-Century Germany," *Past and Present*, no. 118 (February 1988): 25–64; and Staber, *Volksfrömmigkeit und Wallfahrtswesen*, p. 40.

new devotion enjoyed "official" validation, lay reverence could quickly overwhelm the clergy's ability to influence and control it. At Regensburg in the years after 1519, a new cult inspired the most amplified chorus of criticisms of any late medieval mass pilgrimage. The shrine, however, had initially enjoyed the approval of the Regensburg bishop, who laid its cornerstone and consecrated the modest wooden structure hurriedly thrown up to accommodate the pilgrims who flocked to the site. Soon, however, his enthusiasm waned, and he, along with numerous Reformation critics, denounced the cult.

The sudden outpouring of devotion in Regensburg during the years from 1519 to 1525 arose from a bitter legacy of dispute between the city's Christians and Jews, who functioned as interdependent yet distinct communities. In Regensburg as in other German cities, the emperor owned the regalian rights over resident Jews, a fact that granted the group a certain autonomy from local control. In the course of the fifteenth century, the city's economy had declined severely as trade routes shifted in the region. Regensburg's Jews, who had formerly been responsible for dispensing long-distance imperial financial responsibilities, now found their livelihood more circumscribed within the town walls: by the end of the century, they had become primarily lenders and pawnbrokers to the Regensburg populace, serving the city's petty nobility, small merchants, artisans, and lower clergy. In an increasingly impoverished and bleak economy, the town council often heard bitter complaints about the Jews, and in 1478 these tensions had erupted into a protracted ritual-murder trial involving several members of the Jewish community. During the lengthy proceedings the town council tried unsuccessfully to secure the emperor's permission to expel the Jews, and afterward an undercurrent of suspicion and hatred persisted.[21]

21. Concerning the Jews' economic activities in Regensburg in the later Middle Ages, see Wilhelm Volkert, "Die spätmittelalterliche Judengemeinde in Regensburg," *Schriftenreihe der Universität Regensburg* 5 (1981): 135–138. The ritual murder trial is discussed in Hsia, *Myth of Ritual Murder*, pp. 66–85; Raphael Straus, *Die Judengemeinde in Regensburg im ausgehenden Mittelalter* (Heidelberg, 1932), pp. 44, 49ff.; and Peter Herde, "Gestaltung und Krisis des christlich-jüdischen Verhältnisses in Regensburg am Ende des Mittelalters," in *Zeitschrift für bayerische Landesgeschichte* 22 (1959): 381–383. The longterm effects of the ritual murder trial are also examined in Straus, *Die Judengemeinde,* pp. 32ff.; and Leonhard Theobald, *Die Reformationsge-*

In 1516, relations between the Christians and Jews of Regensburg again worsened with the arrival of the preacher Balthasar
Hubmayer in the city. Educated at Ingolstadt in the period of the
Reuchlin controversy over the study of Hebraic texts, Hubmayer
shared the violent anti-Semitism of his mentor, Johannes Eck.[22] In
his sermons as cathedral preacher, Hubmayer dealt at great length
with Jewish crimes, recounting stories of ritual murders of Christian
children, desecrations of the host, and numerous insults against the
Virgin. For three years he used his pulpit to excite latent hatred and
fears, urging burghers once again to approach the town council and
request the Jews' expulsion. In January 1519, in the interregnum
following Emperor Maximilian I's death, the council recognized an
opportunity, and it evicted the Jews, allowing them only five days
to pack up or sell their belongings. In order to prevent their return
should the new emperor reverse their action, the council decided to
raze the ghetto and on the site of the former synagogue erect a
Marian chapel. For this there was ample precedent: Nuremberg,
Bamberg, Würzburg, and Rothenburg ob der Tauber were just a few
of the South German cities in which Marian chapels had been built
on the sites of former ghettos.[23]

Once the expulsion was complete, the Regensburg council employed laborers to demolish the ghetto. During the destruction of
the synagogue, however, part of the roof collapsed, and a mason
named Jacob Kern was buried beneath a pile of rubble. When his

---

schichte der Reichstadt Regensburg, in Einzelarbeiten aus der Kirchengeschichte Bayerns 19 (Munich, 1936), 1:37.

22. Hubmayer was recommended for the Regensburg position of cathedral
preacher by Eck and maintained a close relationship with him after arriving in
Regensburg; see Theobald, *Reformationsgeschichte der Reichstadt Regensburg* 1:39–40.
The "Reuchlin Affair" began in 1509 as a disagreement between Johann Pfefferkorn
and Johann Reuchlin, who were both imperial commissioners charged with inspecting the works of Jews for possible blasphemies. Reuchlin supported preservation
and study of Jewish texts, while Pfefferkorn advocated their destruction. In the
resulting struggle Reuchlin was defended by Germany's humanists, while the Franciscans and Dominicans came to the aid of Pfefferkorn. The controversy is reviewed
in some detail in James H. Overfeld, *Humanism and Scholasticism in Late Medieval
Germany* (Princeton, 1984), pp. 247–297; and Heiko A. Oberman, *Die Wurzeln des
Antisemitismus. Christenangst und Judenplage im Zeitalter von Humanismus und Reformation* (Berlin, 1981), pp. 35ff.

23. Stahl, "Die Wallfahrt zur Schönen Maria," pp. 57–58; Herde, "Gestaltung
und Krisis," pp. 373ff.; and Theobald, *Reformationsgeschichte der Reichstadt Regensburg*
1:39–40.

fellow workers cleared the rocks away, they discovered Kern with blood flowing from his mouth, nose, and ears. He was rushed to his bed and prepared for death, whereupon his wife began praying to Mary, vowing to take his place at the work site if he would be spared. "Immediately," Regensburg's first printed miracle book tells us, Kern recovered and told the group assembled that the Virgin had appeared to comfort him in his unconsciousness.[24] That afternoon Kern's wife went off to help in the demolition of the ghetto, to be joined in a few days by Jacob himself.

As word of Kern's miraculous recovery spread throughout Regensburg, volunteers from every layer of the town—including even the aristocratic canons and the bishop of Regensburg cathedral—joined in the work of razing the synagogue and ghetto. Inspired by their example, one chronicler reported, hundreds of peasants flocked in from the surrounding countryside to cart away the rubble.[25] Thanks to the workers' fervor, the site was quickly cleared and a wooden shrine constructed, which the Regensburg bishop soon consecrated.

Even during the demolition work, a bizarre and carnivalesque atmosphere reigned. One day a group of patrician women proceeded to the site behind a banner emblazoned with the Virgin's image. For several hours they helped cart away stones before turning their attention to the synagogue's cemetery. After tearing down its stone wall and ripping up its tombstones, the women set a herd of pigs to forage through the graves. The tombstones, however, they conscientiously stacked and saved, to be used as the foundation for the future Marian chapel.[26]

Initially the cathedral preacher Hubmayer, Regensburg's bishop,

24. In dysem buchlein seind begriffen die wunderbarlichen zaychen, beschehen zu Regenspurg zu der schoenen Maria der mutter gottes (Nuremberg, 1519), fols. ai(v)–aii(r).
25. "Leonhard Widmanns Chronik von Regensburg," in Chroniken der deutschen Städte 15:31.
26. Stahl, "Die Wallfahrt zur Schönen Maria," p. 63; Theobald, Reformationsgeschichte der Reichstadt Regensburg 1:53ff.; and Carl Theodor Gemeiner, Reichstadt Regensburgische Chronik, ed. Heinz Angermeier, 2d ed. (Munich, 1971), 3:363–365. Ostofrancus, a Benedictine at St. Emmeram's monastery in Regensburg, described the excitement of those who attended the demolition: "Die weil die Synagog iesst zerbrochen war, was das Vorhaben eine Kirche darauff bauen, darum ein solches Arbeiten war von Geistlichen und Weltliche, das unglaublich ist, je einen Tag 3 oder 4,000 Menschen; so schwarkert 4 oder 500 Wagen, die Koth ausfuhrten. Es was schier jedermann toll. Man spricht aber omne ranem carem; vilescit quotidianum" (Gemeiner, Regensburgische Chronik 3:363–364).

and the town council all cooperated to stimulate the cult among burghers and people from the surrounding vicinity. Hubmayer's influence in particular over the cult's early development is detectable in the choice of the chapel's appellation, "Fair Mary" (Schöne Maria), which not only connected Regensburg's Madonna with the triumphalist doctrines of the Immaculate Conception, but also harmonized with the preacher's personal attacks on the Jewish community for their numerous slanders against the Virgin. The title Fair Mary, then, emphasized both the Madonna's purity and her victory over Jewish detraction.[27]

In addition, the dedicatory name Church of the Fair Mary linked the Regensburg shrine with two other famous Marian churches in the adjacent duchy of Bavaria: the Church of Our Fair Lady (Unsere Schöne Frauenkirche) in Ingolstadt and the shrine of Our Lady in Altötting. Indeed, more than just names linked the three sites. Until 1509, a famous golden statue known as the "Fair Mary" had been housed in the Church of Our Fair Lady in Ingolstadt, having come to that church's treasury through a medieval marriage alliance between the Wittelsbach dukes and the French crown. Part of a collection of jewels and regalia known as the "French Treasure," this "Fair Mary" had been pledged to the Altötting canons by the duke of Bavaria-Landshut as security for loans he received during the civil war of 1503–1505. When the duke lost the war, the Altötting canons' hopes of retrieving their money vanished, and in 1509 they claimed their collateral. The "Fair Mary" remained at Altötting for almost three centuries, the most famous and valuable item in the church's possession.[28] Hubmayer had been a student in Ingolstadt during this period and had served for a time as parish priest in the Church of Our Fair Lady. In choosing the appellation for the shrine at Regensburg, the preacher lent his chapel luster by connecting it with a famous object and two already-distinguished sanctuaries.

27. Similarly titled churches are found in medieval France and England. See Stahl, "Die Wallfahrt zur Schönen Maria," pp. 57–58; Stephen Beissel, *Wallfahrten zu Unserer Lieben Frau in Legende und Geschichte* (Freiburg i. B., 1918), p. 108; and Theobald, *Reformationsgeschichte der Reichstadt Regensburg* 1:39ff.
28. Theobald, *Reformationsgeschichte der Reichstadt Regensburg* 1:58; and Stahl, "Die Wallfahrt zur Schönen Maria," pp. 57–58. An inventory conducted in 1782 (shortly before the "Fair Mary" was melted down during the conflicts resulting from the French Revolution) listed the value of the entire "French Treasure" at 41,800 florins; see König, *Weihegaben an U.L. Frau von Altötting* 1:21.

For Hubmayer, the development of a popular pilgrimage within the Regensburg town walls validated the religious truth of his anti-Jewish message. And while the town council certainly shared his prejudices, a number of very practical benefits derived from their decision to transform the site of the former ghetto into a place of religious devotion. Because the expulsion of the Jews had been blatantly illegal, a shrine, especially one confirmed by numerous miracles beyond the original one of Jacob Kern's recovery, vindicated their unlawful action in the name of divine authority. During the first three years of the cult's existence, church scribes assiduously recorded more than seven hundred intercessions;[29] these were then published in multiple editions and sold at the chapel under the auspices of the town council. In addition, the development of a long-term successful pilgrimage promised the enormous benefit of helping to revive the town's sagging economy.

The civic and religious boosterism of Hubmayer and the city fathers soon bore fruit. Indeed, the pace at which the cult grew was astonishing. The miracle of Jacob Kern's recovery had occurred at the end of February 1519, and on March 25 the modest wooden chapel was completed. By June, the Regensburg council had secured a papal indulgence complete with the signatures of twenty-five cardinals. And in less than half a year's time, the Church of the Fair Mary had become one of the most popular pilgrimage sites in South Germany. By September—that is, in the six months following the church's consecration—seventy-four miracles had been reported. Even more amazing was the number of masses that were said during this time: a total of 3,684, or an average of 25 each day. In the first three years of the pilgrimage's existence this daily average decreased only slightly, to approximately 23, with a total of 25,374. The desire of visiting priests to say mass at one of the chapel's altars was said to be so intense that one would begin reciting the service before another was finished. Reports of chaos within the chapel were abundant.[30]

---

29. Stahl includes precise details concerning the printing of the Regensburg miracle books in "Die Wallfahrt zur Schönen Maria," pp. 98–100.

30. A copy of the original indulgence letter is in the collection of the Staatliche Bibliothek Regensburg, Rat. civ. 475. It is also reprinted in Thomas Ried, *Codex chronologico-diplomaticus Episcopatus Ratisbonensis* (Regensburg, 1816), 2:398–399. The indulgence was for one hundred days. The figures regarding masses are appended

Not only priests, but droves of lay pilgrims as well clamored to see the new shrine, their numbers swelling most dramatically on those feast days when an indulgence was available at the church. On Pentecost in 1520, for example, one report estimated that twenty-seven thousand people were in attendance, and that same year on St. George's Day the count was set at fifty thousand.[31] Although early modern chroniclers are commonly accepted as having dramatically overestimated such figures, these estimates may ring more true than modern scholars are willing to admit. After the pilgrimage began, the Regensburg town council commissioned the minting of a commemorative medallion to be sold to pilgrims as souvenirs. Used as amulets against bad weather, the pain of childbirth, and disease, medallions like these were common devotional items at many late medieval German shrines. In 1519 alone, the town council at Regensburg sold more than 12,000 of these objects, and the following year the total climbed to almost 120,000.[32] Given the pattern of particularly heavy pilgrimage traffic on special feast days, these sales figures for medallions suggest that reports of twenty-five thousand, even fifty-thousand people visiting the church on a single day may not be exaggerated.

As attendance climbed, the same reports of abuses and excesses alleged at Wilsnack and Niklashausen began to circulate. Besides the standard complaint that people abruptly dropped all duties to run off to the Regensburg shrine, a variety of enthusiastic and sometimes hysterical behaviors at the chapel were cited as well: of pilgrims who fell suddenly before the statue of the Virgin that stood outside the shrine, prostrating themselves with outstretched arms before it or falling into hysterical fits; of those who danced in groups around the image. Although the prostrate posture was a routinized way of conducting prayers in the late Middle Ages, at least one chronicler reported that at Regensburg, the faithful fell before the

---

to the miracle books published by the Regensburg town council; see Achim Hubel, "Die Schöne Maria von Regensburg, Wallfahrten-Gnadenbilder-Ikonographie," in *850 Jahre Kollegiatstift zu den heiliger Johannes Baptist und Johannes Evangelist in Regensburg, 1127–1927*, ed. Paul Mai (Munich, 1977), p. 202; and Stahl, "Die Wallfahrt zur Schönen Maria," pp. 66ff.

31. "Wilhelm Rems Chronica neuer Geschichten," in *Chroniken der deutschen Städte* 25:132; "Leonhard Widmanns Chronik von Regensburg," ibid., 15:34.

32. Hubel, "Die Schöne Maria von Regensburg," p. 202.

Madonna "as if they had been struck by lightning."[33] Some pilgrims reported apparitions in which the Virgin had assured them that their pilgrimage had freed some family member—father, mother, brother, or sister—from purgatory. Many arrived at the shrine with their work tools still in hand, a sign in some chroniclers' eyes that they were "bewitched." Although the giving of tools as votive gifts was a common practice in medieval rural society, symbolizing the votant through his or her occupation, in reports of the Regensburg pilgrimage the presence of tools became one more proof of the "false" and even diabolic inspiration of the cult.[34]

As at Niklashausen, apocalyptic sentiment was also present at Regensburg, with at least one preacher rising to speak of the world's impending doom. To ward off this imminent event, he commanded his audience to leave behind their hair for the Virgin as a gift.[35] To stop such unsolicited preaching and dampen religious enthusiasm at the site, the Regensburg town council soon enlisted Hubmayer and several monastic orders to circulate in the crowds and provide reassurance. In addition, they hired workers to carry away those who had fainted to places where they could be revived. Despite these precautions, outbreaks of enthusiasm continued to occur, unstoppable by Hubmayer and the other clergy at the shrine.[36]

We will never know whether these accounts are a faithful testimony to what transpired in the city's former ghetto. But the reports that appeared in contemporary historical chronicles and the pamphlets of the early Reformation certainly repeated many of the same criticisms and formulaic accusations regarding late medieval mass pilgrimages. In the case of Regensburg, spread of the shrine's reputation as a host of "pilgrimage fever" seems to have been aided in

33. Sebastian Franck, *Chronica, Zeitbuch unnd Geschichtsbibell von anbegyn biss in dis gegenwertig M.D. XXXVI Jar verlengt* . . . (Ulm, 1536), fol. CCLX; on prostration with outstretched arms as a common way to conduct prayers, see L. A. Veit, *Volksfrommes Brauchtum und Kirche im deutschen Mittelalter* (Freiburg i. B., 1926), p. 20.

34. G. Stahl, "Die Wallfahrt zur Schönen Maria," pp. 69ff., 153ff. On the giving of tools as votive gifts, see Andree, *Votive und Weihegaben*, p. 33; Schreiber, "Strukturwandel der Wallfahrt," p. 88; and Harmening, "Fränkische Mirakelbücher," p. 102.

35. The choice of hair as a votive gift for the Virgin may appear strange, but in late medieval Germany hair was believed to be the seat of the soul; see Hanns Bächtold-Stäubli, *Handwörterbuch des deutschen Aberglaubens* (Berlin-Leipzig, 1927–1937), s.v. "Haar."

36. Stahl, "Die Wallfahrt zur Schönen Maria," pp. 69ff.

part by the Regensburg artist Michael Ostendorfer, who in 1520
published a print of the event that was widely disseminated (fig. 4).
Flying atop the humble Church of the Fair Mary in this picture is a
banner emblazoned with an image of the Virgin and child and the
crossed keys of St. Peter, seal of the city of Regensburg and symbol
of the town council's patronage of the chapel. On either side of the
church the last remnants of the Jewish ghetto can still be seen. Two
processions approach from the right, one of priests and monks, the
other of women. A third group nears from the left, scythes and
sickles rising from the crowded mass. These bands, however, must
stop outside the chapel because of the crush of pilgrims within. In
the print's foreground, another large group, also waiting to enter
the sanctuary, directs its attention to the stone statue of the Virgin
standing in the square. Elevated on a pedestal, Mary holds the
Christ child in one hand and a scepter in the other, a symbol of her
role as the immaculately conceived "Queen of Heaven." Pilgrims
clamor at her feet, some writhing in fits, others prostrating themselves on the ground in prayer.

Such a throng left behind a flood of offerings, including money,
wax, clothing, grain, and livestock. Soon after the pilgrimage commenced, the stock of gifts had grown so vast that the town council
provided Hubmayer with one still-standing Jewish house to use as
a store. From this location, donations that were not needed for the
upkeep of the chapel and its clergy were resold, and the proceeds
saved for the building of a larger vaulted church. By 1525, over
thirty thousand gulden had been collected for this purpose.[37]

Both Hubmayer and the town council had anxiously desired a
successful devotion, yet soon after the processions to their city
commenced the cult appeared a mixed blessing. Not only was the
outpouring of religious enthusiasm at the shrine disturbing, but the
town's preexistent sacred economy and its relations with the resident bishop were also being disrupted by the Fair Mary's success.
The new Marian devotion soon displaced older, more established
shrines in Regensburg, most notably one at the grave of St. Erhard
located in the Lower Münster, an ancient imperial cloister. To preserve their devotion, the Franciscan preachers at the church commissioned a Marian statue and installed it beside the body of Erhard

37. Ibid., p. 79.

to lure pilgrims to the church. Meanwhile, the cloister preacher denounced the shrine of the Fair Mary as an abomination. In his sermons he warned that pilgrims should not seek out the Virgin at the "stinking hole" of the new chapel, since Mary is present everywhere; only within the Lower Münster, however, could the faithful find the body of St. Erhard preserved intact.[38] Yet despite ingenious arguments like these, the Fair Mary's cult continued to grow. The rising tide of pilgrims making their way to Regensburg's former ghetto had introduced the specter of competition into the town's religious life.

The Fair Mary's success also exacerbated long-standing disputes between the town's council and its bishop. It was customary in the later Middle Ages to forward at least a quarter and sometimes as much as a third of the income from pilgrimages to the presiding bishop. Because the town council had acted on its own to expel the Jews and seize their property, it now claimed all rights of patronage over the new church. As early as 1519, their decision to withhold the bishop's customary share of the shrine's income caused a legal dispute that ground on until 1525. It was in these years, prompted in part by the controversies and chaos the Fair Mary caused, that support grew in the council for the evangelical doctrines of the early Reformation.

In the midst of these squabbles, in 1522, Regensburg's councilors approached Luther and requested him to send an evangelical advisor who would aid them in their efforts to reform the local Church and in their ongoing disputes with the bishop. Responding to their inquiry in 1523, Luther stipulated that the destruction of the Fair Mary was an essential prerequisite if Regensburgers desired religious reform. Three years earlier, in 1520, the reformer had already included the Fair Mary in a long list of "devilish" churches that should be razed.[39] Now, when writing to the town council in 1523, he was even more insistent about the devil's role in the cult's creation. After the expulsion of the Jews, he charged, Satan had seized the site of the former ghetto, working false miracles there in

38. Gemeiner, *Regensburgische Chronik* 4:417–418; and Staatsministerium für Unterricht und Kultus, Bavaria, ed., *Die Kunstdenkmäler von Bayern*, 2d ser., 2d ed. (Munich, 1949–), 22:174.

39. Martin Luther, *Address to the Christian Nobility of the German Nation*, in *Luther's Works* 44:185.

the name of the Virgin to deceive the simple. To allow the pilgrimage to continue to prosper, or even to exist, was consequently to aid the devil in his ongoing conjurations at the site.[40]

By 1523, many in Regensburg and in Bavaria appeared ready to agree with Luther's assessment. An outbreak of the plague in the town late in 1521 had already sent the pilgrimage into decline. And although the traffic persisted throughout 1522 and 1523, the numbers had fallen off from the heyday of 1519–1521. By 1525, the shrine was drawing only scattered remnants of the faithful. In the dioceses of South Germany, conservative bishops had forbidden their laity from journeying to the Fair Mary, and in places as distant as Dinkelsbühl and Augsburg preachers actively denounced the cult. Even within Regensburg, the reform-minded now spoke out openly against the pilgrimage.[41]

When assessing the Fair Mary, everyone seemed to agree that it was a "false" cult, yet the pilgrimage's brief life had coincided with the beginning of the Reformation. In these years, the Protestant Reformers worked to popularize their radical critique of late medieval worship and saintly devotion. Although the shrine's pilgrimage evaporated quickly in the wake of the new evangelical doctrines, the Reformation's ongoing war against idolatry was to lend the Regensburg Fair Mary and other mass pilgrimage sites a lingering, if dubious, notoriety. Each of the major intellectual leaders of the early Reformation—Martin Luther, Ulrich Zwingli, Martin Bucer, Heinrich Bullinger, and Andreas Karlstadt—rose in turn to attack pilgrimage, the cult of the saints, and late medieval worship practices generally. They were united in their distaste for shrines like those at Regensburg, yet each advanced varying reasons and motivations for expunging these devotions.[42]

For Luther, people's habit of "running off" to sites like the Church of the Fair Mary was unseemly, a waste of time and money. Pilgrimages sapped society's resources, and because they were intricately linked to the trade in indulgences, they sponsored "false"

---

40. "Luther an Bürgermeister und Rat der Stadt Regensburg, Wittenberg, 26. August 1523," in *Luther Werke*, 4th ser. (Weimar, 1900), 3:141–142.

41. Stahl, "Die Wallfahrt zur Schönen Maria," pp. 77–79; and Lortz, *The Reformation in Germany* 1:100.

42. See Carlos M. N. Eire, *War Against the Idols: The Reform of Worship from Erasmus to Calvin* (Cambridge, 1986), pp. 54–104.

notions of works righteousness. Although widely revered as an act of pious devotion, the pilgrimage was in Luther's mind but another component in a deceived religion which served to increase clerical greed. The image of anxious pilgrims willing to give their time and money encouraged the ecclesiastical hierarchy and the clergy to promote sites that were at best only marginally important, and at worst totally insignificant. Moreover, these journeys, which were thought to aid salvation and offer cures, appeared to provide the simple with an opportunity to barter with saintly patrons. In short, the cult of the saints inspired the widespread misconception that the Christian religion was nothing more than a system of commerce and exchange.

While the Saxon reformer was more extreme than most of his contemporaries in his denunciation of pilgrimage cults, his criticisms were surpassed by the emerging "reformed" theologians. In contrast to Bucer, Zwingli, and Bullinger, who argued for the complete purification of Christianity from these "heathen" idolatries, Luther refused to deny the saints any function in a renewed Christian religion. Dissociated from extravagant and "senseless" displays of religious enthusiasm, from clerical greed, and from "exchanged" miracles and indulgences, the saints could still be a powerful source of examples, helping to inculcate Christian rectitude and behavior. Only in this last sense, however, did Luther judge their veneration to be a matter of "indifference" (*adiaphoron*). Those cults that he found particularly distasteful, like the Regensburg Fair Mary, however, the Saxon reformer denigrated as demonically inspired. By working "false" signs at such sites, he said, Satan was laboring to destroy the last remnants of a pure Christian faith.

In 1523, the same year of his letter to Regensburg's town council denouncing their part in the promotion of the spurious Fair Mary, the reformer entered into a bitter and protracted dispute with the North German diocese of Meissen over the cult of St. Benno, an eleventh-century bishop who had experienced an increase in popularity during the later Middle Ages. Armed with testimonies of Benno's miraculous cures and intercessions, officials of Duke George of Saxony had secured the bishop's canonization from Pope Adrian VI in 1523. The following spring, the conservative George planned an elaborate ceremonial exhumation of the saint. The cousin of Luther's protector Frederick the Wise, George intended

Benno's elevation as a dramatic affirmation of traditional religious practice vis-à-vis the growing Lutheran movement in Germany. He sent invitations to numerous German princes, including Frederick, and requested that the nobles quash criticism of the event. Upon learning of the impending elevation, however, Luther preached a sermon at Wittenberg that denounced the event as an "assault of Satan." He published the treatise under the title *Against the New Idol and the Old Devil Soon to Be Resurrected at Meissen*, thereby opening a tractarian battle over the cult. For Luther, the elevation to be enacted in this diocesan capital was nothing more than a "fool's game . . . , a lie and deceit of the devil."[43] To those who protested that Benno's cult had been confirmed by miracles, the reformer responded that the saint's signs were real, but demonic. Thus, like many later sixteenth-century Protestants, Luther admitted the fact of these miraculous proofs even as he located their origins in diabolic agency.

However reasonable he could be in his attitude toward the saints as pious models, Luther always demonstrated an enormous distaste for "false" outpourings of devotion like those at Meissen and Regensburg. Although the demonic critique of contemporary religious practices was not dominant in Luther's works, he shared it with other early Protestant leaders such as Bucer.[44] In the more generally addressed pamphlets (*Flugschriften*) of early Protestant propaganda, the devil was not cited as the primary reason for the popularity of pilgrimages, though he was sometimes invoked as the ultimate cause of the "false" devotion of the later Middle Ages. In these formulaic statements, rather, the devil usually functioned as a kind of embodiment of mortal failings and credulity, not as a maleficent and cunningly shrewd manipulator of events. Instead early Protestant pamphleteers directed their rage at the social evils of

43. Martin Luther, *Wider den neuen Abgott und alten Teufel, der zu Meißen soll erhoben werden* (Wittenberg, 1524), in *Luther Werke*, 1st ser., 15:170–198, esp. p. 197. In addition, at least one other pamphleteer took up Luther's call against the shrine: Myconius(?), *Von der rechten Erhebung Bennonis ein sendbrief* (1524). Three Catholic responses appeared in the same year. The first was from St. Benno's hagiographer, Hieronymus Emser, and was entitled *Antwurt, Auff das lesterliche buch wider Bischoff Benno zu Meissen, und erhebung der heyligen iungst außgegangen* (Dresden, 1524). The others were anonymous: *Wydder den Wittenbergischen Abtgot, Martin Luther* and *Wyder das wild Geyffernd Eberschwein Luther*. Besides these counterattacks, numerous songs and satires appeared to defend the elevation; see *Luther Werke*, 1st ser., 15:173ff.
44. See Eire, *War Against the Idols*, pp. 89–90.

traditional religion, thus joining their voices to an already powerful strain of anticlerical sentiment. Willing to stop at nothing to bilk credulous lay persons out of their money, they averred, the *clergy* were the true cause of Germany's devotional excesses. In search of riches, bishops and priests had "duped" people into believing that ultimately useless acts like pilgrimage and prayers to the saints produced aid. As for the "pious good works" of the late medieval Church, these were deemed lavish excesses that squandered society's scarce resources. Finally, by teaching people to revere earthly places and objects—shrines, relics, and images—the clergy in effect stressed material things over the things of the spirit. The focus on discrete sites fostered in pilgrims the belief that God could not be approached in prayer everywhere, but had rather to be propitiated at certain places through specific rituals of self-sacrifice.[45]

Though united in their distaste for the "worship" of the saints, Protestant writers of pamphlets sometimes voiced various, even conflicting explanations for the saints' miracles. Here both great theologians and writers of modest tracts faced the same logical problem: if the shrines so scattered throughout the German countryside had indeed provided healing and intercession, how could their saintly patrons now be judged false and impious? Even before the onset of the Reformation, the Renaissance humanist Desiderius Erasmus had provided one answer to this question. In his famous colloquy *A Pilgrimage for Religion's Sake*, he had lambasted the clergy for promoting fraudulent miracles at shrines.[46] Similarly, Protestant propagandists insisted that the reports of wonders that emanated from some sites—the Saxon shrine Wilsnack being one persistent example—were cases of clerical fraud. Within that church's distinguished lineage of critics they particularly celebrated the presence of the condemned heretic and Reformation "precursor" John Huss,

---

45. Ibid., pp. 94–104; Paul Russell, *Lay Theology in the Reformation: Popular Pamphleteers in Southwest Germany, 1521–1525* (Cambridge, 1986), esp. pp. 45, 96, 172, 187; and Ozment, *The Reformation in the Cities*, pp. 67, 77, 83–84, 94, 103.

46. Desiderius Erasmus, "A Pilgrimage for Religion's Sake," in *The Colloquies of Erasmus* (Chicago, 1985), pp. 285–312. For information on the Protestant denunciation of medieval miracles as frauds, see the essays and folk motif catalogue presented in Wolfgang Brückner, ed., *Volkserzählung und Reformation. Ein Handbuch zur Tradierung und Funktion von Erzählliteratur im Protestantismus* (Berlin, 1974). Rudolf Schenda's chapter in this work, "Hieronymus Rauscher und die protestantisch-katholische Legendenpolemik," pp. 179–259, is especially rich in material treating these themes.

whose denunciation of Wilsnack's "miracles" as clerical forgeries was powerful ammunition in the attack on traditional religion.[47]

Despite this frequent charge of fraud, not every miracle could be called clerical artifice. During the decades immediately preceding the Reformation, thousands of intercessions had been reported at various places throughout Germany; indeed, certain miracles possessed veracity precisely because they were so common. As a result, the reformers, in trying to expunge popular appetite for stories of saintly thaumaturgy and divine intervention, were often stopped short by an enduring, conservative belief in supernaturalism. Although they insisted that tangible signs of divine affirmation were unnecessary for those who possessed faith, their audience longed for more concrete testimony of God's approval.

Consequently, among lay Protestants a tendency to equivocate was evident in the first years of the Reformation. In discussing early Protestant iconoclasm, for example, Robert Scribner has observed that conflicting impulses and essentially traditional motivations underlay the popular destruction of religious images, a practice in large part consonant with the medieval exercise of "trying" the saints. When religious paintings and statues had ceased to work intercession in the later Middle Ages, they were often ritually "embarrassed" by being defaced, thrown into a river, or smashed to bits. The image's inability to defend itself against such treatment, in essence, proved once and for all its worthlessness. In the early Reformation, similarly, individual and group iconoclasts would conduct rites of humiliation and trial on once-revered but now denigrated conduits of power. In this sense, iconoclasm was as much a didactic experience for the crowds witnessing these acts as it was a pious exercise and affirmation of the new doctrines for those who waged the destruction. The object was to prove, both to the image breaker himself and to his observers, that the magic that had so recently flowed through the painting or sculpture was impotent when confronted with the power of faith.[48]

47. Huss's *On the Holy Blood* was translated into German and printed at Nuremberg in 1558, several years after a Lutheran pastor had destroyed Wilsnack's holy hosts in 1552. Huss's condemnation continued to spark anti-Roman polemics against miracles in the late sixteenth century. See Breest, "Wunderblut zu Wilsnack," pp. 242–301.

48. Robert W. Scribner, "Ritual and Reformation," in *Popular Culture and Popular Movements*, pp. 103–122.

Inherent in these demonstrations was the belief, not that religious images were ineffective, but that their efficacy had derived
from false, magical sources. The authors of Reformation pamphlets and treatises on the supernatural, then, sometimes had no
choice but to consider the ultimate source of the numinous wonder-
working that had so recently and vigorously functioned in the
German countryside. In one such pamphlet from the early Reformation, for example, the origins of the Regensburg Fair Mary pilgrimage were attributed to a belief in the potency of Jewish magic.
Entitled "A Conversation Between Four People About Their Views
on the Pilgrimage to the Grimmental," this anonymous work from
1523 or 1524 was typical of much early Reformation propaganda.[49]
Based on a "dialogue" between traditionalists and reformists about
various cults, the tract focused on condemning the famous mass
pilgrimage to the Grimmental, which had begun in the 1490s when
a statue of the Virgin had begun to weep. More generally, though,
the work was a catalogue of contemporary religious abuses. At one
point in the conversation, a participant posed the following telling
question: "What do you think of the Regensburg pilgrimage, where
many people came in many different states of excitement, young
and old, women and children, some with banners, others with
sickles?" Another participant, an artisan, theorized that the pilgrimage was probably caused by Jewish magic. By recounting other
instances where Jews had used animal hearts and incantations to
force people to perform bizarre acts, he reasoned that the Regensburg pilgrimage had likely been caused by some kind of spell the
Jews had cast on the site of their synagogue. After that structure's
destruction and the erection of a Christian chapel, this magic had
continued to work miracles and lure pilgrims by the thousand to
Regensburg.

Although this particular tract associated the Regensburg pilgrimage with Jewish sorcery, most mature Protestant polemic pointed to
the devil and the traditional clergy to explain Regensburg's popularity. In the 1536 edition of his famous *Chronicle*, for instance,
Sebastian Franck judged the shrine a product of "the devil's swin-

49. *Ein Gespräch zwischen vier Personnen, wie sie ein Gezänk haben von den Wallfahrt im Grimmental, was fuer Unrat oder Buberei darans entstanden sei* (1523 or 1524), in Otto Clemen, ed., *Die Flugschriften aus den ersten Jahren der Reformation*, vol. 1 (Leipzig, 1906), p. 147.

dling" and clerical greed.[50] Even more vitriolic in his treatment of the cult was Caspar Goltwurm, who made the Fair Mary into a symptom of a disease that Germans had long suffered. In his *Book of Wonders and Miraculous Signs*, published in Frankfurt in 1557, Goltwurm undertook the ambitious project of cataloguing every wonder that had occurred since the beginning of time and classifying each according to its cause.[51] He did not deny the reality of the miracles worked at Regensburg, or in the traditional Church generally. The question was *why* they had occurred. His theory was that Satan had produced them to encourage idolatry. Not the least of these "atrocious public idolatries" was, of course, the Church of the Fair Mary. Although Goltwurm considered the cathedral preacher Hubmayer's original motives in promoting the cult to be pure—for the destruction of the Jewish ghetto was "a Christian work with good intent"—the devil had seized upon this otherwise pious opportunity to work his deceits. "He did not abandon his ancient, cunning style"; indeed, he worked through Hubmayer to draw many mad and senseless people to the church. Soon, however, God had inspired pious Christian teachers to preach against the diabolic cult—a reference to the rise of the Reformation. Dealing the Fair Mary one last polemical blow, the theologian concluded his account of the Regensburg events with the "cleansing" of the sanctuary in 1541, when Emperor Charles V, attending the imperial diet in the city, paid a visit to the now-infamous church. Seeing the numerous votives that the "mad and deluded" had left behind at the shrine, he ordered that everything be cleared away and burnt. Thus the abominable Fair Mary was finally renounced—a conclusion doubly sweet for the Protestant Goltwurm because a Catholic prince had performed the purification rite.

Attacks like these were not confined to theological treatises and pamphlets, for the Reformation quickly adopted a rich visual imagery to convey its message to those who could not read or hear it. In 1542, Duke Ottheinrich of the small but important Upper Palatinate became one of the first princes on Bavaria's borders to introduce a Lutheran church ordinance. In the decades that followed, the terri-

50. Sebastian Franck, *Chronica, Zeitbuch unnd Geschichtsbibell*, fol. CCLX.
51. Caspar Goltwurm, *Wunderwerck und Wunderzeichen Buch. Darinne alle fürnemster Göttliche, Geistliche, Himmlische, Elementische, Irdische, Teufflische wunderwerck . . .* (Frankfurt a. M., 1557), fols. X⁴ff.

tory became an important center for the Protestant movement in southeastern Germany, and actively sought to export the Reformation to her neighbors. Throughout the 1540s and 1550s, Otthein-rich's court artist, Matthias Gerung, published numerous broadsides designed to destroy any residual popular devotion to the Roman Church. The subjects of these prints are often typical of Protestant polemic, showing, for instance, Christ damning the Roman clergy to hell or the devil tearing up an indulgence while welcoming priests into the inferno.

Often, though, Gerung directed his attacks more specifically at the religious practices of Bavaria and South Germany. In several prints, the artist explicitly related Old Testament symbols of idolatry to contemporary shrines. In his "The Worship of the Golden Calf" and "The Destruction of the Golden Calf" (fig. 5), for example, he depicted the famous Old Testament "false" god spoken of in Exodus 32 installed atop a contemporary *Bildstock*, a column on which pilgrimage images and medallions were displayed and venerated in the fields and forests of late medieval Bavaria. Believed to confer protection from harmful spirits like the wandering "poor souls" from purgatory, these picture columns called the faithful to pray to local shrine patrons to watch over the surrounding countryside. Gerung's identification of the Golden Calf with widely diffused contemporary religious practices was not just a condemnation of an abstract "idolatry"; he was raising a battle cry to rid the South German landscape of the magical, heathen cult of pilgrimages, as represented by the *Bildstock*.[52]

In another print entitled "The Threefold Idolatry of the Roman Church" (fig. 6), the artist shows three groups engaged in the worship of false gods. In the left foreground, a group of people kneels before a three-headed beast representing the papacy. To the right, a second group of burghers and nobles worships the goddess Fortuna, who doles out crowns and vestments to her wealthy admirers. Cloven hooves identify the otherwise beguiling woman as

52. Günther Thomann's study of these beliefs in modern Bavaria includes a detailed discussion of their development in the later Middle Ages; see "Die armen Seelen im Volksglauben und Volksbrauch des altbayerischen und oberpfälzischen Raumes: Untersuchungen zur Volksfrömmigkeit des 19. und 20. Jahrhunderts," *Verhandlungen des historischen Vereins für Oberpfalz und Regensburg* 110 (1970): 115–179, 111 (1971): 95–166, and 112 (1972): 173–261.

an evil goddess. In the center of the print, several figures clamor around a statue that recalls Michael Ostendorfer's famous engraving of the Fair Mary of 1520 (see fig. 4). Rather than showing the admiring throng standing before an image of the Virgin, however, Gerung depicts the worshippers gathered around a seminaked male deity with tree boughs for arms and flames billowing from the left appendage. The figure represents the ancient Canaanite god of fertility, Moloch, who required human sacrifice. Pilgrims to his shrines were required to place their hands within a hollow in his breast cavity, an opening that appears in Gerung's depiction. They would then be drawn into the idol by means of a conveyorlike contraption, to be consumed in a fiery immolation.[53] In the background we see the evils that have befallen contemporary society—war, pestilence, and murder—as a result of the worship of "false" gods. While not every viewer will have understood the difficult and often contrived symbolism in this image, Gerung's print drew explicit parallels between the ancient "whoring after false gods" and the contemporary situation. Quoting Ostendorfer's depiction of the extraordinary events at Regensburg made the message clear: revered images, shrines, and pilgrimages did not just deflect attention away from the true God; they were false forms of worship that brought disaster and damnation in their wake.

What impact did attacks like these have in Bavaria, a territory relatively far from the center of religious controversy? Scholars have long recognized a kinship between the Wittelsbach duchy and the Counter-Reformation. Yet while it is true that Bavaria eventually became a bastion of Counter-Reformation Catholicism, Roman hegemony was only achieved by rooting out those who called for the evangelical reform of the Church.

The Wittelsbach dukes, in fact, were among the first German princes to condemn the new doctrines and to punish those who preached or printed them. Already in 1523, a conventicle of Bavarian bishops meeting at Mühldorf adopted measures designed

---

53. Besides representing Moloch, the figure contains some of the attributes of Saturn, who required human sacrifice. Sixteenth-century astrologers credited the dominance of Saturn with producing contemporary disasters. A complete discussion of Gerung's print is included in Werner Hoffmann, *Luther und die Folgen für die Kunst* (Hamburg, 1983), pp. 142–143.

to keep Reformation teaching in check within the territory. Capital punishment, though rarely used, was one means promised to stamp out heterodoxy. In addition, the Wittelsbach princes set themselves the task of eliminating abuses among their own clergy. Concubinage, sacramental and burial fees, and the worst excesses of the indulgence trade were prohibited. Despite the high aims of the reforming program formulated at Mühldorf, however, disorganization and disaffection among Bavaria's clergy quickly plagued its realization.[54] As a result, Protestants continued to multiply in the region during the first years of the Reformation.

Certain general patterns characterize the diffusion of the Reformation within Bavaria's various dioceses. During the 1520s, the new doctrines first found entry into the province through the publication of Protestant books and the wandering of evangelical preachers. This initial evangelical wave was not, as one might expect, a predominantly urban phenomenon. It penetrated deep into the countryside, finding voice as a protest movement against the clergy, against their control over the sacramental system and economy of salvation, and against pilgrimage, fasting, and the mass. In the wake of the Peasants' War of 1525, the Lutheran movement's disavowal of peasant grievances, and the Wittelsbachs' increasingly determined efforts to isolate and root out Zwinglians, Lutherans, and Anabaptists in their territory, support for this first evangelical movement waned.[55]

By 1550, however, a second wave of Protestantism was gaining ground. Bolstered by the adoption of Lutheran church ordinances in many independent territories within and around Bavaria and by the successful Protestant reformations at Augsburg and Regens-

---

54. Bauerreiß, *Kirchengeschichte Bayerns* 6:28–30.

55. The suppression of the Peasants' War produced similar results in other places in Germany; see Franz Lau, "Der Bauernkrieg und das angebliche Ende der lutherischen Reformation als spontane Volksbewegung," *Jahrbuch der Luthergesellschaft* 26 (1959): 109–134. On the Wittelsbachs' opposition to Lutheranism, see Gerald Strauss, "The Religious Policies of Wilhelm and Ludwig of Bavaria in the First Decade of the Reformation," *Church History* 25 (1959): 350–373; and Rüdiger Pohl, "Die 'gegenreformatorische' Politik der bayerischen Herzöge (1522–1528) unter besonderer Berücksichtigung der Bauern und Wiedertäuferbewegung" (diss., Erlangen-Nürnberg, 1972). On the Reformation movement in Bavaria, see Heinrich Lutz, "Das konfessionelle Zeitalter. Erster Teil: Die Herzöge Wilhelm IV und Albrecht V," in Spindler (ed.), *Handbuch der bayerischen Geschichte* 2:295–350; Bauerreiß, *Kirchengeschichte Bayerns*, vol. 6; and Friedrich Zoepfl, *Das Bistum Augsburg und seine Bischöfe im Reformationsjahrhundert*, vol. 2 of *Das Bistum Augsburg* (Munich, 1969).

burg, numerous groups in Bavaria now demanded reform. In contrast to the first stirrings of evangelical sentiment, this second Reformation was concentrated primarily in the Bavarian nobility and among the prosperous burghers, artisans, and patricians of the territory's towns. At Straubing, a Lutheran community was already flourishing in the 1550s, despite the city's function as a center of Wittelsbach state administration. In Munich, Protestants in the town council demanded Lutheran reforms from the Wittelsbach dukes well into the late 1550s. At that time, the Bavarian state's increasing determination to enforce religious uniformity placed the town's elite cadre of Protestants on the defensive, and many later emigrated beyond Bavaria's borders. Although eventually contained at Munich, evangelicals persisted in numerous other towns throughout the territory in the second half of the sixteenth century.[56]

This later reform movement has often been characterized as a "chalice movement" (*Kelchbewegung*), because in 1553 its adherents lobbied the Wittelsbach duke successfully for the establishment of communion with both bread and wine. Besides demanding the lay cup, however, the reformers advocated the abolition of fasting and priestly celibacy and denied the doctrine of the necessity of good works. In short, they criticized and rejected traditional religious practices, including the invocation of the saints, pilgrimages, and various ecclesiastical rites. In all important respects, then, this second wave of the Reformation in Bavaria was not just a "chalice movement," but an evangelical one. During the 1550s and 1560s, many towns in the diocese of Freising and in the Inn River valley (*Innviertel*) of southeastern Bavaria were won over to its program.[57]

Although Bavaria's dukes remained firmly tied to Rome, the Reformation had introduced confusion into the traditional religious life of the territory. For Bavaria's pilgrimages and saints' cults, the

56. On the Protestant movement in Straubing, see Wilhelm Geyer, "Schicksal der Straubinger Protestanten in 16. Jahrhundert," *Beiträge zur bayerischer Kirchengeschichte* 10 (1904): 49–82. Hans Rößler also includes a full prosopographical analysis of the Munich émigrés and the towns in which Protestant factions were active, in *Geschichte und Strukturen der evangelischen Bewegung im Bistum Freising, 1520–1571* (Nuremberg, 1966), pp. 69–77.

57. Rößler, *Geschichte und Strukturen der evangelischen Bewegung*, pp. 9–10; Heinrich Lutz, "Das konfessionelle Zeitalter. Erster Teil."

appearance of the new doctrines was nothing short of disastrous, producing decline and disaffection. Already in 1523, gangs were assaulting peasants en route to Altötting, incited by Luther-inspired preachers in towns around the famous shrine who denounced the cult of the Black Madonna; as a result, the once-popular devotion sank into a recession from which it would not begin to recover until the 1560s. During these years, the shrine's annual revenue declined precipitously and continually, until, in 1560, only seventy-nine florins were collected in the offering box.[58]

The events taking place at Altötting and Regensburg were occurring throughout Bavaria in this period as preachers armed with the new evangelical doctrines rose to attack formerly pious acts like pilgrimage and prayer to the saints. Of course, this criticism did not penetrate Bavaria uniformly; in some places, traditional processions may well have survived relatively unaffected by the Reformation's influence. The general picture, however, is one of decline, as the evidence of miracle records conclusively demonstrates. Of the more than twelve thousand surviving records of miracles from late medieval Bavarian shrines, the overwhelming majority are concentrated in the three decades before 1520. With the coming of the Reformation, this flood of miracle reporting slowed to a trickle.[59]

At only one shrine, that of the Upper Bavarian village of Tuntenhausen, did the clergy continue to print the thin miracle books that were otherwise common in the later Middle Ages. Yet despite the longevity of this publishing enterprise, which persisted throughout the Reformation, a gradual decline occurred in the number of editions produced. During the 1530s, the shrine's books appeared at least annually, but in the 1540s, only two editions were printed, and in the 1550s, only one.[60] These works are instructive of the changes that Protestantism produced in Bavaria.

Beginning in 1530, the redactors of the Tuntenhausen pamphlets introduced an unusual feature which shows that even in this re-

58. W. Sillem, "Zur Geschichte der Reformation in Erzstift Salzburg," *Dorpater Zeitschrift für Theologie und Kirche* 2 (1860): 364–384; Julius Cohen, *Der Kampf der Bayernherzöge gegen die reformatorische Bewegung* (Nuremberg, 1935), p. 31; Wilhelm Maier, *Gedenkblätter und Kulturbilder aus der Geschichte von Altötting* (Munich, 1910), p. 24. On the revenue of the shrine, see König, *Weihegaben an U.L. Frau* 2:50–62.

59. Sargent, "Miracle Books and Pilgrimage Shrines," pp. 469–471.

60. Gierl, *Bauernleben und Bauernwallfahrt*, p. 11.

mote region many were apparently doubting the efficacy of the saints. At the conclusion of each miracle book the church's priests inserted a statement alleging that the wonders reprinted in the book (usually forty-odd) were only some of a much larger number—which they cited exactly—of testimonies recorded during a specific period. Such disclosures appeared in all but one of the miracle books published between 1530 and 1551. According to these figures, Tuntenhausen's Madonna worked a wildly fluctuating number of intercessions in these years, and more than 6,400 in total. Tuntenhausen, however, was not one of Bavaria's great transregional pilgrimage sites; it was a medium-sized shrine located in a somewhat sparsely populated area. This sum, then, is not credible when compared to surviving records of the same time kept at other sites. At the territory's "most miraculous" late medieval shrine, St. Rasso's in Grafrath near Munich, for instance, 5,173 wonders were recorded in the fifteenth and early sixteenth century—over a seventy-two-year period.[61]

Laboring against widespread doubt about saintly intercession, the Tuntenhausen clergy were clearly striving to retain their adherents with an imposing display of numbers. Most clergy elsewhere seem simply to have abandoned their exertions in the wake of general disaffection.[62] Even at Tuntenhausen, the lavish claims of numerous miracles failed to stem the cult's ultimate, Reformation-induced decline, which was furthered after 1550 by the formal adoption of Protestant reforms in several small, independent territories nearby. By 1570, the clerical overseer of this pilgrimage reported to his episcopal superiors at Freising, "The devotion of the people has partly dissolved through Luther's swindling," and the pilgrimage "by which I have been supported has largely disappeared."[63]

61. Sargent, "Miracle Books and Pilgrimage Shrines," p. 458; I have computed the figures for Tuntenhausen's alleged miracles from the statements included in the sixteenth-century miracle books.

62. On the decline of pilgrimages caused by the Reformation, see Rößler, *Geschichte und Strukturen der evangelischen Bewegung*, pp. 205–207; Brigitte Kaff, *Volksreligion und Landeskirche. Die evangelische Bewegung im bayerischen Teil der Diözese Passau* (Munich, 1977), pp. 183, 321; and Staber, *Volksfrömmigkeit und Wallfahrtswesen*, pp. 70–76.

63. Quoted in Gierl, *Bauernleben und Bauernwallfahrt*, p. 17. Anton Bauer also treats the impact of the Reformation on the Tuntenhausen pilgrimage in *Die Marienwallfahrt Tuntenhausen* (Rosenheim, 1930), pp. 15ff.

Indeed, throughout Bavaria the evangelicals' denunciation of miracle promotion, their symbolic inversion of the saints and their shrines into a "false" and demonic perversion of religion, and their scathing attack on the "excesses" of late medieval devotion sent pilgrimage shrines into rapid decline. The scores of simple miracle stories that until then had legitimated shrines no longer drew the faithful to worship.

3

The Rites of State and the Counter-Reformation Resurgence

In the history of Bavaria, the 1560s marked a watershed in confessional politics. During his tenure, Duke Wilhelm IV (r. 1508–1550), prompted by the growing strength of Lutheranism in the empire and among Bavaria's estates, had moved from outright prohibition of Protestantism toward a policy that expressly supported Rome but granted leniency to Protestants. To strengthen the Catholic cause, he had called the Jesuits to the university town of Ingolstadt in 1549. Yet even their early arrival in the territory did not stem the growth of reform sentiment. Hampered by chronic administrative weaknesses and the need to procure the assent of his estates, Wilhelm was unable to impose unified standards on either laity or clergy.

Wilhelm's successor, his son Albrecht V (r. 1550–1579), remained on friendly terms with Protestant and liberal Catholic factions throughout the territory during the first years of his regime. By the late 1550s, however, he had grown distrustful of the Lutheran minority among his nobility, who called insistently for reform. Albrecht, like Wilhelm before him, sensed that evangelical reform was a challenge to his authority. One sign of his growing intolerance came in 1558 when he appointed the uncompromising Simon Eck to serve as his chancellor. Eck and other conservatives in the state councils urged the duke to ignore the pleas of evangelicals and to take strong action to reassert his authority.[1]

Yet another inducement to counter-reform came in the winter of 1563 with the conclusion of the Council of Trent. That body's clear and forceful clarification of Catholic doctrine provided the duke, his advisors, and the growing ranks of counter-reforming clergy in Bavaria with a precise vision of the most important features of the Roman religion. After 1563, state officials and counter-reformers

---

1. W. Götz, *Die bayrische Politik im ersten Jahrzehnt der Regierung Herzog Albrecht V von Bayern, 1550–1560* (Munich, 1896), pp. 110–117.

molded and shaped the pronouncements of Trent to fit their own needs, such that during the next half-century Bavaria emerged as the leader of the Roman resurgence in the empire, pioneering a distinct type of Catholic Reformation that would eventually be imitated in a number of German states.[2]

To reimpose uniformity, Albrecht and his officials relied on a massive application of state power. Although the duke's increasing rigidity had become apparent by the late 1550s, he took the first steps to root out the Protestant opposition in 1563, at a territorial diet held at Ingolstadt. Rejecting the requests for religious reform put forth by his Lutheran nobles, Albrecht dismissed the Ingolstadt diet. He soon learned, however, that many of these nobles were rallying to support the count of Ortenburg, the ruler of a small territory within Bavaria who had recently initiated a Lutheran reformation. Albrecht seized the count—a move that was illegal under imperial law—and opened an investigation of this Lutheran noble faction and their impending rebellion. Having imprisoned the offenders, the duke then used the legal process to deprive them of their lands and estate seats. With this determined stroke the duke managed to destroy the power of the Lutheran nobility and to begin to cow any remaining dissenters into submission. From the suppression of the alleged noble *fronde* of 1564, the Bavarian estates grew progressively weaker as an instrument of constitutional opposition to Wittelsbach hegemony over religion.[3]

Albrecht followed his move against the nobility with a series of measures designed to counteract Protestant influence in Bavaria. Ordinances were enacted that commanded state officials to seize the goods and property of any ducal subject who participated in Protestant worship, the goods not to be returned until the offender renounced evangelical doctrine. Those who crossed the borders of Bavaria to attend Protestant services, a practice common in sixteenth-century Germany, were threatened with fines of fifty to one hundred florins.[4] Booksellers were required to register with the state, and those who had previously been discovered importing

    2. R. Po-Chia Hsia, *Social Discipline in the Reformation: Central Europe, 1550–1750* (London, 1989), p. 41; and Spindler (ed.), *Handbuch der bayerischen Geschichte* 2: 268–294.
    3. Spindler (ed.), *Handbuch der bayerischen Geschichte* 2:340–346.
    4. Rößler, *Geschichte und Strukturen der evangelischen Bewegung*, pp. 12–13.

Protestant books were required to swear that they would never do so in the future.[5]

The Bavarian state's efforts to insure doctrinal purity steadily mounted in the late sixteenth century. By 1570, Lutherans were no longer threatened merely with fines and confiscation: they were required to renounce their beliefs or to emigrate. And in 1571, a ducal decree overturned the concessions that had been granted to the chalice movement, including communion with both bread and wine, the elimination of fasting, and the de facto toleration of clerical marriage and concubinage.[6] One important innovation that helped to accomplish these reforms was the establishment of the Clerical Council at Munich. Comprising both secular and ecclesiastical officials, the council was charged with inspecting the local clergy at regular intervals. In return for obedience in matters of doctrine and religious discipline, clergy were granted the limited function of certifying the orthodoxy of local bureaucrats. By issuing certificates that verified officials' attendance at mass and confession, Bavaria's priests thus became functionaries in a system aimed at establishing conformity and stamping out dissent. In turn, however, the power to examine the religious beliefs and practices of the laity was given not to clerics, but to officials of the state.[7]

The arbitrary efforts of Albrecht to stamp out Protestantism in the territory continued under his successors Wilhelm V (r. 1579–1598) and Maximilian I (r. 1598–1651). Only during Maximilian's regime did the state achieve any real degree of success in rooting out dissenters and in freeing the territory of trade in Protestant ideas. To achieve this, state bureaucrats conducted frequent forays into the countryside to search for Protestant books, and border patrols scrutinized the flow of incoming goods and people more closely than ever before. The movements of Bavarian subjects beyond the boundaries of the state were also carefully monitored. Students

5. Breuer, *Geschichte der literarischen Zensur in Deutschland* (Heidelberg, 1982), pp. 39–42. Bavaria's censorship tradition is treated in greater detail in Helmut Neumann, *Staatliche Bücherzensur und -aufsicht in Bayern von der Reformation bis zum Ausgang des 17. Jahrhunderts* (Heidelberg, 1977); and K. Heigel, "Die Censur in Altbaiern," *Archiv für Geschichte des deutschen Buchhandels* 1 (1876): 5–32.

6. Spindler (ed.), *Handbuch der bayerischen Geschichte* 2:338–344.

7. A discussion of this institution's long and intricate history is included in Richard Bauer, *Der kurfürstliche geistliche Rat und die bayerische Kirchenpolitik, 1768–1802* (Munich, 1971).

who left to study in other territories, for example, were forbidden from attending Protestant universities and required to present proof of their enrollment in orthodox Catholic institutions. Likewise, traveling merchants were expected to attend mass and confession regularly on their journeys and to send back certification verifying their compliance.[8] Innovations like these, of course, necessitated huge infusions of personnel and money, thereby contributing to the steadily rising costs of government in early modern Bavaria.[9]

In their attempt to create a one-confessional state, the Wittelsbach dukes faced strong resistance not only from many quarters of the laity, but from the clergy as well. Concubinage within the priesthood, for instance, remained common long after Albrecht prohibited it. Never well established before the Reformation, clerical celibacy was largely nonexistent during the period 1520–1560 as a result of Protestant attacks.[10] A significant impediment to Wittelsbach plans was the fact that all of Bavaria's cathedral chapters and many of her important monasteries and abbeys were exempt from ducal control. Populated by aristocrats who equated the Counter-Reformation program with an assault on privilege, these institutions often refused to heed Tridentine directives. The decrees forbidding multiple benefices, for example, were roundly opposed. Even such matters as clerical vestments could explode into violent disputes over honor. Refusing to dress in the style required by Trent, the Bavarian higher clergy continued to wear their swords, even while saying mass, as a symbol of their status as well as their defiance of the Counter-Reformation program.[11]

To accomplish the reform of Bavaria's ecclesiastical institutions, Albrecht and his successors relied on the traditional Wittelsbach policy of seeing their sons, relatives, and trusted advisors elected to strategic clerical offices. From these positions of authority, the ducal associates then oversaw the appointment of counter-reforming

8. These measures are described in Rößler, *Geschichte und Strukturen der evangelischen Bewegung*, pp. 12–13.

9. Strauss, *Law, Resistance, and the State*, p. 251; and Spindler (ed.), *Handbuch der bayerischen Geschichte* 2:574–575.

10. A visitation conducted in the diocese of Regensburg in 1548 found that the vast majority of priests were still keeping concubines; see Staber, *Kirchengeschichte des Bistums Regensburg*, p. 120.

11. Ibid.

clergy, who in turn upheld the Tridentine program. And although the Wittelsbachs opposed multiple benefices among the clergy generally, they tolerated and even encouraged it within their own family and among like-minded associates. In 1564, for example, Albrecht secured the election of his eleven-year-old son Ernst as bishop of the large Bavarian diocese of Freising. Later Ernst multiplied his offices to become bishop of Hildesheim, Liège, Halberstadt, and Münster as well as archbishop of Cologne.[12] Picturesquely referred to as "Omnia," Ernst was not the only one of Albrecht's sons to enjoy an unusual career in the Church. In 1567, the duke celebrated another coup: the election of his three-year-old child Philip as bishop of Regensburg. With the diocese thus effectively placed under his regency, Albrecht began the process of counter-reformation by sending a number of trusted priests and Jesuits to Regensburg.[13] By the seventeenth century, persistent Wittelsbach efforts to control elections in ecclesiastical institutions had insured that many of the empire's Catholic dioceses and abbeys were under their control.[14]

The reform of the clergy was a long-term campaign that required several generations to complete. It was also a frequently frustrating enterprise. The Bavarian bureaucracy remained inadequate despite the steady infusion of new officials; its revenues failed to keep pace with the demands of the duke and his officials. And the duke's administration faced a full array of ancient rights and customs that could be invoked to bar government intervention.

These chronic inadequacies also hindered the series of educational reforms that Albrecht initiated in 1569. In that year, the duke wrested control of the territory's primary schools from the territorial estates, to consolidate control over these institutions and so stamp out Protestantism as well as indoctrinate children in the tenets of orthodox Catholicism. But despite the strong moral support that Albrecht and his successors gave the primary education plan, they concentrated their financial resources in building seminaries to in-

---

12. Paula Sutter Fichtner, *Protestantism and Primogeniture in Early Modern Germany* (New Haven, 1989), pp. 53–55.

13. Staber, *Kirchengeschichte des Bistums Regensburg*, pp. 125–128.

14. G. von Lojewski, *Bayerns Weg nach Köln. Geschichte der bayerischen Bistumspolitik in der 2. Hälfte des 16. Jahrhunderts* (Bonn, 1962); Spindler (ed.), *Handbuch der bayerischen Geschichte* 2:595; and Hsia, *Social Discipline in the Reformation*, pp. 42–44.

sure a steady supply of orthodox priests.[15] Albrecht left the raising of funds for the schools to the local communities, who were often unenthusiastic about the plan. The shortage of money and limited supply of orthodox teachers persisted, and Protestants continued to teach in many local schools even into the early seventeenth century. In 1613, Duke Maximilian essentially admitted the failure of the primary education program when he dramatically reduced the number of schools and curtailed their functions.[16]

Like policies calling for an increase in border patrols and inspection of laity and clergy, educational schemes required money and properly trained personnel, resources that were often in short supply in Old Regime societies. For the Counter-Reformers, however, ritual often provided a more effective way of cultivating orthodoxy and religious allegiance than laws, including those that restricted printing and pedagogy. Thus Albrecht and his successors combined their punitive attempts to root out Protestantism with a proliferation of ceremonial rites meant to persuade the wavering and to confirm the orthodox in their beliefs. Their campaign, in short, attempted to wed the arts of prohibition and persuasion.

With court rituals and processions, state and clerical officials propagated the notion of Bavaria as a sacral community united by its ruler and his unfailing allegiance to Rome. Nowhere is this apotheosis of the ducal state more evident than in the dramatically expanded celebration of the feast of Corpus Christi that began during the 1560s. Encouraged by members of the counter-reforming clergy, Albrecht V used this feast to create an imposing portrait of Bavaria and its duke in their role as guardians of biblical and ecclesiastical tradition. Intended to erase doubt through an appeal to the senses and emotions, the amplified celebration of the feast was eventually imitated throughout Catholic Germany and Austria. Enlarged to baroque proportions, Corpus Christi became one of the most important of the German Counter-Reformation's annual rites.[17]

15. See Arno Seifert, *Weltlicher Staat und Kirchenreform. Die Seminarpolitik Bayerns im 16. Jahrhundert* (Münster, 1978).

16. Strauss, *Luther's House of Learning*, pp. 288–291; and Richard Steinmetz, *Erziehung und Konfession. Eine problemgeschichtliche Studie zur kulturhistorisch arbeitenden Volkskunde in Bayern: Spätmittelalter bis Aufklärung* (Frankfurt a. M., 1976).

17. Veit and Lenhart, *Kirche und Volksfrömmigkeit*.

The feast of Corpus Christi, which originated in the thirteenth century, had benefited from the huge late medieval upswing in eucharistic piety. By the eve of the Reformation this celebration had eclipsed even Easter in parts of England and France, where processions often attempted to represent the hierarchy of a city's guilds and occupational groups. The climax of these urban rogations was the host, the body of Christ, which was carried under a canopy and presented as the primary vehicle of social integration. Corpus Christi glorified an image of community as a *corpus mysticum*; its processions were intended to heal fractures in towns and to purify urban space by distributing the host's sacred power.[18]

The celebration of solidarity being its central theme, the feast was a kind of popular sacrament of reconciliation. In England and France, confraternities and guilds were usually responsible for staging these processions, and honor accrued to them for their efforts. Indeed, these groups constantly redoubled their efforts on behalf of the celebration, introducing innovations in the name of corporate honor. In England especially, guilds and confraternities began to build movable floats on which they mimed incidents from the Bible. At their inception, these dramatic scenes were little more than improvised tableaux presented along the processional route; but soon the Corpus Christi "plays" grew into huge cycles that retold the pivotal events of salvific history.[19] In their emplotment the cycles mirrored the outlines of the mass, their narratives following a comic course, that is, with order being brought out of chaos; through a series of episodes man's Redemption was revealed and realized as a consequence of the Fall.[20] In contributing a scene to the cycle, urban occupations and sodalities demonstrated and insured their continuing status within the community.

The myths of Corpus Christi served as inspiration for many fifteenth- and sixteenth-century writers, kings, and rebels. In his

18. Mervyn James, "Ritual, Drama, and Social Body in the Late Medieval English Town," in *Society, Politics, and Culture in Late Medieval England* (Cambridge, 1986), pp. 16–47; and A. N. Galpern, *The Religions of the People in Sixteenth-Century Champagne* (Cambridge, Mass., 1976), pp. 71–78.

19. The classic accounts of English and French Corpus Christi Day cycles are V. A. Kolve, *The Play Called Corpus Christi* (Stanford, 1966); and L. Petit Julleville, *Histoire du théâtre en France: les mystères* (Paris, 1880).

20. O. B. Hardison, Jr., *Christian Rite and Christian Drama in the Middle Ages: Essays in the Origin and Early History of Modern Drama* (Baltimore, 1965), pp. 284–292.

Richard III, for example, Thomas More related the story of the king's violation of the sacraments and the rights of sanctuary by using the dramatic conventions of Corpus Christi cycles. Rather than following the comic movement from Fall to Redemption, or disorder to order, however, More reversed the process. Through a series of Corpus Christi–style scenes he depicted the progressive revelation of the king as a demon and his fall to damnation as a consequence of his wickedness.[21]

The use of the Corpus Christi cycles to portray the story of an evil king would not have appeared at all curious to late medieval English men and women. After all, underpinning the feast's rites was a deep longing for communal solidarity; through violation of the sacraments and sanctuary, Richard had run roughshod over the very forces that sustained the *corpus mysticum*, threatening the kingdom's destruction and producing his own demise. In More's own time, the feast had already provided and still did provide justification for rebellions against landlords, the king's "evil" councillors, and those who through religious heterodoxy threatened to pollute and destroy the body social. Corpus Christi, for example, may well have inspired the peasants' revolt of the Jacquérie in France during 1358, for the rising began in the same week as the feast was celebrated. In England in 1381, the Peasants' Rebellion commenced on Corpus Christi Day, with dissent expressed in a sustained wave of eucharistic processions urging the king to dispose of his advisors.[22] Even into the seventeenth century, the temporal and ritualistic confines of the Corpus Christi festival were invoked as justification for open protest. In 1606, for example, after refusing to repeal laws considered anticlerical by Rome, the Republic of Venice was placed under papal interdict. In response, the city of Venice staged a huge and imposing celebration of the festival to demonstrate its Catholicity and defiance of the evils of Rome.[23]

Corpus Christi, then, represented a powerful ethos of religious and social solidarity that could be called forth in the name of dissent. Inherent within these same rites, however, was also a force

21. Retha M. Warnicke, "More's Richard III and Demonolatry," forthcoming in *Historical Journal* 35, no. 4.
22. Galpern, *Religions of the People in Sixteenth-Century Champagne*, pp. 74–75.
23. William Bouwsma, *Venice and the Defense of Republican Liberty* (Berkeley, 1968), pp. 389–390.

that could be invoked to justify royal authority. Fifteenth-century French monarchs attempted to appropriate the symbols of this important rite of communal and confraternal piety, and the extreme reverence of the host it expressed, to bolster their prestige, in effect transposing the communal ethos inherent in the *fête Dieu* to the higher plane of the nation. Through royal entry ceremonies, for example, monarchy fostered the notion of France as a mystical body united in the person of the king. Appearing at the end of a procession that included a city's saintly relics and its secular and spiritual officials, the French king was carried under a canopy and presented to his subjects just as the host was on Corpus Christi. At royal funeral ceremonies in the late fifteenth century, the practice arose of displaying the king's corpse in tandem with his royal effigy, a practice that underscored his office as "the crown made flesh."[24] In rites such as these, the political and religious doctrine of the "king's two bodies" gained powerful expression: one his earthly presence, and the other the *corps mystère* of the monarchy, which filled the realm with its *praesentia*.[25]

In France, mimetic eucharistic analogies and apologies for the state were common in the sixteenth century. In fact, they appear to have reached a high watermark during the royal entry of Francis II at Paris in 1549.[26] Lasting more than two weeks, the entry incorporated numerous classical and Christian symbols that glorified royalty as a sacramental institution. It concluded with the burning of a group of sacramentarian reformers, highlighting yet another of the monarch's functions as head of the *corps mystère:* the power to protect the nation by exorcizing polluting heretics from the social body.[27]

Although the host and its mystical body provided for sixteenth-century royal theorists, sodalities, and occupational groups potent

---

24. Lawrence M. Bryant deals conclusively with the question of whether the ceremonial rituals of royal entries in fact appropriated the symbols of Corpus Christi, in *The King and the City in the Parisian Royal Entry Ceremony: Politics, Ritual and Art in the Renaissance* (Geneva, 1986), esp. p. 102. On royal funerary developments, see Ralph E. Giesey, *The Royal Funeral Ceremony in Renaissance France* (Geneva, 1960); and idem, *Cérémonial et puissance souveraine: France, XVe–XVIIe siècles* (Paris, 1987).

25. The classic study of this theme is Ernst Kantorowicz, *The King's Two Bodies: A Study in Mediaeval Political Theology* (Princeton, 1957), esp. pp. 221ff.

26. I. D. McFarlane, ed., *The Entry of Henri II into Paris, 16 June 1549* (Binghamton, N.Y., 1982).

27. Ibid., pp. 68–70.

sources of identity, during the Reformation these notions came increasingly under attack. In his study of Corpus Christi Day celebrations in England, Mervyn James observes already in the fifteenth century a waning enthusiasm for the feast in newer quarters of the urban elite. Divorced from traditional sodalities and guilds, the cultured elites of many English towns argued that scripture and edificatory texts should replace the ritualized visual didacticism of traditional feasts.[28]

Eventually curtailed in England with relatively little controversy, Corpus Christi became, beginning in 1562, the focus of some of the bloodiest slaughter during the French Wars of Religion. With its strains sanctifying rebellion, dissent, and community, the feast represented for Calvinists and Catholics alike a unique opportunity for the self-conscious display of religious preference by brute force. In the resulting riots, Catholics enacted their violence upon the persons of the "heretical" French Huguenots, whom they believed to be the source of pollution. Protestants, for their part, concentrated their attention on the "accursed" objects and rites of Roman religion.[29] From Calvin and the Swiss reformers the Huguenots derived an abiding disgust for any religious practice that channeled divine power through the physical. Rather, while retaining a notion of personal and communal sanctification, they intoned the Word as the means for creating godly persons and communities. By attacking the Eucharist in particular, Protestants attempted both to purify the community of the wafer's detrimental effects and to demonstrate to their Catholic opponents that, since it was mere bread, it was ultimately powerless to vindicate itself.[30] Combining their attacks on the eucharistic majesty with a powerful political iconoclasm, which they used to justify the destruction of monuments sanctifying kingship, the Huguenots struck deep at the heart of France's royal and civic religion.[31]

28. James, "Ritual, Drama, and Social Body," pp. 38–47, esp. p. 40.

29. Natalie Z. Davis, "The Rites of Violence," in *Society and Culture in Early Modern France* (Stanford, 1978), pp. 165–172. Davis provides another important assessment of the differing assumptions and attitudes of Huguenots and Catholics toward ritual, urban space, and the sacred in "The Sacred and the Body Social in Sixteenth-Century Lyon," *Past and Present*, no. 90 (February 1981): 40–70.

30. Davis, "The Rites of Violence"; on Calvin's doctrine of idolatry and the proper focus of reverence, see Eire, *War Against the Idols*, pp. 195–233, esp. pp. 212–216.

31. Lionel Rothkrug, "German Holiness and Western Sanctity in Medieval and Modern History," *Historical Reflections* 15 (1988): 199.

Yet when we consider the contrasting development and historical fate of Corpus Christi in Germany, the same kinds of social
mystical or corporatist elements that so marked its celebration in
France and England are not apparent. In both these latter countries,
processions provided a powerful medium for urban groups to compete for the rewards of civic honor. In Germany, however, the
clergy actively worked to exclude sodalities and guilds from participating in the feast. Deemed a jocular assault on the solemnity of the
feast and its host, Corpus Christi Day dramas, with their mumming
and miming, appear to have been performed only in the Rhineland
and the Netherlands, where the numbers and strength of guilds
and confraternities were generally too great for the clergy to resist.
Even in these regions, however, the performance of Corpus Christi
cycles was severely limited, and occurred only after the eucharistic
procession had drawn to a close.[32]

This divergence of festal practice between Germany and its
neighbors to the west appears to have been one result of the proliferation of unsanctioned pilgrimages in the late Middle Ages.
Fearing the multiplication of uncertified shrines dedicated to the
Bleeding Host and the development of other spontaneous cults, the
German clergy used eucharistic processions to instill order into
popular religious life and to redraw more clearly the lines that
differentiated them from the laity. In a study of eucharistic processions in late medieval Germany, Charles Zika concludes that the
host provided a powerful impetus for social and religious discipline
because it was widely perceived, not as a symbolic analogy for
community, but as a kind of holy relic.[33] As such, simply by being
viewed it was efficacious and salvific. In carrying the host through
the streets of towns, the clergy relied on the same visual dimension
of piety that made other salvific displays, like the show of relics, so
religiously potent. In Germany, Corpus Christi consequently lacked
the social, functional aspects of the French and English celebrations;
most often the laity did little more than follow the priests as they
bore the host on its circuit.

The use of the Eucharist as a means of control was widespread in

32. Neil C. Brooks, "Processional Drama and Dramatic Procession in Germany in
the Late Middle Ages," *Journal of English and Germanic Philology* 32 (1933): 141–171;
R. W. Scribner, "Ritual and Popular Religion in Catholic Germany at the Time of the
Reformation," in *Popular Culture and Popular Movements*, pp. 30–31.
33. Zika, "Hosts, Processions, and Pilgrimages," esp. p. 43.

Bavaria, where Bleeding Host and other unsanctioned devotions had multiplied in the fifteenth century. As in other parts of South Germany, the Bavarian clergy resisted the calls of urban groups for representation in the feast's processions.[34] No instance of the laity costuming themselves appears in Bavaria until 1507, when the city fathers at Ingolstadt dressed up to participate in the annual cortege.[35] Biblical costuming thus appeared at Ingolstadt only on the eve of the Reformation, and the practice was not adopted elsewhere in Bavaria until the 1520s.

During the years 1520–1560, a number of towns in and around Bavaria abandoned celebration of the feast in the face of multiplying Protestant attacks. And often in those places where it continued to exist, the number of participants who could be mustered to march plummeted. At Augsburg on Corpus Christi Day in 1560, only twenty people joined the procession, despite the lure of the fiery preaching of the Jesuit Peter Canisius. In Regensburg, the town council permitted processions only in those years when imperial diets were convened in the city.[36] When the Franciscan cathedral preacher Hans Albrecht attempted to revive the procession on an annual basis in 1561, his efforts drew attacks from the city's Lutheran church leaders.[37]

In the Wittelsbach capital of Munich, however, the situation was quite different. Despite the attacks of Protestant reformers, Corpus Christi was celebrated with clockwork regularity throughout the Reformation. In fact, the attacks appear simply to have inspired the Munich town council to double its efforts in support of the feast. By 1523, for example, the council was enlisting the city's guilds and confraternities to prepare living tableaux for the annual procession. By granting these organizations a role in the celebration, the council may have been attempting to satisfy the demands for corporate honor that were such a potent force in sixteenth-century society;

34. Ibid., esp. pp. 33–35.

35. Alois Mitterwieser, *Geschichte der Fronleichnamsprozession in Bayern* (Munich, 1930), p. 19.

36. Ibid., pp. 27–32.

37. Nikolaus Gallus published two tracts attacking the celebration: *Vom Baptischen Abgoettischen Fest CORPORIS CHRISTI oder Fronleichnams Tag genannt, aus den Historien und aus Gottes wort, warer grundtlicher Bericht* (Regensburg, 1561) and *Widerholung unnd bestetigung der waren, noetigen Christlichen Antwort Nicolai Galli, auff des Münchs Thumm Predigers erholete* (Regensburg, 1561).

but in addition, the use of mimed biblical scenes probably had a propagandistic and polemical function, to counter Protestant attacks on the feast as an unscriptural and idolatrous innovation. Whatever the council's reasons for instituting these dramatic tableaux, their decision appears to have been popular. By 1544, the town's occupational and fraternal groups were staging thirty-two living scenes on floats that accompanied the cortege.[38]

During Albrecht's regime, the ducal government dramatically increased both its support for the Corpus Christi processions and its control over the way the feast was celebrated. Protestant attacks on the feast in Regensburg and Augsburg, as well as iconoclastic incidents involving the Eucharist in France and the Netherlands, appear to have prompted Albrecht to use the festival to affirm Catholic truth and demonstrate his support for the Roman cause with a dramatic display. Encouraged by the Jesuits and other members of Bavaria's counter-reforming clergy, Albrecht doubled the size of Munich's Corpus Christi celebration during his reign.[39]

Throughout the late sixteenth and early seventeenth centuries, the festival, which came increasingly to glorify the state and to signify its authority over religion, continued to enjoy strong Wittelsbach support. Several detailed inventories and copies of the processional order have survived from this time period, allowing us to reconstruct the feast's celebration.[40] The 1574 procession, for example, commenced with the standard-bearers of all the guilds of the city making their way through Munich. The duke's stable master followed, escorting members of the elite confraternity of St. George on horseback. Next came a prominent doctor's daughter playing St. Margaret of Antioch, who led a monstrous, yet tamed, dragon. According to legend, the saint was believed to have been swallowed by the animal but was later released when the monster miraculously burst open. At Munich, however, Christian victories over dragons multiplied as St. George, mimed by a nobleman, chased and defeated the animal from behind—a victory tradition-

38. Brooks, "Processional Drama and Dramatic Procession," p. 168, and Mitterwieser, *Geschichte der Fronleichnamsprozession*, pp. 127–132.

39. Mitterwieser, *Geschichte der Fronleichnamsprozession*, pp. 27, 33. On how the new style of festive celebration was received elsewhere in Germany, see Veit and Lenhart's *Kirche und Volksfrömmigkeit*, pp. 84ff.

40. Mitterwieser, *Geschichte der Fronleichnamsprozession*, pp. 34–35.

ally held to be symbolic of the Church's triumph over Satan. Such legends about Christians banishing this monster gave the Counter-Reformation procession an imagery particularly well suited to the attempt to reassert authority in the wake of the Protestant reformers. In the Munich procession of 1574, George, who was also the patron of knights and warriors, was accompanied by a retinue of six knights—a scene which perhaps suggested that military action could also be an effective weapon against the devil.[41]

The next phase of the procession consisted of a series of fifty-five scenes drawn from the Old and New Testaments. Produced by the occupational and fraternal organizations of the city, these living tableaux began with the Creation, as mounted by the fishermen's guild. Subsequent scenes progressed through the Garden of Eden, the Temptation and Fall, the stories of Cain and Abel, the Flood, and so on, and concluded with the depiction of the tortures of Christ, the Crucifixion, the Transfiguration, the descent of the Holy Spirit at Pentecost, and the Last Judgment. All together, 1,439 people were involved in the reenactment of these scenes.

With the biblical history complete, the city's clerics and students in the Catholic schools followed. The ducal trumpeters next raised a blast to announce the nearing of the host, but before it arrived, twelve noble children, reminiscent of the apostles, marched past carrying mock weapons used in the torture and crucifixion of Christ. Finally, two pairs of priests escorted the monstrance with its host, followed by members of the ducal court and the Wittelsbach duke himself, who concluded the procession. Almost two thousand people had participated in this imposing display—a considerable number indeed at a time when the city's population was only about fifteen thousand.

Impressive as this procession was, the numbers of participants rose steadily during the late sixteenth century. By 1582, 3,082 clerics and lay people were recorded marching in the train, and documents from the 1590s suggest a steady increase in intensity, with the Bavarian duke himself providing the processions with costumes, horses' harnesses, and knightly armor. A list of the costumes and regalia compiled in 1592, for example, comes to 178 manuscript

41. David Hugh Farmer, *Oxford Dictionary of the Saints* (Oxford, 1978), pp. 260–261; and Veit and Lenhart, *Kirche und Volksfrömmigkeit*, pp. 85–86.

pages; by 1596, 220 pages were required to catalog the objects used in the procession, and by 1627, 250 pages. To house these items Albrecht had a special warehouse constructed on the grounds of the ducal residence, which his successors were forced to supplement with a second and then a third building to accommodate the steady proliferation of feast-day regalia.[42]

Sumptuous ducal provisioning of the festival, despite the drain on the state's often meager resources, underscored the importance of Corpus Christi as a state function. The undulations of participating confraternities, guilds, and clergy of course delineated the various groups that made up the city of Munich; but the climax of the procession was the sacred host, together with its strongest defenders in the realm: the Bavarian duke and his court. Marching in the procession became an obligation for state officials, insuring at least their outward conformity to the Wittelsbachs' strongly Catholic policies.[43] Those members of the nobility and of Munich's urban organizations who paraded as characters from the Bible were also undertaking a state function, a reality made obvious by the fact that they wore costumes provided by the Wittelsbach dukes.

Besides serving important power functions for the early modern state, the Corpus Christi celebrations taught the religious values of the Counter-Reformation. In the staging of mimed biblical scenes, the Munich processions adopted features from late medieval England and France; the way those features developed, however, proceeded along different lines. Whereas in these countries to the west Corpus Christi miming and living tableaux usually gave way to a kind of spoken street theater, and eventually to huge dramatic cycles performed independent of the procession itself, the Munich Counter-Reformation celebration never adopted the spoken drama; rather, it remained a mute testimony to the truths of Catholicism and its biblical interpretation. This divorce of words and visual display appears to have been a conscious decision, for in the other Bavarian towns that imitated the revamped Munich procession no vernacular dramas were ever staged on the feast day. Only in Dillingen in 1565 and 1602 and at Kösslarn in 1700 do accounts survive of any plays being performed on Corpus Christi Day, but

42. Mitterwieser, *Geschichte der Fronleichnamsprozession,* pp. 36–37.
43. Bauerreiß, *Kirchengeschichte Bayerns* 7:107.

these were Latin, not vernacular, dramas, staged by the Jesuit schools in these towns.[44]

In retaining Corpus Christi as a visual as opposed to an aural experience, the Bavarian counter-reformers were attempting to amplify the traditional importance of *seeing* the Eucharist. As a viewed display, it promoted the notion that the transubstantiation of the host was a kind of theophany, the benefits of which were internalized through the gateway of the eye. Styled as a triumph, the celebration assured onlookers that the Church had weathered and survived numerous trials throughout history, and it imaged the Eucharist as a source of power rising above the crises produced by demons and the "godless." To underscore the living legacy of this battle between the forces of good and evil, costumed demons often circulated along the processional route pelting onlookers with manure, dragons vomited real ox blood, and devils spewed fire.[45] The impulse that caused such a dramatic expansion of the feast during Albrecht's regime was in part polemical, for it was in these years that Calvinists in many places throughout Europe were enacting violent rituals upon the host. But by performing their rites of state and religion in silence, the counter-reformers also set their own theology of the Eucharist as an ultimately incomprehensible mystery against the wordy "prattlings" of Protestants on the subject.[46]

---

44. Brooks, "Processional Drama and Dramatic Procession," pp. 167–168. Efforts to reform processions—to mold them into examples of "correct" piety—were legion in sixteenth-century Europe; see Barbara Wisch, "The Roman Church Triumphant: Pilgrimage, Penance, and Processions Celebrating the Holy Year of 1575," in *All the World's a Stage: Art and Pageantry in the Renaissance and Baroque,* ed. Barbara Wisch and Susan Scott Munshower (University Park, Pa., 1990), pp. 83–118. These reforms, however, were probably more easily accomplished in Bavaria, where traditional celebrations of the festival had lacked a strongly mimetic dimension.

45. Veit and Lenhart, *Kirche und Volksfrömmigkeit,* p. 84.

46. In calling attention to the strongly visual dynamics at work in the Corpus Christi celebration and other elements of late sixteenth-century Catholic religion, I am not suggesting a simple dichotomy of "word" and "image" to explain the differences between Catholic and Protestant reformers. Indeed, the Protestant reformers were intensely visual in their attitudes toward communicating religious truths. See R. W. Scribner, *For the Sake of Simple Folk: Propaganda for the German Reformation* (Cambridge, 1981); and Lee Palmer Wandell, *Always Among Us: Images of the Poor in Zwingli's Zürich* (Cambridge, 1990). Nevertheless, Catholics did charge that Protestant disputes over the Eucharist were simply arguments about words. My attitude toward Protestant visual culture is most similar to that of Kristin Zapalac, *In His Image and Likeness: Political Iconography and Religious Change in Regensburg, 1500–1600* (Ithaca, N.Y., 1990), who suggests that the image was transformed in Lutheranism from a kind of direct immanental "presentation" of religious truth to an *exemplum.* The

In adopting visual spectacle as a primary medium for reestablishing the primacy of the Catholic cult, however, the Bavarian state
and clergy faced a paradox. For even if the new celebration that
radiated outward from Munich was an imposing display, a purely
visual embodiment of religious truth could not answer Protestant attacks on Catholic eucharistic practices. For this reason, the
counter-reformers relied on sermons and the printing press to define more clearly and precisely the significance of their revivified
rites. Such sermons from the 1560s and 1570s still survive, providing insight into the clergy's way of thinking about their renascent
rituals.[47]

Among the most industrious of the defenders of the host and the
feast of Corpus Christi was Johann Nass (1534–1590). A peripatetic
Protestant tailor, he settled in Munich in 1551 and converted shortly
afterward as a result of reading Thomas à Kempis's *Imitation of
Christ*. As a convert, Nass shared a status common among the first
generation of Counter-Reformation propagandists and preachers:
not only was their conversion a victory for the Roman cause that
was often publicly exploited, but as converts these preachers and
polemicists often had an intimate knowledge of Protestant theology, and they, better than those who had been trained as Catholics
from early childhood, knew how to counteract the Reformation's
influence. Shortly after his conversion Nass entered the Franciscan
order, and eventually he began to study at the emerging center of
ultraorthodox Catholicism, the University of Ingolstadt. In addition
to carrying on his activities there in the 1560s, Nass became an
itinerant preacher and traveled in Bavaria and Austria to deliver
sermons at pilgrimage shrines, in fields and city streets, and before
the Wittelsbach and Hapsburg courts. The meaning of the Eucharist
provided one of the most common themes in his preaching, and in
these years he frequently delivered a series of twelve sermons
defending the feast of Corpus Christi. With their strongly mystical

efforts of Catholic reformers in late sixteenth-century Bavaria attempted to return the
laity's vision to an older kind of immanental viewing. But they also aimed to discipline this visual sense by controlling and directing it toward elements of ecclesiastical
ritual like the Eucharist.

47. The Eucharist remained a burning issue in this period because of the Wittelsbach state's attempts to reestablish its orthodox celebration after the interval of
toleration; see Bauerreiß, *Kirchengeschichte Bayerns* 6:237–244.

strains and reliance on an unmediated experience of God in the mass and in the eucharistic procession, these dozen sermons embraced much late medieval German theology about the host.[48] Yet they were also infused with a powerful new sense of Christian history and tradition, one that would find a wide audience in Bavaria. Duke Albrecht encouraged the preacher to publish his sermons, and during the 1560s and 1570s several editions of these works appeared from the Ingolstadt presses. Nass had succeeded in the writer's difficult task of assessing and developing his market.[49]

In his foreword to the 1572 printed edition of the collected sermons, Nass identifies his audience as the "diligent laity and clergy" of Bavaria. Because he often preached in Bavarian towns, he would have addressed students enrolled in the Church's schools, as well as many established clerics and men destined for the priesthood. Consequently, Nass often supported his observations with quotes and allusions to the early Church Fathers and to other theologians with whom such audiences would have been familiar. Running throughout the sermons, however, is a clear and consistent thesis, summarized by frequent repetitions and the use of popular German proverbs and colloquialisms (one is reminded here of his earlier career as an artisan). This mixture of repetitive, aphoristic language and abstruse theological content meant that his preaching combined both theological erudition and more general intelligibility. That is, his sermons were pitched to communicate his message to a broad spectrum of sixteenth-century Bavaria. These twin poles of refinement and vernacular simplicity served yet another practical purpose: they established him as an expert member of the literati, one who had made a detailed study of theological matters but had not surrendered his roots as an artisan.[50]

To defend the powerful immanental and visual dynamics of the

48. Peter Browe, *Die Verehrung der Eucharistie im Mittelalter* (Munich, 1933); Willi Massa, *Die Eucharistie Predigt am Vorabend der Reformation* (Nettetal, 1966), pp. 10–29; and Mayer, "Heilbringende Schau," pp. 234–262.

49. Collected editions published in 1561 and 1565 distributed several of Nass's sermons on the feast, but in 1565, 1568, and 1572 editions of the entire cycle of twelve sermons appeared as well. The 1572 collected edition is reprinted in Richard E. Walker, ed., *The Corpus Christi Sermons of Johannes Nass (1534–1590)* (Göppingen, 1988); see pp. 464–465n.11.

50. This was a common medieval preaching style; see Aron Gurevich, *Medieval Popular Culture: Problems of Belief and Perception*, trans. Janos M. Bak and Paul A. Hollingsworth (Cambridge, 1988), esp. pp. 1–38.

Eucharist and the feast of Corpus Christi, Nass relies on traditional scriptural passages. Like the manna of the Exodus narrative, the host is the "bread of heaven"; but it far surpasses this earlier biblical prefiguration, for it nourishes not just man's bodily need for food, but his salvation. As the physical embodiment of God on earth, the host is placed into ciboria and monstrances that are "framed with precious jewels and gems," a practice also anticipated by the Jews when they enclosed manna in their sacred ark of the covenant. Like this Old Testament shrine, Nass argues, the Eucharist is a holy locus that is displayed on processions so its power can be distributed and suffused to banish evil.[51] But the Eucharist represents a far greater mystery than these pious but outward signs of devotion suggest: it is the one indisputable embodiment of Catholic unity, for, like the body of Christ, it has been preserved inviolate through the ages as the greatest of Christian miracles. The commemoration instituted in Christ's formulas "This do in remembrance of me" and "This is my body" has been performed since the earliest history of the Church. Thus, rather than dwelling on the host's power to sanctify the community or the congregation as part of the body of God, Nass treats the Eucharist like a Christian avatar, preserving its complete separateness. The chief sacrament, it remains an ultimately incomprehensible mystery, and all attempts to explain it in words fail to capture the totality of its meaning.[52]

To explain the attacks of Lutherans, Calvinists, and other Protestant adherents on this eucharistic majesty, the preacher makes repeated reference to the biblical narrative. He argues that two truths emerge from the New Testament: that Jesus was denied, tortured, and crucified, and that he had the power to work miracles.[53] These truths, moreover, can be seen working in the history of the Church, in the way the Savior's detractors have attacked and denigrated the mystery of the Real Presence in the Eucharist. The ultimate perpetrator of this war on the truth, Nass insists, is Satan, who enlisted the Corinthians and Arians in the early Church to attack the Eucharist and who, in modern times, has waged his combat through the various groups of Protestants.

51. Walker (ed.), *Corpus Christi Sermons of Nass*, pp. 23–28.
52. Ibid., pp. 39ff.
53. Ibid., esp. pp. 61ff.

To confirm his observation that the devil never ceases to work against the Church, Nass repeats the late medieval German proverb, "Wherever the Lord God founds a Church, the devil builds his chapels beside it."[54] The battle with Satan and his minions, he says, is visible throughout history in the ongoing skirmishes between the Church militant and the heresies. But for those who seek absolute confirmation of the Catholic religion, they need only look at its historical course: it has been an orderly institution, characterized by harmonious agreement on the central tenets of the faith since its beginnings, while the histories of the heresies have been punctuated with disagreements and disputes.

The universal Church has retained its meticulous doctrinal purity, but not without facing recurring challenges. Against incredible odds and unspeakable hardship, this Church militant successfully accomplished the conversion of the Slavs, the Franks, the Germans, and the Magyars. Even now, Nass reminds his audience, it works to extend its *imperium* over the Indians of the New World and the inhabitants of the Far East.[55] These successes are not mere chance, but the result of a God who continually works dramatic miracles in history to substantiate his truths against the onslaughts of Satan. Nass's entire historical vision can thus be subsumed under the medieval hagiographical forms of *vita* and *miracula:* like the early Christian martyrs and the confessing saints, Christ and his Church have been engaged in constant struggle against Satan and unrepentant mankind, their righteousness proven and made observable in miracles.

In embracing the miraculous as one of the most important proofs of Catholic truth, Nass joined ranks with a number of Counter-Reformation propagandists, who struck vigorously at what they perceived as one of Protestantism's most glaring weaknesses. Despite the Reformation's efforts to destroy the belief in saintly miracles and the efficacy of Catholic rituals, the appetite for wonders remained strong in sixteenth-century Germany. As a result some Protestants, like Ludwig Rabus, tried to convince their preachers and pastors to proclaim the traditional saints as models for a new purified, evangelical piety. In his elaborate, multivolume martyrol-

54. Ibid., pp. 49ff.
55. Ibid., pp. 73–77.

ogy published between 1551 and 1555, this prominent Lutheran church official attempted not simply to condemn false beliefs in the saints, but to reevaluate positively their role in the new religion. He tried, in short, to make the saint over into a model of evangelical piety.[56]

Elite theologians like Rabus might imagine a religion of faith purified of the supernatural, but for most people miracles remained a potent confirmation of religious truth.[57] Thus when trying to promote their tenets to the broadest stratum of sixteenth-century society, the early Reformation propagandists relied on traditional perceptions of sanctity. Indeed, Luther himself had been advertised to the popular audience as someone much like a traditional saint, and as the sixteenth century progressed legends of the reformer's wonders and prophecies multiplied.

For their part, Catholic propagandists possessed the advantage of a long tradition of wonder-working that could be called into play to convince the wavering of the truths of their religion. Nass himself had defended the Real Presence in the host with constant references to the Church's numerous eucharistic wonders and, indeed, the very "miracle" of the institution's survival. Catholic reformers also used stories of contemporary miracles to promote the faith. Beginning around 1560, for example, the Jesuit College at Louvain commenced printing the letters of its missionaries working in Japan and India; filled with accounts of prodigies performed by Society members in the Far East, these missives were printed in pamphlets that saw numerous editions in Germany in the late sixteenth century.[58] Another Catholic convert, Laurentius Surius (1522–1578), too, embraced the use of miracles with enormous enthusiasm. In a polemical chronicle of 1566, this member of the Cologne Carthusians achieved a literary success by recounting a selection of

56. Robert Kolb, *For All the Saints: Changing Perceptions of Martyrdom and Sainthood in the Lutheran Reformation* (Macon, Ga., 1987).

57. Lorna Jane Abray, *The People's Reformation: Magistrates, Clergy, and Commons in Strasbourg, 1500–1598* (Ithaca, N.Y., 1985), p. 173. On the development of the "Luther Myth," see Scribner, *For the Sake of Simple Folk,* pp. 14–36; as well as his "Luther Myth: A Popular Historiography of the Reformer" and "Incombustible Luther: The Image of the Reformer in Early Modern Germany," both reprinted in *Popular Culture and Popular Movements,* pp. 301–322, 323–355.

58. Josef Wicki, *Documenta Indica* (Rome, 1948), reproduces many of these letters. For a large though incomplete listing of this kind of propaganda and its place of publication, see the *National Union Catalogue (NUC)* 284:204ff.

dramatic contemporary miracles worked in the Catholic Church. Through numerous editions in Latin, French, and German, his message of the continuing potency of the Roman tradition enjoyed a wide readership.[59]

Surius's works not only entered into the continuing debate over miracles; they helped to define the saintly piety of the Counter-Reformation as well. In 1571, Surius began to make his most important contribution to this cause with the publication of the first volume of the monumental Latin work *On the Proof of the Historical Saints*.[60] When completed in 1575, the opus totaled six volumes and related the lives of 699 early Christian and medieval saints. In compiling the collection from a variety of sources, Surius departed from the conventions of fifteenth- and sixteenth-century German hagiography. In the late 1400s, hagiographers had typically adopted humanist literary and textual methods to write histories of the saints that stressed their human fallibility. Fantastic miracles were for the most part excluded from these accounts in an effort to promote the saint as a model for piety, rather than as a kind of celestial wonder-worker.[61] The Catholic (but Erasmian) theologian Georg Witzel, for example, had during the 1540s and 1550s published a series of *Lives* that conformed to this mold; by stressing inward contemplation and an individual saint's ability to balance temporal cares with the higher aims of the faith, Witzel used hagiography as a didactic and rhetorical tool to teach proper Christian behavior and values.[62] This humanist skepticism persisted among many Catholics even as Protestant theologians and polemicists attacked the saints and their miracles during the early Reformation.

When we turn to Surius's *On the Proof of the Historical Saints*, its contrast with humanist and Protestant hagiography is striking. Despite the Carthusian's sensitivity to the need to provide source

59. *Commentarius brevis rerum in orbe gestarum ab a. 1500 ad a. 1564* (Cologne, 1566); information on successive editions can be found in *NUC* 577:138ff. On the interesting career of this remarkable counter-reformer, see *Allgemeine deutsche Biographie (ADB)* (Leipzig, 1875–1912), 37:166.

60. Laurentius Surius, *De probatis sanctorum historiis* (Cologne, 1571–1575).

61. Weiss, "Hagiography by German Humanists."

62. Witzel's first martyrology appeared as *Hagiologium seu de sanctis eccleslae* (Mainz, 1541). Numerous abridged forms were published in Latin and German in the 1540s and 1550s. Gregor Richter includes a complete bibliography of the author's works in *Die Schriften Georg Witzels* (Nieuwkoop, 1963); Witzel's theology is treated in Winfried Trusen, *Um die Reform und Einheit der Kirche. Zum Leben und Werk Georg Witzels* (Münster, 1957).

citations to support his claims, he did not shy away from exploring the dramatic, public signs of a saint's celestial power. Surius recognized the strong propagandistic role that miracles had played ever since the time of Augustine, and in his nearly seven hundred lives he recounted an astonishing 6,538 miracles. Rather than presenting his saints as models for pious imitation, he concentrated on their role as Christian magi. Facing ubiquitous trials and tribulations, the holy men and women in Surius's martyrology tirelessly prophesy, combat disease, raise the dead, and bend unyielding nature, harsh circumstances, and even Satan to their wills.[63]

This enthusiastic embrace of miracles achieved an almost instant popularity among Surius's largely clerical readership. In 1574, even before all six volumes had been completed, the Bavarian duke Albrecht V, who sensed in the work a clear and coherent defense of the saints and their miracles, enlisted the preacher Johannes à Via to translate it into German. The first Latin edition was finished in 1575, and just one year later it sold out; immediately a revised edition, complete with a seventh volume, was begun. Over the next two centuries numerous digested versions of the *Proof* were also to appear from the Catholic presses of Germany.[64] In the end, however, Surius's elite and costly martyrology had little direct impact on the religion of many of the Catholic laity, for even in its shorter, digested versions it was beyond their means. Even so, works like this were important in that they codified saints' lives and miracles for their largely clerical readership, thus providing the raw material for many a Counter-Reformation sermon.[65]

Like Nass's Corpus Christi sermons and the resurgent processions of Counter-Reformation Bavaria, Surius's hagiographies

63. They have been catalogued and analyzed for form and content in Hildegard Hebenstreit-Wilfert's "Wunder und Legende: Studien zu Leben und Werk von Laurentius Surius (1522–1578), insbesondere zu seiner Sammlung 'De probatis sanctorum historiis" (Ph.D. diss., Tübingen, 1975), pp. 101ff.
64. Johannes à Via completed the German translation as *Bewerter Historien der liebigen Heiligen Gottes von jrem Christlichen Gottseligem Leben*, 6 vols. (Munich, 1574–1580). Selected editions of this work appeared as *Außzug bewerter Historien der Fürnemsten Heiligen Gottes* (Cologne, 1583, 1592, 1606, 1613, 1617–1618, 1625). Another selected edition prepared by Valentin Leucht was published in numerous editions: *Vitae Sanctorum. Leben, Geschicht, Marter und Todt der Fürnembsten Heyligen, Aller Geschlecht, Ständt, Orden Land, und Zeiten* (Cologne, 1593, 1611, 1660, 1678, 1708, 1751).
65. Paul Holt, "Laurentius Surius und die kirchliche Erneuerung im 16. Jahrhundert," *Jahrbuch des kölnischen Geschichtsvereins* 6–7 (1925): 64ff.; Veit and Lenhart, *Kirche und Volksfrömmigkeit*.

worked to restore credit to the Roman Church as a province in which the divine presence was ceaselessly active. It could be witnessed and experienced. This *praesentia* was confirmed by the unsullied eucharistic theophany and the testimony of saintly miracles. For the propagandists of the Counter-Reformation, the salvific history initiated in the Old Testament was like a vast, unbroken stream punctuated by frequent eddies of apostasy, heresy, and unbelief. With renewed confidence, the Catholic advocates assured their audience that *ecclesia militans* would always emerge victorious from its skirmishes with the "godless." Through its chorus of saints, the purity of its rites, and the reenactment of its pivotal dramatic incidents in mimed biblical procession, the Roman Church testified visibly to its truths. Words could be used to explain its relationship with the divinity; they could also be used to defend its purity and truth. Yet mere language could never capture the limits of this sacred mystery. In its totality, immanence could only be felt and witnessed by those who watched humbly as God embodied himself in the wafer and guided the course of history by means of his miraculous intervention. These were the true signs of an ongoing drama that had commenced in biblical times.

4

The Silent Preacher
Martin Eisengrein and Our Lady at Altötting

The Catholic resurgence that began in Bavaria and in Germany's princely bishoprics in the 1560s achieved stunning successes during the course of the following century. By the conclusion of the Thirty Years War in 1648, approximately one-third of the lands lost to Protestantism had been officially reconverted to Catholicism. State power and imperial politics were certainly factors in this renewal. But in an age when governmental authority was habitually weak, Counter-Reformation princes and clerics fused force and prohibition with a massive propagandistic campaign designed to convince and confirm. In this offensive, the notion of the Roman religion as an unbroken heritage punctuated and proven by miracles provided state and church officials with a powerful appeal. Vitriolic disputes, polemical preaching and printing, the perceived threat of political insurrection, iconoclasm, and religious wars—all these came after the rise of the Reformation. In assessing the contemporary situation, therefore, many found the idea of following time-honored practices justified by supernatural sanction to be more appealing than the new departures of *sola fide* and *sola scriptura*, which seemed to produce only controversy and bitterness.

Protestant theologians and preachers recognized the allure of custom and precedent as well, and from the days of Luther's earliest teaching the reformers had argued that they were not departing from tradition but, rather, restoring it to its pristine state. The charge was to ring increasingly hollow in the late sixteenth century as the numbers of various, competing Protestant ideologies swelled. Within Lutheranism alone, disputes over the Eucharist, justification, prebaptismal exorcism, and the issue of "indifferent things," or *adiaphora*, multiplied following Luther's death in 1546. The clamor only increased in volume when Calvinism entered the empire.

An "illicit" religion according to the Peace of Augsburg settlement of 1555, the Genevan reformation gained its first German foothold in the small but powerful Palatine Electorate. In 1563, the Rhenish elector Frederick III violated the terms of the peace by adopting the Heidelberg Catechism. Soon the relatively puritanical doctrines of this reformed religion were being promoted in the dynasty's various holdings throughout the empire. One of these territories, the Upper Palatinate, lay directly north and northwest of Bavaria. Here the new ecclesiastical leadership initiated a war on popular "superstition," discouraging religious beliefs and practices that were not explicitly of biblical origin. Calvinist officials and ministers were not concerned only with ridding the territory of such traditions as prebaptismal exorcisms, high altars, and religious art; they sought the complete moral reformation of their congregations. And in their offensive they attacked some of the oldest cultural features of the region.

The enthusiasm with which the Calvinists labored can be gleaned from their efforts to modify traditional death customs. To purge the territory of its funerary "unrighteousness," they razed charnel houses and abolished chantries. Ordinances forbade those attending the sick from carrying candles, crosses, and rosaries, objects that traditionally were used to ward off the influence of the poor souls from purgatory and demons who fought at the deathbed over the fate of the dying. To transform the funeral into a rite of familial piety, officials insisted that corpses—widely believed to be polluting—be kept at home until being conveyed to the cemetery. They drastically shortened the period between death and burial and required that each household in a village send one mourner to the graveside, a duty traditionally shunned because of the danger lurking at the moment of interment. The ringing of bells, the use of perpetual lights on graves, and the circuitous procession that the family made with the corpse to the cemetery—similarly believed to protect against evil spirits—were all prohibited as well.[1]

In the Upper Palatinate especially, these extreme attempts to eradicate age-old customs condemned the Calvinist reformation to unpopularity. Both Lutheran and Catholic beliefs and practices re-

1. See Walter Hartinger's study of death practices during the Reformation and Counter-Reformation in the Upper Palatinate: . . . *Denen Gott genad! Totenbrauchtum und Armen-Seele-Glaube in der Operpfalz* (Regensburg, 1979), pp. 16–21, 36–42.

mained firmly entrenched; indeed, the survival of the latter helped to pave the way for the recatholicization of the territory in the early 1600s.[2] For three centuries, the Calvinist ascendancy survived in the folklore of the region as a brief yet terrifying cataclysm.[3]

At the same time Calvinist moral police were waging their assault in the Upper Palatinate, a very different kind of reformation was under way in the neighboring duchy of Bavaria. Like the movement endorsed by the Palatine electors, the Counter-Reformation in the Wittelsbach territory bore the inspiration and imprint of state authority. At its inception, though, this Catholic effort was not against traditional beliefs and practices; rather, the aim was to appropriate them along with the emotional appeal inherent in the idea of *traditio* and so defend the Roman Church, its sacraments, and its ceremonial rites. In place of the Protestant vision of the church as an institution to be organized according to the unchanging terms of scripture, Bavaria's counter-reformers juxtaposed their own notion of the true Church as itself a visible text that was constantly developing, assisted by providential guidance. Nevertheless, at the center of this Catholic tradition were certain unchanging rites, such as the seven sacraments, and a variety of benedictory formulae, prayers, and customs, all of which had been blessed by God, as testified by miracles. Touring countryside and towns, figures like Johann Nass proclaimed the miraculous nature of the Roman tradition, and through the publication of printed pamphlets these men attempted to broaden their address to the literate minority. The state-supported production of martyrologies also endeavored to rehabilitate the saints as repositories of supernatural power. Finally,

2. Robert Döllinger, *Das Evangelium in der Oberpfalz* (Neuendettelsau, 1952), pp. 60–70; and Johann B. Götz, "Die große oberpfälzische Landesvisitation unter dem Kurfürsten Ludwig VI" (pt. 1), *Verhandlungen des Historischen Vereins für Oberpfalz und Regensburg* 85 (1935): 148–244. One Calvinist official from the Rhineland Palatinate charged with supervising the reforms was actually murdered by a crowd of townspeople at Tirschenreuth, and the culprits were allowed to escape; see Johann Brunner, "Die Ermorderung des kurfürstlicher Stiftshauptmanns Valentin Winsheim zu Tirschenreuth a. 24. Feb. 1592," *Verhandlungen des Historischen Vereins für Oberpfalz und Regensburg* 80 (1930): 173–199.

3. Tales of church desecration and iconoclastic attacks worked by Calvinists survived in the region long after its recatholicization. A nineteenth- and early twentieth-century Catholic almanac, for example, frequently included these legends to pious effect when it treated various villages and churches throughout the Upper Palatinate. See *Sulzbach Kalendar für katholische Christen* (Sulzbach, 1840–), 1848:82–84, 1857:84–89, 1872:69–70.

the amplification and resurgence of traditional feasts like Corpus Christi advertised the Roman Church and the Wittelsbach state as two pillars of authority that mediated and distributed the supernatural presence of the Eucharist to the laity.

In a conservative society like Bavaria, the appeal to tradition and miracles could be a powerful means of reviving enthusiasm for the Catholic Church. But to be truly effective, tradition could not be confirmed only in terms of wonders worked and recorded in the past. To convince those who still doubted the efficacy of the ancient rites, contemporary miracles needed to be proclaimed and promoted so that *traditio* could be seen as a continuous legacy and a living, dynamic principle. In the late sixteenth century, therefore, Bavaria's counter-reforming clergy turned once again to publicizing contemporary miracles. Most Bavarians could not read the statements that poured from the Catholic presses at the time, nor was the resurgence inherent in the new rites of Church and state visible to all. Most people lived far from the urban centers where brilliant orators like Johann Nass preached their sermons. But through proclamation at local pilgrimage shrines, publication in modest pamphlets, and oral circulation, the dramatic testimony of neighbors and countrymen provided a continuing confirmation of the *praesentia* of the Catholic Church.

Although Protestant attacks had discouraged for a time the appeal of local shrines, the fundamental living conditions that had once nourished the popularity of the saints had not changed. Despite the Reformation's stated objectives, even Lutheran pastors had been unable to prevent the borrowing of medieval notions of sanctity and intercession by practitioners of their reformed religion. Social and demographic realities—the ever-present specter of disease, famine, and epidemic, the lack of insurance, and the instability caused by crime and accidents—gave the saints a powerful and enduring role. Protestantism may have devalued the traditional saints, yet in popular and elite perceptions alike they retained a fundamental appeal: the ability to address situations in which human justice, economics, and medicine proved inadequate.[4]

4. A point also made in Thomas, *Religion and the Decline of Magic;* and in Brown, *Cult of the Saints,* p. 63 and passim. An incisive review of Thomas's functionalism appears in Natalie Z. Davis, "Some Tasks and Themes in the Study of Popular Religion," in *The Pursuit of Holiness,* ed. Charles E. Trinkaus and Heiko A. Oberman

The counter-reformers astutely sensed that restoring luster to the saints' reputation as wonder-workers was often all that was necessary to revive a particular devotion. Miraculous testimonies were thus one of the first tools Bavarian propagandists used in their attempts to revivify traditional religion and local pilgrimages. The collections of miracles proclaimed and recorded at early modern shrines in Bavaria often grew to incredible lengths, even when compared to the dramatic florescence of the late Middle Ages. Between 1600 and 1800, for example, over 12,000 miracles were recorded at the shrine of Neukirchen bei Heilig Blut;[5] and at Bettbrunn, the clergy may have compiled more than 16,500 accounts for the period 1573–1768.[6] A study by Hermann Bach shows that these collections, prodigious as they are, were not unusual.[7]

Besides these manuscript compilations, the Counter-Reformation clergy renewed the use of printed books to publicize their cults. Two trends typified this revival: a reliance on thin miracle books similar to those published in late medieval Bavaria and, in addition, the appearance of apologetic and theological works designed to defend pilgrimages from Protestant attack and to deepen and discipline the experience of peregrination.

In the century or so before the Counter-Reformation was launched, only three shrines—all Marian pilgrimages—had published the first sort of work. Their precocity in distributing miracle records was due to the devotion's relative novelty within Bavaria: because Marian shrines often appeared suddenly and inexplicably, they lacked the relics, images, and long traditions of wonder-

---

(Leiden, 1972), pp. 307–336. Here the application of the functionalist interpretation is not without its problems: it fails, for instance, to explain why belief in the efficacy of the saints had been called into question in the first place. Nevertheless, as a reason for the resurgence of miracles and pilgrimage, its application appears especially warranted. As I have tried to show, Protestant attempts to expunge the cult of the saints failed because no equally compelling explanations for inexplicable phenomena were provided as a replacement. Moreover, there was not one mutually agreed upon "Protestant" attitude toward miracles and the supernatural, but only a confusion of voices; this only compounded the problem.

5. Walter Hartinger, "Die Wallfahrt Neukirchen bei heilig Blut: volkskundliche Untersuchung einer Gnadenstätte an der bayerisch-böhmischen Grenze," *Beiträge zur Geschichte des Bistums Regensburg* 5 (1971): 157ff.

6. See Alois Döring, "St. Salvator in Bettbrunn: historisch-volkskundliche Untersuchung zur eucharistischen Wallfahrt," *Beiträge zur Geschichte des Bistums Regensburg* 13 (1977): 175–176.

7. Bach, "Mirakelbücher bayerischer Wallfahrtsorte."

working and legend-weaving that other sites used to attract the faithful. The printing of miracles thus gave the clergy at these shrines a unique opportunity to promote their cult.[8] With the coming of the Counter-Reformation, however, an increasing number and variety of cults began to use printing to promote their saintly wonders.

At first, these modest miracle pamphlets remained remarkably similar to those published in the late Middle Ages. Their terse formulaic style, modest vocabulary, and simple illustrations allowed them to be cheaply produced, distributed, and purchased by the broadest possible audience in Bavaria. Throughout early modern Catholic Europe, in fact, this literature of contemporary miracles enjoyed a strong appeal. Assessing France, Roger Chartier has termed the miracle pamphlet one component of a "true popular literature," meaning that its audience comprised tradesmen, artisans, and even some peasants, though clerics, patricians, and other burghers would also have read these tracts.[9] In Bavaria, the miracles publicized in these slim volumes continued to exemplify the relationship of exchange between votant and saint, just as the pamphlets from the late Middle Ages had done. Their dependable content and remarkable profusion suggest that for many—probably the majority of those inclined to believe in the power of the saints—the Reformation had had little long-term impact.[10]

But in the 1560s a new class of worshipers was emerging for whom miracles alone would not suffice to justify Bavaria's local shrines. These "diligent laity and clergy," to use Johann Nass's description, had as their goal to understand the deeper, interior meaning of Catholic practices. When this new devotional movement first appeared, its composition was distinctly elite and literate, consisting largely of students at Bavaria's Church schools and the university at Ingolstadt, Wittelsbach officials, highly placed bur-

8. Josef Staber, "Religionsgeschichtliche Bemerkungen zum Ursprung der Marienwallfahrten in Bistum Regensburg," *Beiträge zur Geschichte des Bistums Regensburg* 7 (1973): 41–61; and idem, *Volksfrömmigkeit und Wallfahrtswesen*, pp. 40 and passim.

9. Roger Chartier, "Publishing Strategies and What the People Read, 1530–1660," in *The Cultural Uses of Print in Early Modern France*, trans. Lydia G. Cochrane (Princeton, 1987), pp. 145–182; and idem, "The Hanged Woman Miraculously Saved: An *Occasionnel*," in Chartier (ed.), *Culture of Print*, pp. 59–91.

10. This point is also made by Steven Sargent in "Miracle Books and Pilgrimage Shrines," pp. 470–471.

ghers, and the clerical elite. These pious displayed a fervent devotion to Roman rites and practices from the outset. From the position of the Church hierarchy, however, their zeal also presented a certain danger; for by striving toward the internalization of piety they—like late medieval groups such as the Beguines and Beghards before them—threatened to make superfluous the rites and sacraments of the institutional Church. Certainly, Bavaria's Catholic reformers recognized that the Reformation itself had roots in this piety: the ideas of Erasmus, Luther, and other early Protestant leaders had all, after all, been nurtured in an outpouring of lay and clerical spirituality. In the late sixteenth century, then, Bavaria's Counter-Reformation theologians and clerical officials began to concentrate on institutionalizing the religiosity of the new devout within the structures of the Roman Church (a movement that pious confraternities were eventually to contain and discipline).[11]

Because many of those searching for a deeper piety were also literate, Bavaria's foremost theologians began to produce a new kind of printed work, propaganda in the true, original sense of the term: incorporating apologetic, polemical, and devotional strains, this was a literature intended to revive, define, and discipline the emerging religion of the Catholic Reformation—truly, to propagate the faith. While many in the new devotional movements were drawn from the social, political, and clerical elites of Bavaria, few were well schooled in the traditions of scholastic theology. As a result, the tone of much of this writing is distinctly "middle-brow."

Pilgrimage was one of the first traditional religious practices to receive the special attention of Bavaria's new propagandists, and thanks to their efforts it eventually became an important vehicle for the expression of Catholic religiosity. In the 1560s, the Ingolstadt theologian Martin Eisengrein (1535–1578) published the first of many works aimed at reviving local shrines. These early contributions, which were crucial to the later development of a distinctive peregrinational theology, provide a valuable glimpse at the tactics of Bavaria's clerical hierarchy.

Like most members of the first generation of Counter-Reformation propagandists, Eisengrein was a convert. Born into a wealthy Lutheran family in Stuttgart, he had spent his student years attend-

11. Chatellier, *Europe of the Devout*, pp. 14–46.

ing the universities of Tübingen, Ingolstadt, and Vienna. It was in the last city that he converted, sometime in 1558 or 1559, and there he began to study theology. By 1560 he had been ordained a priest and assumed the powerful position of cathedral preacher at the city's St. Stephen's Cathedral. From the start Eisengrein was rigorous in his devotion to Catholic orthodoxy, and he soon became involved in a plan, ultimately unsuccessful, to purge the University of Vienna of its Protestants. His participation in this scheme prepared the way for his move to Bavaria, for at Ingolstadt the rector of the university, Friedrich Staphylus, learned of Eisengrein's efforts and asked Duke Albrecht to invite him to become priest and preacher at the university's St. Moritz parish.[12]

From his arrival in Ingolstadt in 1562 until his death in 1578, Eisengrein dedicated himself completely to the cause of Catholic reform, not just in the university town, but throughout Bavaria. His career exemplifies the blurring that occurred between state and clerical functions as the Wittelsbachs worked to establish their hegemony over religion. Although called to serve as a parish priest, Eisengrein soon joined the theological faculty of the university, and in this capacity he united with other counter-reformers to rid the institution of its Protestants. For his successes in enforcing doctrinal uniformity, the Wittelsbach duke entrusted Eisengrein with a variety of governmental and ecclesiastical functions. He was sent on preaching missions to regions of Bavaria that had adopted evangelical reforms, participated in commissions established to oversee the territory's local clergy, and went to Rome to negotiate the election of the duke's son Ernst as bishop of Freising. In his frequent correspondence with the duke, Eisengrein encouraged Albrecht to pursue strict policies to root out Bavaria's Protestants. For his efforts, the duke rewarded the theologian with a number of benefices: besides his priestly and professorial offices at Ingolstadt, Eisengrein was granted the position of provost of the collegiate churches in

---

12. On the life of this remarkable but largely unrecognized counter-reformer, see Luzian Pfleger, *Martin Eisengrein (1535–1578). Ein Lebensbild aus der Zeit der katholischen Restauration in Bayern*, in *Erläuterungen und Ergänzungen zu Janssens Geschichte des deutschen Volkes*, ed. Ludwig Pastor, vol. 6, pt. 2 (Freiburg i. B., 1908); Wilhelm Kosch, *Das katholische Deutschland* (Augsburg, 1933–1939), 1:607; and M. Buchberger, *Kirchliches Handlexikon*, vol. 1 (Munich, 1935), no. 1262.

Passau, Moosburg, and Altötting, and in 1570 he became superintendent of the University of Ingolstadt.[13]

Actively engaged in the administrative duties of Church and state, Eisengrein was also a powerful orator whose sermons and teaching helped to shape the devotional and theological climate of the Counter-Reformation. At Ingolstadt, he instructed many of the students who subsequently entered the ranks of the territory's counter-reforming clergy. His preaching missions allowed him to present his clear and forceful defense of the Catholic tradition in those Bavarian towns where Protestants had long been tolerated. In these endeavors, Eisengrein, like Johann Nass, often defended the Catholic Eucharist, transubstantiation, and the Real Presence from Protestant attack. In one polemical sermon published shortly after his arrival at Ingolstadt in 1562, he praised the amplified celebrations of Corpus Christi that were just then beginning to appear.[14] He encouraged Albrecht in letters to continue to protect the faith by means of orchestrated processions like those at Munich, and throughout his life he actively defended the holiday as an imperative. While on a mission in 1569 to the Hapsburg court in Vienna, for example, he became embroiled in a controversy over Corpus Christi. Upon learning that the university's predominantly Lutheran faculty refused to participate in the procession, he convinced the emperor's officials to require them to take part. And although he was bedridden with an attack of gout at the time, he left his confinement to march triumphantly in the cortege.[15]

At its core, the remodeled Corpus Christi procession of the Counter-Reformation was an attempt to revive a sense of awe and humility before the host. Pilgrimage to local shrines, too, could have a similar effect, and in his sermons, printed works, and pastoral ministrations Eisengrein strove to resurrect and reform the religious life of Bavaria's shrines. In 1563, the theologian journeyed from Ingolstadt to the nearby shrine of Hohenwart, where he was impressed with the piety of the "common people" who still made

---

13. Pfleger, *Martin Eisengrein;* and idem, *Martin Eisengrein und die Universität Ingolstadt,* Historisch-politische Blätter 134 (Munich, 1905); and Spindler (ed.), *Handbuch der bayerischen Geschichte* 2:268–294.

14. Spindler (ed.), *Handbuch der bayerischen Geschichte* 2:124–132.

15. Pfleger, *Martin Eisengrein,* pp. 69–71.

their way to the place. Returning home, he preached a sermon that
stands as one of the first counter-reformational defenses of the cult
of the saints and pilgrimage; published in 1564 as *A Christian Sermon
Concerning the Reasons Shrines Are Held in Such High Esteem in the
Catholic Church*, it became one of Eisengrein's more widely distributed works, with at least seven editions printed before 1600.[16]

In his sermons Eisengrein presents numerous traditional defenses for the veneration of the saints, repeating some of the same
arguments that were being voiced around the same time at the
Council of Trent.[17] Quoting the Tridentine decrees, for example, he
argues that saintly veneration is "good and useful" for several
reasons. First, God has ceaselessly worked miracles through the
saints, their relics, and their images, demonstrating his approval of
these devotions and providing aid to those who place their prayerful requests before the saints. Second, the relics, images, and lives
of the saints are all powerful memorials, reminding the faithful of
these figures' past holiness. Further, Eisengrein delineates the differences between the worship of God and the veneration of the
saints, turning for support in this matter to the early Church fathers—including Jerome, Clement, Eusebius, Basil, and Augustine—rather than the medieval Scholastics; he uses the antiquity of
their arguments to refute the Protestant charge that the cult of the
saints was a late medieval innovation.[18]

Eisengrein also sets forth a theology of immanence and a vision
of Christian history that are reminiscent of Johann Nass's defense of
the Catholic Eucharist. For this he cites Matthew 9, the story of
the woman relieved of a twelve-year hemorrhage. In this passage,
he reminds his audience, the woman was not healed directly by
Christ, but by touching the hem of the Savior's garment, in which

16. *Ein christliche predig Was vom Hailthumb, so im Papstumb in so grossen ehren, zu
halten sey* . . . (Ingolstadt, 1564); the work was reprinted at Ingolstadt in 1565, 1583,
and 1598; a Latin translation appeared in 1565; one additional German edition
appeared at Constance in 1599. See Pfleger, *Martin Eisengrein*, p. 125; and Stalla,
Bibliographie der Ingolstädter Buchdrucker, nos. 444, 474, 918, and 1214. I cite a seventh
edition which was included as part of a pilgrimage book published for the shrine of
Bettbrunn entitled *Sanct Saluator zu Bettbrunn* (Ingolstadt, 1584).
17. Hubert Jedin, *Geschichte des Konzils von Trent*, vol. 4, pt. 2 (Freiburg i. B.,
1975), pp. 183–187. The Tridentine decrees on saintly veneration were adopted
during the final days of the Council in 1563.
18. *Ein christliche predig*, pp. 22–55, includes a long excursion through the works
of the fathers.

act God demonstrated his tendency to work through intermediary agents. Even today, Eisengrein states, the Lord operates through the saints to cure specific diseases at certain times and locations; relics and shrines thus remain two of the divinely ordained media through which God grants grace and intercession.[19]

To explain the Protestant rejection of this outpouring of divine generosity, Eisengrein, again like Nass, argues that "godless" heretics have always waged a persistent war against the saints and their devotions. Arians, iconoclasts, Hussites, Lutherans, and Calvinists—each is invoked as another link in a long chain of heresies, inspired by Satan to destroy true devotion to the saints. In one particularly effective polemical passage, Eisengrein connects the rejection of the belief in the saints with a host of other heresies:

> Then we are well aware by the grace of God that the enemy of our Savior, the grievous Satan, uses these artifices [heresies] when he wants to sow contempt in the people for something in which they have put their trust. So he begins by deriding and despising these [beliefs]; because they cannot be destroyed on the grounds of truth, he seeks to reduce them by means of disgraceful slanders. Thus he mocks the Holy Trinity through the unbelievers [who ask] how it is possible that three different persons can be a single nature. Thus he mocks the sacrament of baptism in which we believe that through such exterior washing, we are cleansed and washed internally of our sins. Thus through his servants he mocks the sacrament of the altar in which we believe that the body and blood of Christ are actually present. Thus he has mocked many other salvific parts of our Christian faith. Therefore, it is not only at this time, but from time immemorial, that he has undertaken to mock relics.[20]

In this and similar passages Eisengrein, attempting to demonstrate the illogicality of the Protestant (especially the Lutheran and Bucerian) attack on the veneration of the saints as demonically inspired delusion, leads his audience through a series of heretical attacks on Catholic belief. First, he refers to the devil's attempt to destroy the universal doctrines of the Trinity and baptism, both practices accepted and defended by Lutherans and Calvinists. Next he refers to attacks on belief in the Real Presence, a doctrine also

19. Ibid., p. 64.
20. Ibid., p. 21.

affirmed by the Lutherans. And he concludes with the Protestant renunciation of the cult of the saints. The point toward which Eisengrein's argument has been moving now becomes explicit: while Protestants have correctly affirmed Satan's enormous power to cultivate heresies against the Trinity, baptism, and the Eucharist, they have been deluded by that same enemy into rejecting the truth of the Catholic saints.

In the remainder of the sermon, Eisengrein devotes considerable attention to proving the antiquity of saintly veneration. He points to the bones of the Old Testament Elijah, the raiment of Christ, and the cults of the Roman martyrs as confirmation that these beliefs originated among the Jews and were imported into the new Christian religion.[21] As with all dimensions of godly religion, however, demonically inspired heresies have uninterruptedly assaulted the divinely ordained practice of saintly veneration. While warning that Satan's power is enormous, Eisengrein assures his audience that the saints will always prove more powerful. The *Christian Sermon* concludes with ringing passages praising the saints' continued victory over heresy and unbelief.

This perception of the saints as part of a visible legacy of skirmishes between truth and falsehood was to reappear and find its broadest audience in the pilgrimage book Eisengrein published to defend the cult of Our Lady of Altötting. In 1567, the theologian was appointed provost of this shrine's ancient collegiate church, and his efforts on behalf of the cult show that he regarded this position as integral to his efforts to reform the Bavarian Church.[22] By the 1560s, this once-great pilgrimage had declined precipitously; the shrine now lay in the center of a region where evangelical ideas and practices had attracted a wide following.[23] In this setting, which was often openly hostile to the shrine's revival, Eisengrein worked to reform the shrine's collegiate church and to encourage the pilgrimage.[24]

21. Ibid., pp. 25ff.
22. Pfleger, *Martin Eisengrein*, p. 72.
23. König, *Weihegaben an U.L. Frau von Altötting* 1:50ff.
24. The shrine was vandalized on several occasions during the late 1550s; see ibid., pp. 58ff. On the Reformation's impact in and around Altötting, see Bauerreiß, *Kirchengeschichte Bayerns* 6:215, 232; and Spindler (ed.), *Handbuch der bayerischen Geschichte* 2:338–344.

To achieve this renewal Eisengrein began by appointing like-minded reformers to the church's benefices, and he worked to eliminate concubinage among the older canons. He also preached sermons to those few processions of devotees that still visited the site.[25] But his most significant achievement in defense of the pilgrimage was the apologetic book *Our Lady at Altötting;* first published in 1571, the book was reprinted at least ten times before 1625, making it a vernacular best-seller and helping to stimulate the shrine's revival.[26]

Eisengrein dedicated the book to Altötting's neighboring towns that had adopted evangelical practices like the celebration of communion with both bread and wine,[27] a practice that they, however, had had to abandon following forcible reconversion to orthodoxy in the late 1560s. Thus, while it is doubtful that convinced Protestants would have purchased or read Eisengrein's book, the dedication does perhaps reveal his fervent hope that Catholicism would be successfully reestablished in the vicinity. It betrays, moreover, the self-consciousness of his decision to promote the renewal of a once-popular pilgrimage in a region populated by evangelicals.[28]

To convince his readers of the shrine's power, Eisengrein relies on a "myth" to transform the pilgrimage site into a key link in the Almighty's plan for Bavaria. The legend he tells is epic in proportion, for he begins his tale not with the development of the pilgrimage in 1489, but with the peopling of Bavaria by the descendants of Noah after the Flood.[29] Drawing upon Johannes Aventinus's humanist history of Altötting of 1519, Eisengrein recounts the first settlement of the region by the heathen Bajuwaren, and includes a detailed biblical-styled genealogy of the tribes' kings.[30] Successive

25. Pfleger, *Martin Eisengrein,* p. 75.

26. Eisengrein, *Unser liebe Fraw zu alten Oetting.* In his *Bibliographie der Ingolstädter Buchdrucker,* Gerhard Stalla lists the following editions: 1571 (2 printings), 1581 (2 printings), 1587, and 1588. The Bavarian State Library also has copies printed in the following years: 1598, 1601, 1613, and 1625. From the publication of Eisengrein's books until the 1630s, offering revenue at Altötting steadily rose; see König, *Weihegaben an U.L. Frau von Altötting* 2:471.

27. Eisengrein, *Unser liebe Fraw zu alten Oetting,* "Vorrede."

28. Chatellier treats the geographical intentions of the counter-reformers evocatively in *Europe of the Devout,* pp. 49–52.

29. Eisengrein, *Unser liebe Fraw zu alten Oetting,* pp. 1–5.

30. Johannes Aventinus, *Der hochwirdigen und weit berumten Stifft Alten Oting loblich herkomen . . .* (Ingolstadt, 1519), in *Sämmtliche Werke* 4(2):31–59.

chapters treat the Roman occupation and the expulsion of the Bajuwaren from Bavaria to the lands north of the Danube. Under Roman rule, Eisengrein relates, Altötting assumed great strategic importance because it guarded a bridge spanning the nearby Inn River. During the Barbarian invasions of the fifth and sixth centuries, the town was frequently the scene of heavy fighting and looting, until it was finally annihilated in 520. Christian Romans watched helplessly as marauding Bajuwaren led by Duke Dieth invaded their churches and pillaged their relics. Eisengrein draws parallels between these incidents and the contemporary assault of Protestants, especially iconoclastic Calvinists, on the possessions of the true Church:

> But because he [Duke Dieth] and his army were unbelievers at that time, they set out to destroy, desecrate, and burn the churches and Christian houses of the Lord. They robbed these of their relics and treasures. They did so while the clergy were still before their altars at the divine office, even in front of Bishop Lupus himself. Their conduct was not much better than that of the unchristian bloodthirsty Huguenots and Calvinists in the Netherlands and France in our day, who have committed all kinds of murder and ecclesiastical thievery wherever they have gained the upper hand.[31]

The modern reader may see little relation between this long and colorful narrative and the later pilgrimage to Altötting. But by beginning with the Flood and progressing through a series of conquests, invasions, and desecrations, Eisengrein establishes a kind of convergence between Bavaria's history and the Bible, in which the territory's pre-Christian development reads like a kind of Old Testament narrative. Before the advent of modern modes of criticism in the eighteenth century, the practice of locating one's origins within the biblical story was common. As Hans Frei once observed, "Christian preachers and theological commentators . . . envisioned the real world as formed by the sequence told by the biblical stories." It was thus the historian's and the biblical commentator's "duty to fit himself" into this narrative and "to see . . . the shape of his own life as well as that of his era's events as figures of that storied world."[32] This is precisely Eisengrein's purpose in *Our Lady*

31. Eisengrein, *Unser liebe Fraw zu alten Oetting*, pp. 7–16, esp. p. 12.
32. Hans Frei, *The Eclipse of Biblical Narrative: A Study in Eighteenth- and Nineteenth-Century Hermeneutics* (New Haven, 1974), pp. 1, 3.

of Altötting. Having recounted the history of the region from biblical days to the very eve of its Christianization, the author turns his attention more specifically to the history of the chapel of Our Lady at Altötting.[33] The shrine of Our Lady, with its numerous miracles and its dramatic history, is namely both the continuation and the fulfillment of the biblical story in Bavaria.

The chronicle that Eisengrein fashions for Altötting is brilliantly calculated for maximum propagandistic effect. In considering the Christianization of Bavaria, for instance, he relates that the first missionaries arrived following the marriage of the marauding iconoclast Duke Dieth to the Frankish princess Regentraut. Because the town of Altötting was at the time home to the Bavarian court, St. Rupert, the duchy's "apostle," came there to preach the Christian message. To provide his converts with a place of worship, Rupert consecrated a chapel: the future pilgrimage shrine. In Aventinus's early sixteenth-century chronicle of the site, the chapel of Our Lady was described as a structure hurriedly erected after these first conversions.[34] In Eisengrein's account, the Altötting church becomes a preexistent heathen temple put to Christian use upon St. Rupert's consecration. To grant this observation a kind of historical veracity, Eisengrein says that according to a legend told by the town's "common folk" the pre-Christian shrine had been used for the worship of the seven planets, noting that seven holes carved in the walls of the sanctuary—perhaps used for viewing the stars—point to its truth.[35]

It is not just the building at Altötting that was of pre-Christian origin; rather, Eisengrein alleges that pilgrimages, too, were a rite common to the ancient heathen Germans: long before their conversion, the Bavarians were fond of journeying into their forests to conduct devotions to their gods. The transformation that St. Rupert effected at Altötting, then, relied on the prior affection of the Bavarians for this site, but it redirected and employed that emotion "to better use."[36] By making Altötting over into a pre-Christian devotion, moreover, Eisengrein attempted to answer a common Protestant charge regarding saintly pilgrimages: that these were innovations of the late medieval Church. That is, Eisengrein transformed

33. Eisengrein, *Unser liebe Fraw zu alten Oetting,* pp. 1–126. This narrative encompasses the first ten chapters of the book.
34. Aventinus, *Sämmtliche Werke* 4(2):31–59.
35. Eisengrein, *Unser liebe Fraw zu alten Oetting,* pp. 24–25.
36. Ibid., pp. 22–31.

both Altötting specifically and pilgrimage generally into symbols of Bavaria's Christianization. The metamorphosis that St. Rupert accomplished at Altötting was essential to all Bavaria's salvation, he argued, for it destroyed the pagan, pre-Christian devotions of the Bajuwaren and transferred their attentions to the worship of the true Christian God.

In addition to its obvious polemical dimensions, Eisengrein's history also extols the apotropaic importance of verbal formulae. In his view, the words that Rupert repeated in consecrating Altötting's chapel were charged with the power to expel the heathen "devil and his mother and every idolatrous sacrifice" from the site and to invoke Mary's protection and patronage for all time.[37] To emphasize the exorcistic power of words repeated in consecratory rites Eisengrein tells a story from Gregory of Tours concerning the reconsecration of a church following the expulsion of Arian heretics. As the relics of SS. Agatha and Sebastian were brought into the building and the rite of consecration commenced, the assembled congregation witnessed the devil fleeing the church in the form of a pig. Like the expulsion of the heathen "devil and his mother" worked by St. Rupert at Altötting, this Arian demon could not stand to be in the same place where Christian saints and worship were present.[38]

In medieval Europe, a lush variety of private and public incantations and benedictions had served to call down the protection of the saints on communities, individuals, and property. Pre-Reformation theologians and Church officials had often attempted unsuccessfully to eradicate those extra-ecclesiastical saintly conjurations they judged to be most "magical" and "superstitious" and to locate the saints' power more firmly within the institutional Church and its clergy.[39] Then, in the decades when the Reformation's impact was most widely felt, Protestant theologians and pastors extended the offensive to include all saintly supplication, waging their battle even more rigorously. Though ultimately unable to change an entire set of religious and social assumptions that marshaled supernatural power for the benefit of daily life, the Protestant assault prompted

37. Ibid., p. 30.
38. Ibid.
39. Scribner, "Cosmic Order and Daily Life" and "Ritual and Popular Religion"; and Adolf Franz, *Die kirchlichen Benediktionen im Mittelalter,* 2 vols. (Freiburg i. B., 1909).

Catholic reformers like Eisengrein to renew efforts to stamp out the "unofficial" use of conjurative language. His account extolled the awesome potential that resided in St. Rupert's sixth-century consecration, stressing the enormous subsequent benefits it provided Altötting and Bavaria. An implicit warning, however, reposed in Eisengrein's praise of Rupert's act: performed by ordained priests for the benefit of all Catholics, rites like these were not to be appropriated by the laity for personal needs.[40]

In the remainder of his history, Eisengrein demonstrates how the Virgin's patronage and divine protection have preserved and blessed Altötting for more than one thousand years. During this time, he argues, the shrine has been a continuing focus for both the German emperors' and the Bavarian dukes' devotion. The Carolingian emperors, for example, maintained a residence in the town, conducted pilgrimages to the holy chapel, and lavished the site with rich endowments, including a Benedictine abbey. Two descendants of Charlemagne died at Altötting, and, Eisengrein notes, masses for their souls were still said for them in the shrine.[41] Whereas in other parts of the Christian world Arians, iconoclasts, Cathars, Hussites, and now Lutherans and Calvinists attacked the true religion of the saints, Bavaria, its dukes, and the empire had remained faithful to Our Lady's presence in the tiny chapel of Altötting. Repeating a common miraculous topos, Eisengrein states that although marauding hordes of Magyars entered Altötting in the tenth century and set fire to the settlement, burning everything including the imperial residence and monastery, the flames were incapable of consuming Our Lady's chapel.[42]

To prove the Virgin's continuous protection over the site, Eisen-

40. John Bossy touched on this theme in a European context in his "The Counter-Reformation and the People of Catholic Europe," *Past and Present*, no. 47 (1970): 51–70. See also Virginia Reinburg, "Popular Prayers in Late Medieval and Reformation France" (Ph.D. diss., Princeton University, 1985), esp. pp. 284–360. Counter-Reformation efforts to reform popular prayers will also be treated at greater length in Prof. Reinburg's forthcoming book, to be published by Cornell University Press.

41. He is referring to Carloman, king of Bavaria (876–880), and Arnulf, king of the East Franks (887–899) and emperor (896–899); Eisengrein, *Unser liebe Fraw zu alten Oetting*, pp. 47–50; see also pp. 33–36 for a description of the above-cited material.

42. Ibid., pp. 53 and 66–116 passim. On the relationship between fire and hagiography, see R. Freudenthal, *Das Feuer im deutschen Glauben und Brauch* (Berlin, 1931); and Veit, *Volksfrommes Brauchtum und Kirche*. Lutherans, too, drew upon the topos of incombustibility; see Scribner, "Incombustible Luther."

grein also adapts the legends of other popular shrines, such as Andechs and Hohenwart, that celebrated the "miraculous" rediscovery of relics or a saint's grave and so connected these local sites to the popular myth of St. Helen's unearthing of the True Cross in fourth-century Palestine.[43] Eisengrein, in this mold, notes that during the Magyar attacks Altötting's relic treasury was spirited away for safekeeping in Passau. There it was walled into the cathedral, and in the ensuing chaos became forgotten and neglected. After more than 450 years, however, it was miraculously rediscovered, to be returned in triumph to its true home.[44]

Eisengrein's Altötting history is thus a story of perpetual reverence in the face of constant challenges and trials, the tiny chapel of Our Lady becoming a mute emblem of the entire sweep of the territory's history. As Bavaria's "first church," its survival over a thousand years is the best testimony to Catholic truth. It is the duchy's "silent preacher," revered through the ages not only by ordinary "common folk," but by the German emperors, nobles, and important clergy as well. Protected by God, it is like a seal set to the duchy's special covenant:

> Therefore, you chosen, beloved Bavarians, heed the silent preacher God has sent you and which He has miraculously preserved for your good for such a long time, namely, the ancient and holy chapel of Our Lady at Altötting. Do not hastily renounce it. Hold it no less in honor than your pious forefathers who left to you a strong argument and a sharp sword against any opposition to the faith. You yourself are a continual reminder and sermon for the ancient Catholic faith which St. Rupert preached in this chapel a thousand years ago. In this [faith] you have been baptized, as all Christian Bavarians of the present and previous times were, and in it you will remain confirmed in your graves. And do not let yourselves be separated from it in any way, so that you will without a doubt receive and possess eternal joy and holiness after this transitory life. Amen.[45]

By making Altötting a visible yet silent attestation of Catholic truth, Eisengrein relied on the same pious sensibilities that underpinned such rites as Corpus Christi. As in that event's pompous processions, his rhetoric appealed to an emergent Bavarian cultural

43. Sargent, "Miracle Books and Pilgrimage Shrines," p. 463.
44. Eisengrein, *Unser liebe Fraw zu alten Oetting*, pp. 127ff.
45. Ibid., pp. 98–99.

identity. In the late fifteenth century, humanist hagiographers had often used the lives of native saints to resolve an abiding sense of Pan-Germanic cultural inferiority and symbolize imperial unity.[46] Certainly by Eisengrein's time, hopes of finding such an iconic embodiment of imperial unity in a saint's cult had become futile; in his account, therefore, Altötting represents more narrowly the Bavarian duchy's increasingly self-conscious alliance with Rome. While he grants the shrine a primacy of place in the territory's *Heilsgeschichte*, moreover, he omits any discussion of the life and piety of its patroness; rather than serving as a model for human imitation, she stands in the background of the drama enacted at Altötting. Her ability to protect the site, her personal triumph over sin, and her saintly demeanor, after all, are superhuman attributes incapable of mortal simulation. Hence, by ignoring the human and concentrating on the protective dimensions of the Virgin, Eisengrein undertakes to renew reverence and humility before her shrine.

To deepen this awe, the theologian includes idealized portraits of the piety and spirituality that the faithful demonstrate at the chapel. He describes the joy and excitement on the faces of peasants as they first view Altötting. Rather than falling into fits of ecstasy or hysteria, Eisengrein's pilgrims approach the chapel feeling unworthy. They hesitate before entering the Virgin's presence; many, he writes, remain outside, falling to their knees to recite the Stations of the Cross. After a time they rise and enter the church, where they confess their sins, participate in the mass, partake of the Eucharist, and leave their offerings. Some maintain a nightlong vigil outside the shrine, singing songs of praise to Mary and Christ.[47]

By emphasizing the pronounced psychological unworthiness that sin produces in those who come into the shrine's presence, the theologian strove to establish a more rigorous kind of discipline over pilgrimage. In a now-classic essay on Counter-Reformation penance, John Bossy argues that the Tridentine Church moved to promote a new personal conception of wrong-doing. While scholastic theologians argued that sin was first a product of the human mind, in practice, Bossy observes, the late medieval Church had attacked the outward consequences and divisions that it created in

46. Weiss, "Hagiography by German Humanists."
47. Eisengrein, *Unser liebe Fraw zu alten Oetting,* p. 159.

communities. By contrast, the counter-reformers promoted a new technology of confession that underscored the penitent's interior failings. Through the adoption of private rather than public penance, the use of confessional boxes, and a ritualized regimen emphasizing the interior dimension of sin, confession became an act of intense, inward psychological self-examination.[48]

Others have presented a different picture of the progress of penance in early modern Europe. Jean Delumeau and Emmanuel Le Roy Ladurie, for example, overturn evidence that an internalized sense of *metanoia* already existed among broad segments of European society as early as the thirteenth century.[49] Thomas Tentler's study of confessors' manuals, moreover, shows that late medieval priests excavated, enumerated, and attacked sins for both the personal and the social evils they produced.[50] But despite their differing characterizations of the appearance and development of a distinctly Western guilt culture, all these scholars are agreed that the various reformations of the sixteenth century did intensify the personal, interior conception of sin. Both Luther and Calvin articulated some of the most pessimistic assessments of human depravity in the Western tradition. And while the views propounded at the Council of Trent were slightly more optimistic, they were hardly a ringing endorsement of human potentiality.

In his account of the Altötting devotion, then, Eisengrein connected the practice of pilgrimage to this increasingly despairing debate on human frailty. Convicted by the knowledge of their sinful nature, the faithful who entered into the divine presence at Altötting were, like Old Testament figures, struck dumb by a "tremendous and fascinating mystery."

This effort to lodge pilgrimage within the Catholic Reformation's discourses on sin is also interesting because of its chronology. The Counter-Reformation regimen of penance pioneered in Italy by Charles Borromeo was to be adopted only slowly in Germany. As late as 1630, the private confessional was viewed in many dioceses

48. John Bossy, "The Social History of Confession in the Age of the Reformation," *Transactions of the Royal Historical Society* 25 (1975): 21–38.

49. Jean Delumeau, *Sin and Fear: The Emergence of a Western Guilt Culture, 13th–18th Centuries,* trans. Eric Nicholson (New York, 1990); and Emmanuel Le Roy Ladurie, *Montaillou: The Promised Land of Error,* trans. Barbara Bray (New York, 1978).

50. Thomas N. Tentler, *Sin and Confession on the Eve of the Reformation* (Princeton, 1978).

as entirely optional, and the rigor of the new penance was not generally established until the late seventeenth and early eighteenth centuries.[51] Long before the new type of penitential discipline became the standard, figures like Martin Eisengrein were beginning to link extrasacramental practices such as pilgrimage to the examination of conscience, and to insist that these institutions could deepen knowledge of an individual's unworthiness.

Humility and awe before Altötting are not extolled just because of the shrine's venerable age, its eminence as Bavaria's "first church," or past miracles worked at the site. In the final chapters of his book Eisengrein includes numerous accounts of contemporary miracles worked there to prove the shrine's continuing power. The longest and most thoroughly expounded of these stories relates Peter Canisius's exorcism of a young noblewoman, Anna von Bernhausen, in 1570, an event Eisengrein did not personally observe but reconstructed from the testimonies of witnesses.[52] An exorcism provided an ideal way to rebut Protestant attacks on shrines as inspired by Satan; for if the shrine's patron could cast out demons, pilgrimage could hardly be judged diabolic worship. Eisengrein's publicizing of the Altötting event, however, was more than a simple counterattack in the Protestant-Catholic debate over pilgrimage; it was also, apparently, an attempt to convince his readers of the reality of demons.

A complex series of events had preceded the exorcistic drama recounted by Eisengrein in his pilgrimage book, and evidently shaped his exploitation of the incident. In 1568, the noble Fugger family at Augsburg believed that evil spirits had infested their house. Two women, one a young maid named Susanna and the other a noble lady-in-waiting, Anna von Bernhausen, had begun to exhibit all the "classic" signs of demonic possession, including the eating of glass. To cure the women, the Fuggers approached the rector of the local Jesuit college, Paul Hoffaeus, and requested the services of an exorcist. The rector appointed a young Jesuit to perform

51. W. M. Ploechl, *Geschichte des Kirchenrechts* (Munich, 1966), 4:149; and Henry Charles Lea, *A History of Auricular Confession and Indulgences in the Latin Church* (Philadelphia, 1896), 1:396.

52. Eisengrein, *Unser liebe Fraw zu alten Oetting*, pp. 248ff. The list of those who witnessed the event begins on page 264 and includes two canons of the Altötting collegiate church, the shrine's preacher, the organist, an imperial notary, a Wittelsbach notary, a monastic canon, and university students from Stuttgart and Ingolstadt.

the task, but stipulated that he not exorcise his patients at night, in public, or more often than once a week. At the time, approximately 90 percent of Augsburg's population was Protestant, and by adhering to these cautious measures Hoffaeus hoped to avoid criticism from the locals. His prohibitions against nocturnal exorcisms especially were likely intended to protect the young priest from charges of sexual impropriety.[53]

The Jesuit took up residence in the Fugger household, but despite frequent attempts he was unable to free the women from the spirits. Soon others were enlisted to try their hand. In the midst of this confusion, a spirit appeared to Ursula Fugger with the message that the maid Susanna would be cured of her possession only by making a pilgrimage to Loreto and Rome. The Jesuit fathers, who had been laboring against the spirits now for almost two years, agreed that a pilgrimage might prove successful. Thus in 1569 Ursula and Johann Fugger and the young Susanna set out on their journey, accompanied by their Jesuit exorcist and an impressive entourage. But as Hoffaeus had feared, the public spectacle created by their departure drew reaction from Augsburg's Protestants, who circulated broadsides mocking the pilgrimage and the Jesuits.[54]

The pilgrims made their way to Rome via the Holy House at Loreto, and on their arrival in the Holy City they were welcomed in audiences with the pope and Augsburg's absent bishop, the Cardinal Otto Truchseß von Waldburg. The pope arranged for several Jesuits to conduct Susanna's exorcisms, and after a few attempts in the church of S. Maria dell'Anima the spirits fled her body in March 1570. With the young girl cured, the Fuggers prepared to return to Augsburg; but before their departure Cardinal Truchseß learned that Johann Fugger harbored a "false opinion" concerning the possession: he believed that no demon had bewitched her, but rather that God had sent the spirit of a dead, poor soul from purgatory to reside in Susanna's body, and, to proclaim his divine majesty, he had allowed the devil to torture the spirit before redeeming it.[55]

Since at least the fifteenth century, the activities of these name-

53. James Brodrick, *St. Peter Canisius* (Chicago, 1962), pp. 695–697.
54. Otto Braunsberger, *Beati Petri Canissii Societatis Jesu Epistulae et Acta* (Freiburg i. B., 1896–1923), 6:641–651; and Brodrick, *St. Peter Canisius,* pp. 695–697.
55. Franz Zoepfl, *Geschichte des Bistums Augsburg und seiner Bischöfe im Reformationsjahrhundert* (Munich, 1969), 2:404.

less poor souls had been feared in the Bavarian countryside, where, condemned to wander in search of the prayers and pious good works of the living, they were believed to congregate in cemeteries and shrines. Sometimes they assumed the form of huge toads to threaten people into performing some good work, a pilgrimage, the giving of alms, or the recitation of prayers to aid their redemption. At Bavarian shrines, female pilgrims offered votives in the shape of frogs to protect themselves from the "bearing mother," a spirit that bit women, threatening their fertility and pregnancies. And in late medieval and early modern miracle books, accounts appear of those who witnessed some affliction flee their body in the form of toads or snakes.[56] These phenomena seem to share more than a structural similarity, and they reveal the intimate role that the purgatorial dead could play in Bavarian religion.

Whether Johann Fugger associated Susanna's pilgrimage to Rome and Loreto with the exorcism of reptilian spirits is not known, but he does seem to have believed that a poor soul in need of the pious good work of a pilgrimage had inhabited the woman's body before being redeemed. To Cardinal Truchseß, however, such an opinion was an "old and damnable heresy." On two occasions in 1570, in fact, he wrote Duke Albrecht in Bavaria to alert him of the dangers inherent in Fugger's views, assuring the duke that God had no need to use possession to proclaim his majesty and that the pope had denounced the confusion of poor souls with true demons.[57]

In attributing possession to a purgatorial spirit sent by God to be tortured in Susanna's body, Johann Fugger had raised one of the great questions inherent in Christian exorcism: What part did God play in possession? As master of the universe, did he play only a passive role in allowing Satan to torment human bodies, or was his role more directive? The official position of the Roman Church on possession was subtle, insisting that God's role was similar to that

56. See Andree, *Votive und Weihegaben*, pp. 129–132; Gierl, *Bauernleben und Bauernwallfahrt*, p. 125; Rudolf Kriss, *Das Gebärmuttervotiv. Ein Beitrag zur Volkskunde* (Augsburg, 1929); and Peter Assion, "Das Krötenvotiv in Franken," *Bayerisches Jahrbuch für Volkskunde 1968*, pp. 65–77. On the *Armeseelen*, or poor souls, see *Reallexikon zur deutschen Kunstgeschichte*, ed. Otto Schmidt, vol. 1 (Stuttgart, 1937), s.v. "Armeseelen"; and Bächtold-Stäubli (ed.), *Handwörterbuch des deutschen Aberglaubens*, s.v. "Armeseelen." Günther Thomann includes a discussion of the late medieval and early modern cult of the dead in "Die armen Seelen."
57. Zoepfl, *Geschichte des Bistums Augsburg*, p. 404.

in the trials of Job; that is, he merely permitted Satan to torture Christians. But the use of exorcism to prove points of doctrine was common among both Catholics and Protestants in sixteenth-century Europe. In France in 1566, a famous case had occurred when the young Nicole Obry was exorcised daily for over two months in the cathedral at Laon. This "miracle of Laon," which may have been witnessed by as many as 150,000 people, sparked a whole series of dramatic, propagandistic exorcisms in France that theologians of both persuasions used to affirm their own doctrinal positions.[58]

When priestly footsoldiers headed off into the field to implement such a powerful device as exorcism, fine theological distinctions often disappeared. In several of the French cases of propagandistic exorcism, the possessing devils insisted that they had been sent directly by God to preach Catholic truth.[59] Fugger, too, had committed this error by judging Susanna's possession too explicitly a work of God. But he had also expressed a more serious opinion by insisting that the souls of the departed were not actually consigned to purgatory, but were free to roam the earth and to torture human beings in search of good works and godly intervention. Such an assessment of the divine plan, clearly, could cause serious disruption of orderly Catholic relations with the dead.

It is not known whether Duke Albrecht relayed Cardinal Truchseß's concerns regarding these heretical purgatorial beliefs to Martin Eisengrein. Although relations among Truchseß, Canisius (the final player in this drama, the man who would exorcise Anna von Bernhausen), Eisengrein, and the Wittelsbach duke were close, a lacuna occurs in the correspondence between Eisengrein and Albrecht during 1570.[60] Perhaps Eisengrein learned of Fugger's "errors" from Canisius or some other third party. In any case, when the Ingolstadt theologian arrived at the story of Anna's exorcism in the Altötting chapel, his understanding of how Bavaria's purgatorial beliefs deviated from the official position of the Church came into

---

58. D. P. Walker, *Unclean Spirits: Possession and Exorcism in France and England in the Late Sixteenth and Early Seventeenth Centuries* (Philadelphia, 1981).

59. Ibid.

60. More than forty-five letters passed between the duke and Eisengrein during 1568–1569, but only three survive from 1570. See Pfleger, *Martin Eisengrein,* pp. 150–161.

play.[61] He was concerned, in other words, not only to use the event to refute Protestant attacks on shrines; he also sought to demonstrate that demons, rather than poor souls, had inhabited the young woman's body.

As the first group of Fugger pilgrims was traveling to Loreto and Rome in search of a cure for the possessed maid Susanna, the condition of Anna von Bernhausen worsened. When she began to exhibit the signs of a more serious multiple possession,[62] her caretakers, Mark and Sybilla Fugger, appealed to the Jesuit Peter Canisius, at the college in nearby Dillingen, to come to Augsburg and exorcise the woman. He accepted and, late in 1569, announced that he would perform the exorcism publicly in Augsburg's cathedral as a vindication of Catholicism. Martin Eisengrein began his account of Anna's rescue with these public rituals, during which, he related, Canisius was able to expel six demons, but a seventh stubbornly remained.[63] Then one evening the Virgin appeared to Anna to tell her that this last demon would be exorcised only if she made a pilgrimage to Altötting and there presented a chalice as a votive gift. Immediately, the Fugger family prepared to make the journey to the shrine with a small entourage that included Canisius.

Arriving at Altötting late on January 21, 1570, the group, before retiring, hurried to the chapel to recite the Laurentian litany—a collection of prayers connected to the shrine at Loreto—"in order to make a good beginning."[64] During the late sixteenth and early seventeenth centuries, the popularity of the Loreto devotion had been steadily rising in Catholic Europe. Canisius himself had introduced the Laurentian prayers to Bavaria with a German translation published at Ingolstadt in 1559, and his benefactor, Cardinal Truchseß, maintained a special affection for the shrine also.[65]

61. Earlier, notably, he had published two treatises that promoted Church teaching concerning purgatory and prayers for the dead: *Ein frey, christlich, unpartheyisch und allgemain Concilium* (Ingolstadt, 1567) and *Beschayden und diser Zeyt sehr nothwendige erklärung dreyer Hauptarticul* (Ingolstadt, 1568); Latin ed.: *De certitudine gratiae tractatus apologeticus* (Ingolstadt, 1569), reprinted under the title *Euthanasia sive de firma spe ac fiducia in Dei misericordi* (Cologne, 1576).
62. Eisengrein, *Unser liebe Fraw zu alten Oetting*, pp. 248–249.
63. Ibid.; and Brodrick, *St. Peter Canisius*, pp. 695–697.
64. Eisengrein, *Unser liebe Fraw zu alten Oetting*, p. 345.
65. Nikolaus Paulus, "Die Einführung der lauretanischen Litanei in Deutschland durch den seligen Petrus Canisius," *Zeitschrift für katholische Theologie* 26 (1902): 574–600; Bauerreiß, *Kirchengeschichte Bayerns* 6:342–343; and Barbara Leslie Wollesen-

According to legend, angels had rescued the Virgin's house in Palestine from impending doom at the hands of infidels, transporting it to Loreto in northern Italy. It was thus an extension of this story to assume, as many did, that prayers discovered in that house, a place preserved from the attack of the godless, possessed the power to protect against evil spirits.[66] Indeed, prayers discovered in holy places, mostly at pilgrimage shrines, were thought to be qualitatively superior to the many other types of prayers in circulation. Those found in the Holy Sepulcher in Jerusalem, for example, evoked the site itself and allowed supplicants to imagine themselves at the actual place where the greatest of Christian events had occurred.[67] In the Fuggers' case, however, by directing their prayers to the Loreto Madonna, the entourage desired not only to evoke an image of the holy house, but also, and more importantly, to elicit the Virgin's protection and presence. Because they believed their house to be under attack from evil spirits, perhaps Our Lady of Loreto would look favorably on their entreaties and resolve their household crisis in Augsburg.

The next morning, the pilgrims heard two masses consecutively, and each confessed to Canisius and received the sacrament. In the afternoon the Jesuit priest began to lead the group in the rosary, but the devil inside Anna would not allow her to repeat the phrase "Holy Mary, Mother of God." Instead he began to speak in the deep, throaty voice often described as typical of demons. He would not be silenced until Mark Fugger picked the girl up and placed her before the chapel's main altar.[68]

Realizing that the time had come to begin the ritual of exorcism, Canisius ordered the demon to flee the woman's body. Then he proceeded to interrogate the devil, asking who had sent him. The demon responded that he was the seventh and final spirit sent by

Wisch, "The Archiconfraternità del Gonfalone and Its Oratory in Rome: Art and Counter-Reformation Spiritual Values" (Ph.D. diss., University of California, Berkeley, 1985), pp. 319–320.

66. G. G. Mersseman, "Der Hymnos Akathistos im Abendland" (pt. 2), *Spicilegium Friburgense* 3 (1960): 53–63; Walter Pötzl, "Loreto in Bayern," *Jahrbuch für Volkskunde* 2 (1979): 187–218; Stephen Beissel, *Geschichte der Verehrung Marias im 16. und 17. Jahrhundert* (Freiburg i. B., 1909).

67. Reinburg, "Popular Prayers in Late Medieval and Reformation France," pp. 300–313.

68. Eisengrein, *Unser liebe Fraw zu alten Oetting*, p. 252.

Satan to torture Anna. Canisius continued the examination, asking him how much longer he would plague her. The devil replied that he would be allowed to stay two days longer so that he might torture her twenty-four times: seven times for her sins and those of her mother and father, seven times for the sins of her lineage, five times for the trespasses of the Fuggers, and five times more because "it was commanded of him."[69]

Having revealed his agenda, the demon proceeded with his twenty-four tortures. Eisengrein's account emphasizes the physical battle being waged for the young girl's body between Mary and the demon, and the narrative is divided into the four scenes of multiple tortures outlined by the demon. To mount his counteroffensive, Canisius recited a variety of prayers, to which the devil responded by levitating the woman's body and then sending her crashing to the floor. She would then succumb to fits so severe that not even five men could hold her down. Only when a small statue of the Virgin was held behind the woman's head or the cross placed before her eyes would the attacks stop, and the demon would cry out, "Let go of me, you whore! Why are you trouncing me so hard?" The devil addressed the exorcist as a "dog torturer," to which the priest responded on more than one occasion that he would indeed torture him like the "devilish hound" he was.[70]

After nineteen of these fits, Anna slipped into a deep state of unconsciousness in which the Virgin appeared to her, flanked by two angels clad in white. Our Lady told the woman that the devil would be allowed to torture her another five times but then would flee. Before leaving her body, however, the demon should be commanded by Canisius to perform a ritual of submission: he should kneel, recite five Our Fathers, five Hail Marys, and finally kiss the ground of the chapel seven times. The events proceeded as the Virgin had foretold and prescribed, and following the demon's show of submission he let out one last blood-curdling scream and fled the site.[71]

With the woman freed from her possessing spirit, Canisius

---

69. Ibid., p. 255; this is a recurrent topos in exorcistic accounts. See D. Walker, *Unclean Spirits*, pp. 8ff.

70. Eisengrein, *Unser liebe Fraw zu alten Oetting*, p. 254.

71. Ibid., p. 258.

spoke to those assembled about the meaning of the event, reminding them that as witnesses to this great miracle they should elect to change their own lives. Echoing the concerns of many Jesuits, the priest recommended frequent confession to his listeners. It had been Anna's fate to suffer not only for her own sins, but for those of her mother and father, her lineage, and the Fuggers. Frequent confession, he said, protects one and others from this kind of diabolic attack.[72] In addition, the Jesuit exhorted the witnesses to be careful in their speech: they should guard against swearing or repeating any conjurative formulae that contained the devil's name. Three years earlier, he said, the young Anna had vainly and impiously uttered the name of the devil in an oath, and it was at this very moment that demons had begun to torment her. Attributing possession to an oath was common in medieval legends;[73] its inclusion in Eisengrein's account, however, served to reinforce his previous statement concerning the power of words and incantatory formulae.

Canisius's remarks at the conclusion of the Altötting exorcism in particular, then, painted a portrait of a Satan who used every weapon at his disposal—right down to a carelessly uttered word— to ensnare poor Christians. For Canisius and Eisengrein both, the battle lines between a divinely instituted Church and the Prince of Darkness were clear. Indeed, medieval theologians generally had long insisted that only two types of spirits had been loosed upon the world, angels and demons, of which the latter were more plentiful. Beyond clerical ranks, however, the topography of the spiritual otherworld was more diverse, peopled not just with angels and devils, but with a variety of other maleficent and potentially harmful spirits, including the wandering damned, those who suffered untimely deaths, the unburied, and the poor souls.[74]

In Eisengrein's account, therefore, this story of demonic possession was in part an attempt to recast this realm of spirits in terms of the black-and-white polarity of angels versus demons. Such efforts

---

72. Ibid., p. 263. Drawing the lesson of confession from this exorcism is consonant with the general program of the Jesuit order to renew penance at all costs; see A. Lynn Martin, *The Jesuit Mind: The Mentality of an Elite in Early Modern France* (Ithaca, N.Y., 1988), pp. 69–83.

73. Gurevich, *Medieval Popular Culture*, p. 189.

74. Scribner, "Cosmic Order and Daily Life," p. 8.

were in fact common in sixteenth-century Europe, where Protestant and Catholic theologians alike considered it important to eradicate belief in a continuing intercourse between the dead and the living. Certainly Eisengrein was not the last to use this device to invoke spiritual bipolarity. Still, accounts of demonic possession could not have been very effective in this endeavor, for although the mostly elite readers of Eisengrein's pilgrimage book may have accepted that the evil forces all around them were demonic, others continued to believe in an otherworld full of all sorts of maleficent spirits, including once-mortal "poor souls."[75] Publicly staged exorcisms might not erase such beliefs; however, they apparently raised the general level of fear and anxiety concerning the devil—a desirable outcome from the counter-reformers' perspective.[76]

More important, by including the exorcism in his pilgrimage book, Eisengrein hoped to assure readers that Catholicism possessed a multitude of defenses to combat the Satanic menace. In some French cases of demonic possession, the Eucharist was the sole exorcistic medium, making these events fertile ground for the Huguenot-Catholic dispute over the Real Presence.[77] Although the focus of *Our Lady at Altötting* is somewhat diffuse, its purpose is not. At first glance, young Anna's pilgrimage to Our Lady's chapel appears to be the decisive act that produced the cure; but the rite of exorcism was also posed as a dramatic struggle that employed a variety of intermediating agents to accomplish its ends. The pilgrimage, the mass, the Laurentian litany, an image of the Virgin, the rosary, confession, the cross, and the demonic adjuration—all were combined and channeled in the routinized charisma of an ordained, Catholic priest working in a consecrated sanctuary. By the very multiplicity of its defenses, this retelling of the incident advertised the Roman Church as an institution that alone had the tools necessary to conquer the devil.

75. Concerning the increasing dualism of the Protestant and Catholic reformers' cosmos, see Erik Midelfort, "The Devil and the German People: Reflections on the Popularity of Demon Possession in Sixteenth-Century Germany," in *Religion and Culture in the Renaissance and Reformation*, ed. Steven Ozment, Sixteenth-Century Essays and Studies 11 (Kirksville, Mo., 1989), pp. 101–103. The persistence of the "poor soul" cult in Bavaria is treated in Günther Thomann, "Die armen Seelen im Volksglauben und Volksbrauch."

76. Erik Midelfort, "The Devil and the German People."

77. D. Walker, *Unclean Spirits*, pp. 19–42.

Eisengrein's inclusion of Canisius's remarks to the exorcism's witnesses are revealing in another sense as well. Certainly the best way to conquer Satan, this Counter-Reformation account intones, is to avoid confrontation with him altogether. Through confession, Christians rid both themselves and the community of sins, thus preventing Satan's attempts to claim what is, without sacramental intervention, a flawed and damned humanity, which is his by right. Care in speech is another way to immunize oneself from diabolic attack. Canisius's prescription, then, involves reforming the individual and community in a way that directs both their inward and outward acts toward God—a theme that stands as an important component of Counter-Reformation and Jesuit piety.[78] In recent years, historians have characterized the fifteenth and sixteenth centuries as a period in which laity and clergy alike devoted themselves to the pursuit of both personal and communal holiness with new vigor. The connection that Canisius and Eisengrein drew between such sanctity and the need to protect oneself from demonic attack demonstrates that negative forces, perhaps as much as positive ones, were contributing to this lay and clerical reassessment of piety.

In the final chapter of his book, directly following the account of the exorcism, Eisengrein relates the other miracles that the Virgin has worked at Altötting. Presented thematically under headings specifying seven kinds of intercession, the miracles read like a catalogue of responses to sixteenth-century despairs: revival from death and near death, and cures from mental illness, kidney stones, crippling diseases, deafness, and blindness.[79] Although the terse, formulaic literary style typical of the late Middle Ages has been abandoned here in favor of a more complete narrative, the kinds of intercessions are similar to those reported at late medieval shrines. Since the dramatic climax of the book has already appeared in the account of the exorcism, these thaumaturgic wonders are transformed into logical, relatively undramatic continuities in a history filled with fantastic events. For what reader, having been convinced that Our Lady possessed the power to make the devil kiss the floor

78. Bossy, "The Counter-Reformation and the People of Catholic Europe"; H. O. Evennett, *The Spirit of the Counter Reformation* (Notre Dame, Ind., 1970), pp. 23–42; and Martin, *Jesuit Mind*, pp. 72ff.

79. Eisengrein, *Unser liebe Fraw zu alten Oetting*, pp. 293ff.

of her chapel, could doubt that she could also cure gout or rheumatism, or even revive the dead?

Like the host in Johann Nass's defense of Corpus Christi, Eisengrein's Altötting propaganda metamorphosed this tiny church into an immutable locus in a dramatic historical procession, an immanental anchor and a repository of "graces" to be sought out and revered. Originally the focus for heathen devotion, the chapel became Bavaria's first church, the place in which the sacrifice of the mass had first been celebrated. Preserved inviolate through the centuries, despite the attacks of "godless" Magyars and the presence of heresies all around Bavaria, this site had sent forth a steady stream of testimonies to its miraculous and salvific powers. Unspoiled for more than a thousand years, its very survival validated the truths of Roman *traditio.*

In total, then, Eisengrein's pilgrimage book extolled piety for the mute and humble faithful who came to view the silent witness of Our Lady's shrine, sought to understand its sacred mysteries, and strove to apply the spiritual insights they attained there toward improving their lives. The Altötting myth that he created answered the Protestant charge that shrines were the superfluous innovation of the late medieval Church and that they encouraged diabolic idolatry.

It also resolved a tension over the meaning of the Altötting shrine specifically. Before 1489, in fact, no pilgrimage to Altötting had existed, and when miracles first began to be reported there and pilgrims—including the German emperor and the Wittelsbach duke—flocked to the site, conflicting explanations for the shrine's origins and present purpose were also advanced. Jacob Isseckemer, in 1497, reasoned in his *Little Book of Mary* that the Virgin had established herself at Altötting, a church constructed by Charlemagne, to create a fortress in the center of the Holy Roman Empire; she had been displaying great graces to gather the faithful in preparation for the imminent arrival of the Antichrist and the Apocalypse.[80] A little over two decades later, in 1519, Johannes Aventinus, in humanist, patriotic fashion, transformed the chapel into a structure hurriedly erected by the Christianized Bajuwaren; displaying the humanist's cautious attitude toward miracles, however, he failed to make ex-

---

80. Jacob Isseckemer, *Das Buchlein der Zuflucht zu Maria.*

plicit the connection between the site's antiquity and its current miraculous power.[81] During these same years, Bavaria's dukes had
showered the site with a reverence reserved for only a few of their
territory's most important shrines. Until the 1520s, in fact, Altötting
remained one of the most important shrines in a landscape crowded
with such sites. Still, there were few signs in these early decades that
the tiny chapel would eventually become Bavaria's spiritual capital.

As Martin Eisengrein attempted to revive the shrine from its
Reformation-era decline, he skillfully crafted a new identity for the
cult. Like Johannes Aventinus before him, the theologian searched
for meaning in the past rather than in the vision of an imminent
Apocalypse, and he pushed his sights well into antiquity, into the
dark days of Bavaria's heathen past. Unlike Aventinus, however,
Eisengrein embraced Altötting as the visible embodiment of an
ever-expanding, organic tradition, in which the relationship between past and present bore no trace of humanist disjunction.
Eisengrein's work brilliantly evokes the power of myth. And with
the extravagant legendary identity thus conferred on the shrine, the
site was set to be raised, by both the Wittelsbach state and Bavaria's
counter-reforming clergy, to ever greater preeminence within the
ranks of the duchy's holy places.

81. Aventinus, *Sämmtliche Werke* 4(2):30–59.

Fig. 1.   Title page of Jacob Isseckemer's 1497 Altötting miracle book, *The Little Book of Mary, God's Mother's Refuge in Altötting*.

Fig. 2.   A pilgrimage broadside advertising the Passau Bleeding Host miracle of 1478.

Von aim grossen wunderzaychen das vnser

fraw gethan hat vor dem birg in aim dörflin Scheffaw genant nach bey Etal. Darnach von den
vier walfarten wie sy creutzweyß ligen im mittel Etal.

Marie lob wil ich breysen
Mit vil wunderzaychñ weysen
Die yetz geschehen uberal
Die all zuschreiben ist on zal
So vil thůt sy wunderzaychen
Das vns der glaub nit kan laychen
Auns ich yetzund euch wil sagen
Das gschehen ist bey den tagñ
Vordem birg nit weit von Etal
Waust menger mensch uberal
Ist ain dörflin Aschach geñant
Des hat der Abt in gwalt vnd hant
Zů Etal do sind brüder drey
Die haben ain gůt schweig dabey
Zů sich ward graf ain gůte geseß
Ziehen sich haben milch vnd keß
Was sich geben hat in dem jar
Will ich euch machen offenbar
An dem abent deß aufferttag
Das ist kain mer ain ware sag
Hat der hirt auf getryben frů
Ist kömen ain klains knäblin herzů
Wolffgang nun fierthalb jar alt
Hat noch seiner vernůft kain gwalt
Kain her auff ain stecken gritten
Nach jung vnd kintlichem sitten
Kam weyt mit dem hirten hinauß
Er maint es wer wider zůhauß
Hindersich baim von jm gegangen
Das was nit gar groß verlangen
Hetten vatter vnd můter bald
Vmb jr liebs kind hetten sy groß laid
Sůchten das allenthalben uberal
Gar vil nachpauren one zal
Am andern tag wards nit funden
Hanns heutner sein vater von stunden
Entbieß das zů vnser frawen
Das sy mit jr gnad wer schawen
Auff jren hertzenliebsten son
Das jr den behüte gar schon
Von stund an trost er uberkam
Seins hertzens groß traurig nam
Maria die hailigst junckfraw
Die mit gnad raicht zů scheffaw

Nit weit von dem er̄ elegen
On zweyfel sy hat geptlegen
Vnd das kind in der wüst bewart
Des můter sich auch kymmert hart
Der vater die můter trost wol
Dañ sy was aller traurung vol
Nun hört zů an dem dritten tag
Kam allenthalb die groß klag
Von meng ward gesůcht das kind
Durch schrofen weld wasser gswind
In wolf bern hiln grüben auch
Allen menschen zesůchen was gauch
Ob es im wasser ertruncken wer
Oder vertragen wolf oder ber
Vil wasser lauffen do gar gschwind
Noch kund niemand finden das kind
Auf abent verzweyflet die schar
Ain grosses volck aber nit gar
Ain man der gieng neben auß weit
Do ain filzmoß mit heggen leyt
Vber das moß gugt er hinein
Er ersach das haupt des kindelein
Vber ain staudenies sich duckt
Es sich verbarg do hinder schmuckt
Doch er der stauden wol acht nam
Er zů dem kindlin gar bald kam
Maria on zweyfel in wiß
Das er das kindlin fand so gwiß
Grosse fröd der man do empfieng
Das kindlin ain weil mit jm gieng
Er trůgs kind sein not ermessen
Er fragt liebs kind wo hast gessen
Es sprach mit meiner můter dranck
Hab ich jm die speyß vnd den tranck
Můter maria geben hab
Also ward gefunden der knab
Vater můter groß fröd hetten
Och alle menschen sy tetten
Ain loblich opffer gen scheffaw
Do mit zaychen r···
Die on zweyfel das kind hat bhut
Mit jr grosser gnad milter gůt
Die behüt vns allesam hie
Helff vns auß aller angst vnd mie

Ain anders hör vnd weyter mer
Damit der můter gottes eer
Werd gmeret brisen in allem land
Sich wie sy in der figur stand
Auff das creutz du gar eben lůg
Ich hab das erfunden gar klůg
In vnsers lands Geographei
Aller stet beschreybung fand frey
Fier grosser hauptkirchen walfart
Die zesůchen sich meng nit spart
In Prabant ist aine haifft Ach
In schweytz Ainsidelen darnach
Im patt land Etting, jm welschland
Ich Mariam sant loret fand
Die ist ain capell mit groß zieret
Die die engel gottes hand gefürt
Vber mör vnd ist die capell
Do der ertzengel Gabriel
Verkündet englischen grůß
Do ist ablaß für pein schuld büß
Der grof Karel hat auch erleicht
Gottes hand Ainsidel hat gweicht
Sant Karel kayser bawen hat
Ettingen nach der gůten tat
Do er die haiden gar erschlůg
Vor Regenspurg gwan das mit füg
Kayser Ludwig zů Rom lag lang
Der Bapst thet jm an groß zwanr
Der Bapst jm kron nit wolt geben
Der Karser het traurigs leben
Ain minch bracht jm ain merge bild
Er sprach Karser weist du thůn wild
Was ich dich haiff so wirst versönt
Mit dem Bapst: auff den tag krönt
Das gschach der minch hieß jn reiten
In teutschland nit lenger beyten
Auff ain eben reim finster wald
Seins oidens Kloster bawen bald
Das thet er, hyeß Etal do stat
Das bild das jm der minch gebn hat
Sůcht ert all·h·lb vnser frawen
So wils in nde auff euch scha·ven
In mittel des Creutz stat Etal
Billich ist es auch an der zal

Fig. 4. Michael Ostendorfer's 1520 depiction of the contemporary events transpiring at the *Schöne Maria* pilgrimage in Regensburg.

Fig. 5.   Matthias Gerung's "Destruction of the Golden Calf" (ca. 1550),
showing the image installed on a "picture column" (*Bildstock*).

Fig. 6.   Matthias Gerung's "Threefold Idolatry of the Roman Church" (ca. 1550).

Fig. 7. A 1570 Augsburg prodigy depicting a shower of grain in Zwipalen and Ried that occurred on June 14 in that year.

Fig. 8. The "four-footed" hare. A prodigy printed in Calvinist Heidelberg showing an abnormal hare caught on 28 April 1583 in the Palatinate.

Fig. 9.   A 1578 prodigy printed in Catholic Cologne relating the story of the birth of a "cyclopslike" boy in the Netherlands.

Fig. 10.   A 1569 broadside telling of a Jesuit who tried to frighten a young
girl into relinquishing her faith by costuming himself as a demon.

Fig. 11. Lucas Cranach the Elder's depiction of "The Origins of the Papacy," printed in Luther's *The Papacy at Rome, Founded by the Devil* (1545). The work shows the pope being born of the devil's shit and being suckled and reared by demons.

Fig. 12.   A broadside (ca. 1670) showing Munich's recently acquired St. Benno silhouetted against the city's skyline.

Fig. 13. A seventeenth-century broadside advertising the Altötting pilgrimage. The print depicts the central square of the town with its pilgrimage chapel of Our Lady and the ancient collegiate church of Sts. Philip and James. In the foreground, all three patrons are shown doling out rewards to the faithful.

Fig. 14. Frontispiece to Fortunatus Huber's 1671 Neukirchen pilgrimage book, *Ripe Pomegranate*. The print shows the Virgin floating in an ethereal setting while a knife cuts the pomegranate beneath her. The inscription cites Canticles 4:3, "Thy temples are like a piece of pomegranate." In the text Huber explained that it was only by being subjected to the knife that the Virgin of Neukirchen sent forth the precious garnetlike drops of her blood. Neukirchen was located in a border region between Bavaria and recently recatholicized Bohemia, both states being depicted on globes that the lions present at the bottom of the print. Notice, however, that the Bavarian globe is placed above that of the once-Protestant Bohemia.

5

Our Lady at Altötting

A Late Reformation Dispute

Protestant reaction to Martin Eisengrein's *Our Lady at Altötting* was immediate; the swiftness with which the debate commenced still astonishes after more than four centuries. Eisengrein had published the manuscript early in 1571, less than a year following Canisius's soon-to-be notorious exorcism, and the book was displayed at the Frankfurt book fair during Lent. When the Protestant response came, it appeared on the far western fringes of the empire at Strasbourg. Having received his copy of Eisengrein's book soon after its Frankfurt unveiling, the theologian Johann Marbach rushed to complete a four-hundred-page response, *On Miracles and Wondrous Signs*, in time for it to be sold at the fall book fair in the same year.[1] This fury of activity came at a time when he was president of the Lutheran church at Strasbourg and was expected to fulfill a variety of administrative and pastoral functions. His polemic dissected almost line-for-line Eisengrein's claims for the Altötting pilgrimage, revealing the urgent fears that Catholic miracles raised among Protestant theologians. It is doubtful that he ever thought his attack on Eisengrein's pilgrimage book would discourage Bavaria's counter-reformers from using miracles to publicize the power of their church. His aims were more indirect: by engaging in a debate with his rivals, he hoped to convince his Protestant readers of the false, even satanic deceptions that the Jesuits and members of the resurgent Catholic priesthood were perpetrating.

Disputes like these plagued almost every major theologian who wrote during the late Reformation, as polemical activity rose to

1. Martin Eisengrein's *Unser liebe Fraw zu alten Oetting* appears in the Lenten register of the Frankfurt book fair. See *Die Messkataloge Georg Willers*, Die Messkataloge des 16. Jahrhunderts (Hildesheim, 1970), 1:[358]. Johann Marbach's reply, *Von Mirackeln und Wunderzeichen. Wie man sie auß unnd nach Gottes Wort fuer waar oder falsch erkenen soll* (Strasbourg, 1571), appears in the fall Frankfurt catalogue. (*Messkataloge Georg Willers* 1:[394]).

address the increasingly divided and confused religious situation. During the early Reformation Protestant propagandists, faced by a generally disunited, often confused Catholic opposition, had often targeted a distant Roman Antichrist in their printed campaign.[2] By the second half of the century, the Protestant opposition moved to attack the more locally resurgent Catholicism of Jesuit missionaries and openly Catholic states like Bavaria. But now it was Protestantism that was badly disunited as within the empire various brands of Lutheranism and the newly imported Calvinism competed for primacy not only against the Catholics, but among themselves as well. In this complex and heightened confessional atmosphere, any doctrinal pronouncement, whether voiced by Lutheran, Calvinist, or Catholic, was more likely than ever before to stir comment and engender attack.

The Reformation itself had created a market for the debate that poured from German presses during the second half of the century. Printers and booksellers rushed to serve this audience, with the semiannual book fairs in the city of Frankfurt becoming the primary venues for circulation. By 1564, the Augsburg printer Georg Willer had begun to produce catalogues of the books displayed at the fair, a development that allowed theologians and booksellers throughout the empire to track the course of current religious controversies.[3] The presentation of theological ideas at Frankfurt had become highly politicized; town councils and state governments now supervised and sometimes commissioned the works that their local church officials sent off to be displayed at the fairs. As cities and territories jockeyed to gain advantage, to maintain allies, and to criticize enemies, books became an important weapon in imperial politics.[4]

But the disputes that raged between theologians—disputes that can often be traced in the Frankfurt book fair catalogues—were also

2. Scribner, *For the Sake of Simple Folk*; Mark U. Edwards, *Luther's Last Battles: Politics and Polemics, 1531–1546* (Ithaca, N.Y., 1983); and idem, "Catholic Controversial Literature, 1518–1555: Some Statistics," *Archiv für Reformationsgeschichte* 79 (1988): 189–205.

3. On the history of the Frankfurt book fair as a distribution point for Reformation propaganda, see Febvre and Martin, *The Coming of the Book*, pp. 228–233.

4. See the remarks of Abray in *People's Reformation*, pp. 134–135; and Febvre and Martin, *Coming of the Book*, pp. 192–194.

highly personal attacks. Polemicists contented themselves not only with discussing theological issues; they also denigrated their opponents' looks, demeanor, and intelligence. Seething controversies could be maintained for decades, and disputants enlisted their closest associates to enter the fray in their defense. Converts were numerous among the ranks of first-generation counter-reformers and Calvinists, and in many disputes both sides were linked by an intricate web of personal affiliations, participants having studied at the same university or lived and worked for a time in the same city. With the consequent opportunity to monitor enemies' activities and writings over time, polemicists' attacks often included an entire catalogue of the opposition's abuses and "heretical" deviations.

The increasing tendency for theologians on both sides to articulate extreme positions can be seen in the persisting debate over the cult of the saints and pilgrimage. Among the early Protestant leaders, Luther and Bucer were among the two most outspoken. They had attacked saints' shrines for a number of reasons: for promoting a misplaced faith in works, detracting attention away from the parish, wasting time and money, and allowing the faithful to use vows to bargain with saintly patrons. In pondering the mass pilgrimages of the late Middle Ages, both Luther and Bucer had adopted even more extreme positions. Recognizing that the appeal of these places rested firmly on miracles, they denounced the wonders the clergy promoted at shrines like Regensburg and Altötting as "works of the devil." There was in fact little novelty in the charge, since late medieval bishops and ecclesiastical officials had also denounced devotions they judged undesirable and "superstitious" as products of Satan. The prestige and popularity of the early reformers, however, certainly gave the attack more weight.

While the critique of the reformers was for a time successful in discouraging devotion to the saints, it did not completely destroy it. And in the late sixteenth century, as a new class of counter-reforming bishops, theologians, and preachers labored to renew shrines and pilgrimage, Protestant attacks became more persistent, relying increasingly on the idea of diabolic inspiration. In Reformation literature, a topos was developing that characterized pilgrimage shrines as havens of the devil, where Satan worked false miracles to delude and deceive simple people. A corollary motif involved the warning that the clergy who promoted such places were in fact magicians, witches, and sorcerers.[5]

In Strasbourg, Johann Marbach sincerely believed and repeated these charges in his denunciation of Eisengrein's pilgrimage book. Addressing his work to "pious Christians" in Augsburg and Bavaria, Marbach appealed to his readers to remain free of the false religion that "Jesuits and Mammelukes" were promoting in the region. (This reference to the Mamelukes, a politically powerful Egyptian military class occupying the sultanate from 1250 to 1517, occurred frequently throughout the work, only one of many derisory terms Marbach used in describing the activities of the Jesuits.)[6] He commences his attack on *Our Lady at Altötting* by summarizing Eisengrein's principal arguments in defense of the shrine, including its venerable age and survival through the centuries, the numerous pilgrims, among them princes and nobles, that had revered the site, and the miracles that the Virgin had performed there. By applying the Protestant razor of the Scriptures, Marbach summarily dismisses these claims: because the religion practiced at Altötting is unbiblical, Our Lady's cult must be false and superstitious.[7] Thereafter, Marbach undertakes to expose the human and satanic deviations of the Roman Church, cataloguing a host of miracles that the "papists," "the devil's accomplices," have promoted throughout history. Sometimes the Catholics have produced their wonders fraudulently—here he recalls the by-now famous case of the weeping Grimmental Madonna, a statue that each day was made to cry by pouring oil through holes drilled in its head.[8] In addition, Marbach attacks as lies and deceits the traditional miracles attributed to such venerable figures as Saints Benedict, Dominic, and Francis. Like Luther and Bucer he locates the source of all these deceptions in the devil; however, he is unwilling to call the Roman clergy merely confused, deluded by Satan into accepting the divine inspiration of these events. Rather, the Catholic clergy are drawn as active accomplices in perpetrating false miracles. Eisengrein's contemporary account of the Virgin's miracles at Altötting thus

5. Brückner (ed.), *Volkserzählungen und Reformation*, pp. 892–897.
6. Marbach, *Von Mirackeln und Wunderzeichen*, title page; Ludwig Koch, *Jesuiten-Lexikon* (Paderborn, 1934), p. 1153.
7. Marbach, *Von Mirackeln und Wunderzeichen*, p. ii and. fols. ai(r)–aiiii(r).
8. Ibid., fol. diii(v).

emerges in Marbach's polemic as a resurgence of a dangerous "long and mostly forgotten" diabolic idolatry.[9]

The fact that this resurgence of false faith came just when the Lutheran gospel was proclaimed is utterly vexing to Marbach. In twenty-two chapters—more than three-quarters of his account—he devotes himself to a detailed examination of the Ingolstadt theologian's claims for the shrine, with particular attention to the account of Canisius's exorcism.[10] After faithfully recounting the story of Anna von Bernhausen's possession and exorcism as told by Eisengrein, he undertakes to prove the diabolic origins of Canisius's prodigy, emphasizing in particular the multiple apparitions of the Virgin to the young woman. In so doing Marbach transforms the priest Canisius into a demonic sorcerer who conjures up evil spirits not only to possess Anna, but also to assume the form of the Virgin and tell the young woman of Altötting's curative power. He then turns to the Old Testament, comparing Canisius's "false Mary" to the witch of Endor's conjuration of Samuel before Saul:

> The Papists, especially Eisengrein who published the miracles at Altötting, should recognize that this story sounds exactly like the false appearance described in 1 Samuel 29. This Mary of whom he [Eisengrein] speaks was not the holy Virgin Mary, Christ our Lord's Mother. Rather she was a false Mary whom the Jesuits conjured up with the form and the appearance of the Holy Virgin Mary. [This they performed] through their sorcery and the company that they keep with the devil. Just like the devil's whore and soothsayer conjured up through her swearing and magic not Samuel, but the devil himself brought up from hell in the form of Samuel.[11]

Thus Marbach transforms the biblical witch of Endor story, in which no hint of diabolism appears, into a case of black magic. The witch had been a practitioner of necromancy, the conjuring of the spirits of the dead, an art that was enjoying a certain degree of popularity among European elites even as Marbach wrote.[12] The theologian's association of this skill with witchcraft, however, reflects the persistent efforts of Protestants to hinder intercourse with the dead by

9. Ibid., fols. dii(v)–hiii(r).
10. Ibid., fols. nii(r)ff.
11. Ibid., fol. kii.
12. See Jean Seznec, *The Survival of the Pagan Gods* (Princeton, 1972), pp. 37–82, esp. p. 62.

labeling any such effort as satanic conjuration. Whereas for Martin Eisengrein and Peter Canisius, the exorcism in Our Lady's chapel had provided an opportunity to evoke the reality of certain spirits—those of demons and saints—while at the same time denying the presence and potency of the poor souls, Marbach judged all traffic with the spirit world a form of demon worship. As proof he called attention to such incantations and repetitious prayers as the rosary and the Laurentian litany. The Virgin of Altötting must be a demon, he reasoned, for only a demon could inspire the idolatrous outpourings of those who gathered in the tiny chapel.[13]

To inoculate his readers against these idolatries, Marbach sets forth a purified Lutheran theology of miracles. First, he dismisses the doctrine of mediating agents used by Eisengrein to explain the power of holy places, the saints, and consecrated objects and rites.[14] Denying that God has ever worked through the bones or possessions of the saints, he attributes all miracles in the Christian tradition directly to God, his angels, the apostles, and the prophets. These last two classes of wonder-workers, moreover, were mortal, not celestial, and while God granted them the power to perform fantastic feats to confirm his message while living, they were never able to perform miracles from their graves. Thus, all the reports of saintly miracles recorded after the deaths of the apostles, Marbach concludes, are "false" and demonic.[15]

Although he admits that contemporary miracles do occur, Marbach defines them as distinctly different from those recorded in the Bible or the history of the apostolic Church. To the apostles was given the power to heal or to raise the dead so that the Gospel message might be confirmed and proven to the first Christian converts. In the contemporary world, however, God performs miracles of grace and salvation to reveal his plan and confirm his divine majesty. The greatest of these wonders, Marbach intones, is the Lutheran Reformation itself. God sent Luther as a prophet to proclaim his truth, and despite the opposition of the Antichristian

13. Marbach, *Von Mirackeln und Wunderzeichen,* fol. qi(v).
14. Ibid., fols. [2]aiii(v)ff.
15. Ibid., fols. [2]aiii(r)–2bii(r). This charge, the first gleaning of a doctrine of the cessation of miracles, was also appearing around the same time in Calvinist theological works; D. Walker, "The Cessation of Miracles," in *Hermeticism and the Renaissance: Intellectual History and the Occult in Early Modern Europe,* ed. Ingrid Merkel and Allen G. Debus (Washington, D.C., 1988), pp. 111–124.

papacy, the evangel has been preserved, proclaimed, and established in the world. In addition he cites as contemporary miracles the establishment of the true message of faith in Europe, the translation of the Bible into German and other languages, and its distribution to the people.[16]

For those inclined to believe in the direct physical intercession of God in the world, recorded daily in tales of earthquakes, strange births, and other horrors, Marbach's recourse to the "miracles of faith" probably seemed a curious way to affirm Protestant truth. Thus, even as he labored to discourage the appeal of Catholic miracles, his opus helped produce the opposite result in Bavaria and at the Frankfurt fair, granting Eisengrein's pilgrimage book greater attention than it might otherwise have had. Book merchants rushed to purchase the Ingolstadt theologian's tome; during 1571, two editions had to be printed to meet demand.[17]

Marbach's polemic also elicited a response from Bavaria's Catholic reformers, and it bore the stamp of the Wittelsbachs. Within the ducal household, the Catholic convert and court preacher Dr. Johann Jakob Rabus (1545–after 1585) received a copy of Marbach's *On Miracles and Wondrous Signs* shortly after its appearance at the Frankfurt book fair in the fall of 1571. Like Marbach himself, Rabus rushed to issue a rebuttal. By November 30 of the same year, he had completed and sent to press his *Christian Refutation of "On Miracles and Wondrous Signs."*[18]

This Catholic reformer already bore battle scars from several previous combative engagements with Protestants, each of which he appears to have relished. He had, for example, recently opposed Johann Marbach's plan to secularize Catholic Church property in Strasbourg.[19] His interest in preserving the city's Catholic establishment was partly personal, for he had been born in Strasbourg and maintained connections with some of its burghers. Rabus was also the son of one of Germany's more eminent late Reformation theolo-

16. Marbach, *Von Mirackeln und Wunderzeichen*, fols. [2]li(v)–[2]lii(r).
17. Stalla, *Bibliographie der Ingolstädter Buchdrucker*, no. 851.
18. Johann Rabus, *Christlicher und wohlgegründeter Gegenbericht von Mirackeln und Wunderzeichen* (Dillingen, 1572, 1573). Listed in Frankfurt book fair catalogue *Messkataloge Georg Willers 1*, pp. 470, 527.
19. The relevant printed exchanges in this dispute are Johann Marbach, *Von dem Bishofflichen Ampt unnd eines Bishoffs Tugenden* (Strasbourg, 1569); and Johann Rabus, *Christliche und bescheidene ablehnung der vermeinten Bischofspredigt* (Cologne, 1570).

gians; he had been educated in the very heart of the Lutheran movement at Wittenberg before receiving a doctorate in theology from Tübingen. In 1565, dissatisfied with Lutheranism, he had traveled to Augsburg to receive theological instruction from the Jesuits. Fearing that he had been sent as a spy, the Society cautiously accepted the young man as a student, requiring numerous affirmations of his sincerity before finally allowing him to convert.[20] The Wittelsbach duke Albrecht V awarded him generous funds to finance his studies at the Jesuit colleges of Rome, Trent, Cologne, Louvain, Mainz, and Dillingen, and ultimately made him court preacher.

Doubts about Rabus's sincerity apparently persisted, because the preacher continued to make grand gestures of displaying his Catholicity. In Bavaria, for example, he avidly collected Protestant books, smuggled in by traveling merchants, and used them to flesh out his sermons denouncing the heresies of the Reformation.[21] In 1570, he went so far as to turn on his father as a means of proclaiming his support for the Roman cause: when a letter to the elder Rabus explaining his conversion was returned unopened, the new court preacher had it printed to publicize his decision and embarrass his eminent Protestant father. At the same time, he addressed a pamphlet to his father's Ulm parishioners encouraging them to renounce Protestantism and return to the true Church.[22]

Such disloyalty created bitter feelings in Protestant theological circles. At Strasbourg, Johann Marbach denounced Rabus as a sensualist who had managed to find satisfaction only by surrendering himself to the pleasures of "lascivious" papism.[23] In a poem published anonymously, "Night Raven," one of Marbach's associates, Johann Fischart, compared the counter-reformer to a bird of prey

20. *ADB*, s.v. "Rabus, Johann Jakob"; and Hans J. Utz, "Johann Jakob Rabus," *Jahresbericht des Historischen Verein für Straubing und Umgebung* 78 (1975): 53.

21. Karl Schottenloher, ed., *Rom. Eine Münchener Pilgerfahrt im Jubeljahr 1575* (Munich, 1925), p. xix.

22. Johann Jakob Rabus, *Jo. Jac. Rabus etc ad Ludovicum patrem virum clarissimum pro fide Catholica ac suo ad eam accessu epistola apologetica* (Cologne, 1570) (listed in the *Messkataloge Georg Willers* 1:[269]); his pamphlet to his father's parishioners, *Christliche und treuhertzige Vermanung an seine liebe Landsleute alle katholischen Ulmer Daß sie sich von der heiligen Allgemeiner Apostolischen und Papstlichen Kirche nicht abwendig machen lassen* (Cologne, 1570) (*Messkataloge Georg Willers* 1:[288]).

23. Adolf von Haufen, *Johann Fischart. Ein Literaturbild aus der Zeit der Gegenreformation* (Berlin, 1921), 1:105.

feeding upon poor, unsuspecting Christian souls. The 3,700-plus-line poem was particularly caustic in including detailed descriptions of Rabus's exterior ugliness, which Fischart used to confirm his internal corruption. Attacking his "sunken ears baked like cobblestones" and his "chewed-up, poisoned mouth that stinks like a plow horse," "Night Raven" was exceptional in its virulence, even at a time when bitter personal attacks were common.[24] And Rabus remembered the insult: in his counterattack in the dispute over Catholic miracles, he credited Marbach with writing the poem.[25]

But it was more than personal rivalry with Marbach that inspired the court preacher to publish his defense of Martin Eisengrein's pilgrimage book. His father, Ludwig Rabus, had led a Lutheran program to "purify" the saints of their miracles and install them as paragons of a new faith-centered piety. Beginning in 1552, the elder Rabus had issued an eight-volume martyrology intended for use by ministers in composing sermons and for the devotional edification of the elite. In this work the saints, mostly comprising early Church martyrs and confessors, are praised for the strength of their faith rather than for their miracles. In 1571, even as the younger Rabus was writing his defense of the saints and their miracles, his father's martyrology was being reprinted.[26] Rabus's treatise was consequently a denunciation of his father's efforts to cleanse the cult of the saints of one of its traditional appeals.

In the style of much sixteenth-century polemical literature, Johann Rabus draws parallels between biblical incidents of idolatry and contemporary events to discredit Marbach's *On Miracles and Wondrous Signs*, which becomes a "sacrifice to Baal . . . and the whore of Babylon."[27] Though argumentative in tone, Rabus's response does set forth a reasoned defense of Catholic miracles as something other than diabolic sorcery. Like Nass and Eisengrein he agrees that throughout history, from Old Testament times until the present, God has worked spectacular feats by the hands of a host of

24. Johann Fischart, "Nacht Rab oder Nebelkräh" (Strasbourg, 1570), in *Sämtliche Dichtungen*, Deutsche Bibliothek, vol. 8, pt. 1 (Leipzig, 1866), pp. 1–98.

25. Johann Rabus, *Christlicher Gegenbericht*, fol. bii(v).

26. Ludwig Rabus, *Der Heyligen außerwöhlte Gottes Zeugen, Bekennern und Martyrern*, 8 vols. (Strasbourg, 1552); republished as *Historien der Martyrer*, 2 vols. (Strasbourg, 1571). On Ludwig Rabus, see *ADB*, s.v. "Rabus, Ludwig"; and Kolb, *For All the Saints*.

27. Johann Rabus, *Christlicher Gegenbericht*, fol. b(r).

prophets, apostles, and saints.[28] But, he admits, the devil too possesses the power to work miracles. His supernatural theology thus includes "true godly wonders" worked by holy men and "false devilish ones" performed by Satan and evil human beings.

Like Marbach, then, Rabus saw human society as poised between the opposing forces of good and evil. Both the Protestant and the Catholic writer, moreover, took pains to provide readers with a means of testing the spirits to discern whether an event was of divine or demonic origin. Marbach looked to Scripture for his test, for only in a church that followed the Bible's dictates could true, divine miracles occur. Rabus devised a more complicated, and more flexible, four-step method for determining the nature of supernatural intervention. First, he writes, divine miracles always serve to display God's majesty and omnipotence. Second, godly miracles produce lasting results, while the devil's are fleeting. Third, the form, matter, and agents through which the wonder occurs differ according to its origins: the devil works his miracles "through sorcerers, practitioners of black magic, witches, evil spirits, godless, crazed people, and heretics," while God works through the Catholic Church to produce prodigies in the martyrs and the saints. And fourth, godly miracles serve a useful purpose, while devilish ones have no practical end.[29]

Having outlined these rules, Rabus is free to prove that the miracles that have occurred within the Catholic Church are godly. Like Eisengrein, he recounts a number of miracles worked in the early and medieval Church to demonstrate both the antiquity and continuity of God's intervention. But he also decries the complete lack of godly miracles in the Lutheran tradition: after more than fifty years, Rabus charges, the reformers had failed to produce any dramatic affirmations such as appeared with such abundance in the Catholic tradition.[30] Moreover, despite frequent attempts by the Lutherans to exorcise evil spirits, their results had not proved lasting. This was hardly surprising, he reasons, since they stand outside the true Church and its apostolic succession; they are thus both deluded by Satan and lacking the raw materials to combat him. As a consequence of their failed exorcisms, they perceive the devil's

28. Ibid., fol. 15(r).
29. Ibid., fols. 20(v)–21(r).
30. Ibid., fol. 157(r).

power to be greater than it really is. To demonstrate his point, Rabus includes stories of Lutheran exorcisms, two of which involve Luther himself. In one case, a possessed girl was brought from Meissen to Wittenberg for Luther to exorcise. Try as he might, Luther was unable to release the woman from her torturer. Finally, the devil slammed the doors and windows of the room in which the event was occurring. Petrified by fear, Luther tried to leave the room, but without success; he was freed only when someone standing outside seized an axe and chopped through the door.[31] Another story comically satirizes the theologian Bugenhagen's exorcism of a butter-robbing devil from his wife's kitchen. Enraged, the pastor sat on top of the butter dish, adjuring the "butter devil" and his "magical whore" to flee. The message of these incidents, Rabus explains, is clear. Even Luther was unable to bend the devil to his will; and to provide themselves the illusion of being victorious over the devil, Luther's followers trivialize exorcism by fighting imaginary "butter devils."[32]

With the circulation of Rabus's *Christian Refutation* at the Frankfurt book fair early in 1572 the battle lines were clearly drawn, with Satan at the center of the controversy. Both sides feared the devil immensely, interpreting any threat to their missionary and pastoral efforts as a case of demonic intervention. Before their laity, however, Catholic reformers like Canisius, Eisengrein, and Rabus emphasized that he could be controlled by means of Catholicism's outward rituals, its consecrated objects, and its priestly caste. In their eyes, miracles proved the divine authority of their mission. For orthodox Lutherans like Marbach, in contrast, the most effective mechanisms against Satan were an internal faith, a pious life, and the Scriptures. These men argued that Catholic miracles were often cases of diabolic magic, usually attributing this sorcery to the Jesuits or some other counter-reforming religious order.

The debate over Eisengrein's pilgrimage book persisted for more than four years, yet little new entered into the dispute. To stress

---

31. Ibid., fol. 157(v). The story was told to him by the Catholic convert Friedrich Staphylus who was allegedly present at the event.

32. Ibid., fol. 158(r). Rabus reproduces a story circulated among Lutherans; it appeared in Sebastian Fröschel, *Von dem heiligen Engeln, Von Teufel und der Menschen Seele. Drey Sermon* (Wittenberg, 1563). The work is described in Johannes Janssen, *History of the German People at the Close of the Middle Ages*, trans. M. A. Mitchell and A. M. Cowie, 16 vols. (1896–1925; reprinted New York, 1966), 14:474.

to their own flock the dire portent that the resurgence of Catholic miracles represented, Strasbourg's Protestant leaders staged a mock disputation in 1574 that debated and disproved the claims of Rabus's counterpolemic, which Marbach's associate Johann Pappus transcribed and published. And in Bavaria, Rabus, as soon as he received his copy, wrote yet another reply, which he had printed in Strasbourg and in two Munich editions. Like the other entries in this battle of volley and countervolley, Rabus sent his response off to be displayed at the fall 1574 Frankfurt book fair.[33]

The opinions expressed by Lutherans and Catholics in this debate on divine and diabolic intervention were far more than academic theological positions. The evidence suggests that fear of the devil was significantly greater in Lutheran territories during the second half of the sixteenth century than it was in Catholic Germany. A wave of apocalypticism had accompanied the Reformation from its earliest appearance. For Luther, God had abandoned contemporary society to the devil, who was being allowed to confuse and delude mankind before the renewal of gospel preaching and the final Judgment Day. Such apocalyptic fears fueled the propagandistic needs of the early reformers and contributed an urgency to the Protestant call to cleanse Germany of its magical idolatries.[34] Nor was apocalypticism limited to theological elites; the demands of peasants and the urban poor voiced in the Peasants' War of 1525 and the Revolution of the Münster Prophets in 1535 also relied on apocalyptic expectations. A flood of cheap broadsides and prophetic pamphlets thus multiplied theories about the Antichrist's identity and provided reckonings for the imminent date of the Last Judgment. For Lutherans, more than for Catholics or Calvinists, the rising influence of Satan and the coming apocalypse provided a means of explaining their own movement's failures and gave a sense of stability and order.[35]

33. The text of the Strasbourg disputation was published as *Propositiones de dono miraculorum: contra mirabilios* (Strasbourg, 1574). Rabus's response appeared as *Adversus theses a° 1574 publice disputatas contra Sacrarum reliquiarum miracula velitatio succincta* (Strasbourg, 1574; Munich, 1574, 1576). See Utz, "Johann Jakob Rabus," p. 56, for a discussion of the book. The 1574 edition was displayed at the Frankfurt book fair (*Messkataloge Georg Willers* 2:[70]).

34. Scribner, *For the Sake of Simple Folk*; and Heiko A. Oberman, *Luther. Mensch zwischen Gott und Teufel* (Berlin, 1983).

35. Robin Barnes, *Prophecy and Gnosis: Apocalypticism in the Wake of the Late Lutheran Reformation* (Stanford, 1988). Militant apocalypticism also accompanied the

Satan was feared in Lutheran Germany not just as an ominous abstraction but because of the enormous intimacy he could enjoy with the interior person. During the 1550s, a new genre of "devil books" (*Teufelbücher*) had begun to appear in Lutheran Germany. Intended for the layperson, these books placed the blame for human vices on demons, transmogrifying human frailties and short-comings into specific kinds of possession. By 1570, these pamphlets had captured a 10 percent share of the Protestant book market. Presses in Lutheran Germany churned out books on the "marriage devil," the "drunkenness devil," and the "magician's devil," with instructions on how to exorcise the demon that inspired the particular vice or problem.[36] Although intended for personal edification and sanctification, works in this genre blamed Satan for all human frailty. Readers of devil books were consequently taught to fear the devil's activity even in their most intimate thoughts.[37]

Devil-book production was one of the great successes of the sixteenth-century press, with some Protestant printers even establishing their fortunes in this burgeoning market. In 1563, for example, one Sigmund Feyerabend arrived in Frankfurt and began pirating editions of devil books from other printers. By 1568 he had established himself as a highly successful merchant in the field, selling 1,200 copies of his varied stock at the Frankfurt book fair. The following year he became an innovator when he published his *Theater of the Demons*, a work that gathered together twenty separate

---

appearance of the Religious Wars in France; see Denis Crouzet, *Les guerriers de Dieu: la violence au temps des troubles de religion*, 2 vols. (Paris, 1990), esp. chaps. 13–15.

36. On the "marriage devil," see Andreas Musculus, *Wider den Ehteuffel. Ein sehr nützliches Büchlein wie man den heimlichen listen damit sich der leydige Satan wider die Ehestifftung aufflehnet . . .* (Frankfurt a. d. O., 1556), of which seven editions were printed in the sixteenth century. On the "drunkenness devil": *Wider den Sauffteuffel. Etliche wichtige Ursachen Warumb alle Menschen sich für dem Sauffen hüten sollen* (Leipzig, 1552) (eight editions in the sixteenth century). On the "magician's devil": Ludwig Milichius, *Der Zauber Teuffel. Das ist Von Zauberey, Warsagung, Beschwehren, Segen, Aberglauben, Hexerey und manchereley Wercken des Teuffels* (Frankfurt a. M., 1563) (four editions in the sixteenth century). For more on these three works, see Keith L. Roos, *The Devil in Sixteenth-Century German Literature: The Teufelsbücher*, European University Papers, ser. 1: German Language and Literature 68 (Bern, 1972), p. 118.

37. Roos, *Devil in Sixteenth-Century German Literature*; Midelfort, "Devil and the German People," p. 102; Max Osborn, *Die Teufelliteratur des XVI Jahrhunderts* (Berlin, 1893). A selection of many of the devil books published in sixteenth-century Germany appears in Ria Stambaugh, ed., *Teufelbücher in Auswahl*, 5 vols. (Berlin, 1970–80).

devil books within a single edition.[38] By 1574 Feyerabend's preeminence was assured when he sold 3,411 copies of his various demonic publications to one book dealer alone.[39]

Books of this sort taught simply that human failings were demonically produced, but other works, like Jodok Hocker's *The Devil Himself*, published in 1568, focused more directly on providing a complete portrait of Satan in all his guises. Like Marbach, Hocker charged that the devil possessed the power not only to inhabit human bodies but also to use myriad arts of cunning and black magic to deceive and damn mankind. He also, like so many late sixteenth-century Lutherans, judged the thaumaturgy and saintly intercession of the traditional Church as satanic sorcery.[40]

Works like these were the product of a society in which the devil was offered up ever more frequently as an explanation for human misery and misfortune. But it was not just in the press that German Lutherans displayed their pervasive fears of demons; in the decades following 1550, exorcisms rose dramatically in Lutheran Germany, especially in the territories of the North. In that region, indeed, a particular kind of demonomania would sometimes grip a village with a pack of evil spirits possessing groups of 40 or even 150 people. The cause of this tremendous fear, Erik Midelfort suggests, lay in the decades-long pastoral condemnation of sin as demonically produced, coupled with the insistent Lutheran call to faith and the perfect life.[41]

In contrast to Canisius's elaborate spectacle in the Altötting shrine, Lutheran doctrine posed faith as the primary medium of exorcism, and the exorcistic ritual was simpler, relying on prayer, hymns, and Scripture. Certainly in both regions exorcisms were used propagandistically: they were intended to convince people not only of the omnipresence of the devil, but also of their particular confession's ability to combat Satan. In Lutheran Germany, how-

38. *Theatrum Diabolorum, Das ist Ein sehr Nutzliches verstenndiges Buch* . . . (Frankfurt a. M., 1569).

39. See *ADB*, s.v. "Feyerabend, Sigmund"; Roos, *Devil in Sixteenth-Century German Literature*, pp. 62–69, 115–116, 122, 123, 125; and Heinrich Grimm, "Die deutschen 'Teufelbücher' des 16. Jahrhunderts: ihre Rolle im Buchwesen und ihre Bedeutung," *Archiv für Geschichte des Buchwesens* 16 (1959): 1733–1790.

40. Jodok Hocker, *Der Teufel selbs. Das ist Warhafftiger bestendiger und wolgegründter bericht von den Teufeln, was sie sein, woher sie gekommen, und was sie teglich wircken* (Ursel, 1568).

41. Erik Midelfort, "Devil and the German People," pp. 98–119.

ever, exorcism also fulfilled important pious functions, in that it was used explicitly to call the faithful to live an ever more perfect life. Possessions might recur, and whole congregations were vulnerable; pastors, therefore, continually redoubled their efforts to combat Satan by warning their flocks to flee sin.[42]

Given the contrasting styles and purposes of Lutheran and Catholic exorcisms, Johann Rabus's charge that Lutherans granted Satan too much power because of their inability to combat him assumes greater meaning. In the Catholic regions of South Germany exorcisms remained an extraordinary testimony to the physical and spiritual defenses of the Roman Church. Cases like Canisius's exorcism of Anna von Bernhausen in the Altötting shrine were thus freely publicized as dramatic tours de force emblematic of Catholic truth. In 1582, for example, Georg Scherer trotted out a battery of Catholic armaments in his successful exorcism of a young woman in the cathedral of Vienna, expelling a legion of 12,652 demons.[43]

Such dramatic testimonies of Roman truth remained few. Yet when they occurred, the Catholic exorcist relied on a variety of external devices—the cross, the saintly image, the demonic adjuration, penance, the Eucharist, blessed prayers, and the charismatic mediation of his own priestly station—to accomplish the demon's expulsion. Preachers like Canisius might use their exorcisms as vehicles to exhort their audiences to lead more perfect lives, but when they faced the possessing spirits, they applied a host of external medications. Their remedies, clearly, were well suited to an enduring religious culture in which tangible objects and conjurative formulae—not internalized beliefs or perfect lives—were needed to channel supernatural power to protect against evil spirits.[44]

It may have been obvious to contemporaries that Lutherans suffered more demonic attacks than their Catholic or Calvinist counterparts. Yet despite this wave of unprecedented devilish activity, Lutheran officials continued to urge only faith and piety as antidotes. The sheer number of cases of Lutheran possession likely

42. Ibid.
43. Ibid. Scherer preached on the incident and published a popular account describing it entitled *Christliche Erinnerung bei der Historien von jüngst geschehen Erledigung einer Jungfrauen, die mit 12652 Teufeln besessen gewesen* (Vienna, 1583). On Catholic exorcism in the sixteenth century, see Cécile Ernst, *Teufelaustreibungen. Die Praxis der katholischen Kirche im 16. und 17. Jahrhundert* (Bern, 1972).
44. Midelfort, "Devil and the German People," p. 103.

prompted many to question, as Rabus did, the effectiveness of faith alone against a mounting demonic onslaught. Could faith, the Scriptures, and hymns be sufficient to war against demons? In fact, the unchanged survival of amulets, potions, and even prayers addressed to the devil is well documented in Lutheran Germany even after decades of Reformation teaching, suggesting that many continued to use physical objects and the force of conjurations to combat Satan's influence.[45]

In his attack on Canisius's exorcism, Marbach, too, sensed this affinity between the counter-reformers' methods and enduring religious perceptions. Although he had addressed his original polemic to Augsburgers and Bavarians, the mock disputation at Strasbourg and his continued monitoring of the Bavarian reformers show that he was quite concerned with the possibility of a Catholic resurgence in his own city. In the 1570s, in fact, the fate of Strasbourg's Lutheran Reformation was still in doubt. Unlike in Nuremberg or Augsburg, where Lutherans had enjoyed a definitive triumph early in the Reformation, in Strasbourg various kinds of Protestants, humanists, and spiritualists had all competed to gain advantage. The town council eventually sided with the Lutherans, but Catholic and, later, Calvinist minorities remained active in the city. As president of the Lutheran church, Marbach had gradually established control over the city's religious life, but his grip remained tenuous. For him and his orthodox Lutheran pastors, the election of a counter-reforming Catholic bishop to head the Strasbourg diocese in 1569 was a crucial turning point. Soon the Jesuits were at work in the city, and the Protestant clergy feared a full-fledged Catholic resurgence.[46]

Most Strasbourgeois remained Lutheran, but Marbach and his ministers sensed that Catholic exorcisms and miracles both represented a particularly dangerous threat to the primacy of their religion. Catholic polemicists often attacked the Reformation at its most vulnerable point, charging that the reformers had failed to produce any stunning miracles of confirmation. Their Protestant opponents responded that true miracles were those, like the Reformation, that confirmed, increased, and multiplied faith. Among

45. Strauss, *Luther's House of Learning*, esp. pp. 303–304.
46. See Abray, *People's Reformation*, pp. 91–92, 116–126.

their own laity, however, there existed an unquenchable appetite for signs of God's direct intervention in the world. Even some members of the Protestant leadership shared this desire and publicized miracle stories to prove the Reformation's divine authority. In the decades after 1520 and into the seventeenth century, for example, Protestant propagandists promoted Luther as something like a medieval saint, with stories of his miracles and prophecies. And cults of Luther images, which perhaps wept or were preserved inviolate from fire and attack, survived in Lutheranism until the late 1700s.[47]

Beyond the bounds of this often officially sanctioned and promoted Luther cult, elaborate stories about God's unmediated intervention in the world continued to circulate in Protestant Germany. The late medieval world—in which sixteenth-century Protestants remained firmly embedded—had not only known the miracles of the saints and the diabolic magic of Satan; in its cosmology, natural events were also signs that revealed the Almighty's providence. Comets, earthquakes, floods, visions seen in the clouds, deformed births, and bizarre creatures belonged to a tertiary category of miracles, which Jacques Le Goff has termed the "marvelous" and which German scholars often label as "prodigies."[48]

Accounts of strange, sometimes horrifying events had circulated orally for centuries among the people, been retold in the sermons of medieval preachers, and been recorded in collections of exempla.[49] Beginning in the late fifteenth century, however, the press began to record and extend the circulation of prodigies, satisfying the popular appetite for news of sensational, even "miraculous" events. Hundreds of illustrated prodigies produced in a modest single-leaf format have survived, revealing a tradition of miracle storytelling that ran counter to the aims of Protestant reformers. While oral modes of communicating these tales certainly remained dominant

47. Scribner, "Luther Myth: A Popular Historiography of the Reformer" and idem, "Incombustible Luther." See also Scribner's *For the Sake of Simple Folk*, pp. 14–36.
48. See Jacques Le Goff, "The Marvelous in the Medieval West," in *The Medieval Imagination* (Chicago, 1988), pp. 27–46. Traditional motifs in German prodigy literature are catalogued in Brückner (ed.), *Volkserzählung und Reformation*. See also Rudolf Schenda, "Die deutschen Prodigiensammlungen des 16. und 17. Jahrhunderts," *Archiv für Geschichte des Buchwesen* 4 (1962), cols. 37–710); and idem, *Die französische Prodigienliteratur in des 2. Hälfte des 16. Jahrhunderts* (Munich, 1961).
49. Gurevich, *Medieval Popular Culture*.

in sixteenth-century Germany, the printed broadside allows us to
see how the laity interpreted the inexplicable events occurring
around them.

Unlike the theological polemics that issued from the empire's
great printing houses, the illustrated prodigy had humble origins.
At Augsburg, for example, more than fifty small printers conducted
a busy trade in broadsides during the period 1550–1750, three-
quarters of these shops being located in one of the city's poorer
suburbs. Often the purveyors and producers of these works clus-
tered around a city's gates, where they could sell their wares not
only to the poor artisans who lived in the suburbs but also to
traveling peddlers and merchants. Cheaply produced in editions
ranging from several hundred to about 2,500, these broadsides
were sold for a modest price—about four to six pfennigs—that
remained constant into the early seventeenth century.[50] Sometimes
the sheets were distributed by merchants who sold other kinds of
dry goods. At Leipzig in 1588, for example, the inventory of the
shopkeeper Cornelius Caimax included everything from bonnets,
belts, and daggers to the illustrated broadside.[51]

Printed prodigies, in short, were a product of market forces, with
printers competing to produce accounts that would most excite
curiosity and generate sales. Their output thus followed formulae,
and illustrations were sometimes modeled after those in more ex-
pensive chronicles.[52] Whole accounts published in other cities could
also be plagiarized. But despite their formulaic nature, the vast
profusion of these works indicates that many people in both Protestant and Catholic territories were eager to learn about contemporary
cases of divine intervention. More than four-fifths of the prodigies
that survive from the late sixteenth century tell of apparitions,
comets, meteors, and related incidents of abnormal births, the appearance of strange new species of animals, and the discovery of
freakish flora and fauna. The remaining one-fifth tell of floods,
storms, and other natural disasters, with a small number reporting

50. Wolfgang Seitz, "The Addresses of Augsburg Broadsheet Makers," in *The German Single-Leaf Woodcut, 1600–1700* (New York, 1977), 3:827; and Walter L. Strauss, ed., *The German Single-Leaf Woodcut, 1550–1600* (New York, 1975), 1:1–9.

51. Strauss (ed.), *German Single-Leaf Woodcut, 1550–1600* 1:5.

52. One important source in codifying the illustrations produced in these broad-sheets was Conrad Lykosthenes' *Prodigiorum ac Ostentorum Chronicon* (Basel, 1557). It included more than 670 illustrations of comets, abnormal births, and meteorological phenomena.

a variety of strange incidents, such as inexplicable murders and cases of women who survived without eating.[53]

Whether published in Lutheran, Calvinist, or Catholic regions, prodigy accounts were remarkably similar. The following cases are typical of those in circulation around the time that Johann Marbach and Strasbourg's Lutheran pastors were denouncing Catholic miracles. In 1570, a printer in Protestant Augsburg told of a "miraculous" shower of grain that had occurred in several places in Bavaria and Austria (fig. 7).[54] A four-footed hare discovered in the Calvinist Palatinate provided the subject of a Heidelberg printer's account in 1583 (fig. 8).[55] And in Catholic Cologne, a 1578 prodigy relayed the story of the strange birth of a Dutch boy with multiple cyclopean heads and the legs and feet of a centaur (fig. 9).[56] The message of these three cases was essentially the same: the "miraculous" shower of grain, the four-footed hare, and the cyclopean Dutch boy were all, their promoters proclaimed, "wondrous signs" sent by God as both a warning and a testimony to his mercy. They were intended to call people to repent and to live pious lives. The apocalypticism that was often so cogent in Lutheran theological pamphlets and books is notably absent from these prodigy accounts. While printers sometimes included the vague eschatological observation that the celestial apparition or strange plant or animal being described was a sign "of the last times," the explicit prophetic reckonings and astrological forecasting typical of late Lutheran theology rarely appear.[57] Perhaps more important, however, is the relatively small explanatory role that Satan plays in these accounts; in only a very few cases is some contemporary event attributed specifically to the devil.[58]

53. Dorothy Alexander and Walter L. Strauss, eds., *The German Single-Leaf Woodcut, 1600–1700* (New York, 1977), 1:20–21. The editors' comments defend their selection of prints as typical of those in circulation at the time.

54. *Ein warhafftige doch wunderseltzame geschicht so gesehen ist worden . . . in dem Ländlein ob der Ens dem Hauß Osterreich zugehörig . . . ,* reproduced in Strauss (ed.), *German Single-Leaf Woodcut, 1550–1600* 2:666.

55. *Dieser Hase hierunder contersey ist im Jar M.D. lxxxiii. zu Türckheim an der Hardt LS. Aprillen gefangen . . . ,* reproduced in ibid., p. 771.

56. *Warhafftige Contrafactur einer erschrecklichen Wundergeburt eines Knebleins, welches recht am newen Jarstage dieses jetztlauffendern 1578. Jars . . . ,* reproduced in ibid., 3:892.

57. See Barnes, *Prophecy and Gnosis.*

58. See also Miriam U. Chrisman, *Lay Culture, Learned Culture: Books and Social Change in Strasbourg, 1480–1599* (New Haven, 1982), p. 260; and Barnes, *Prophecy and Gnosis,* pp. 73–74.

The prodigy, then, reflected an enduring religious mentality that was resistant to Protestant reformers' efforts to blame contemporary woes and horrors on Satan. For the purveyors and readers of this literature, the earth was like a vast book in which God, not the devil, was continuously working strange and horrific marvels to call the faithful to repentance and the pious life. These were not the miracles of faith and grace that Johann Marbach and his Lutheran pastors recommended as the true wonders of the contemporary world. Rather, they were cases where God intervened directly in the natural order to produce visible testimony to his anger and mercy. And if four-footed hares or malformed human births were such potent signs of God's power, surely the miracles that Eisengrein and other Catholics were promoting would exert even greater pull: more than a mere pronouncement of divine authority, Catholic thaumaturgic and exorcistic miracles actually helped people. No wonder the Lutheran leadership at Strasbourg attacked the resurgence of Catholic miracles so vigorously.

To inoculate the laity against the allures of this Catholic renascence, Protestant propagandists throughout Germany produced their own "anti-prodigies," tales by which they endeavored to convince their audience of the deceits and trickery of the Roman Church. Such stories, indeed, were characteristic of both Reformation and Counter-Reformation propaganda. One thinks immediately of Luther's *Table Talk*, which was filled with tales fulfilling the didactic, apologetic needs of the Reformation. On the Catholic side, the Jesuits in France gathered some particularly remarkable, farfetched stories about Protestant crimes of ritual murder and bizarre sacrilege.[59] In Germany, stories set into circulation through sermons, modest broadsides, and pamphlets proved an important means of discrediting competing confessions.[60] Although Marbach's and Rabus's printed polemics had likewise placed Catholic and Protestant deceits and trickery before their readers, their tales were pointedly intended to summarize and validate doctrinal positions. When the goal, however, was to appeal to the laity en masse, stories often assumed a more autonomous role.

59. Martin, *Jesuit Mind*, pp. 95–98.
60. See Janssen, *History of the German People* 8:346–375, 14:182–190; and Schenda, "Hieronymus Rauscher und die protestantisch-katholische Legendenpolemik."

Unlike other kinds of theological argument to which Protestant and Catholic theologians and preachers had recourse—the appeal to Scripture, to an abstract tradition, or to logically fashioned principles like the *sola fide*—stories provided a unique propagandistic opportunity, for they described concrete events. By retelling these tales, preachers, pamphleteers, and producers of the popular Reformation broadsides hoped to immunize both literate and illiterate lay people against the appeals of the Catholic resurgence. The allegations of crimes like ritual murder and diabolic sorcery that Catholics and Protestants flung at one another were certainly not beyond the bounds of sixteenth-century credibility. For more than two centuries, after all, German society had been conditioned by equally fantastic tales of ritual sacrifice and host desecration to hate the Jews. The sexual crimes attributed to the Beguines and the Brethren of the Free Spirit had been colossal but, for many, completely credible. And even as monstrous tales about the crimes of Protestants and Catholics circulated, much of Northern Europe was being taught to fear the onslaught of witches, which one inquisitor warned numbered in "the thousands everywhere" and were "multiplying upon the earth even as worms in a garden."[61]

The legends that Protestant propagandists promoted about the reforming orders of the Counter-Reformation, the Catholic Church, and its miracles repeated many of the same accusations that had long been associated with Jews, witches, and heretics. Indeed, a kind of "black legend" concerning the Roman Church was steadily intensifying in the late sixteenth century. In a series of pamphlets published during the early 1560s, for example, the Lutheran preacher Hieronymus Rauscher dissected the lives of the saints, transforming them into lies promoted by the devil and the "papists" to "damn simple people and lead them to the abyss of hell." Widely circulated in numerous editions, Rauscher's pamphlet polemics had a profound influence on the later stories told by Protestant writers and preachers about the Catholic Church.[62]

61. Henri Boguet, *An Examen of Witches,* ed. Montague Summers, trans. E. A. Ashwin (London, 1929), p. xxxiv; cited in Alison P. Coudert, "The Myth of the Improved Status of Protestant Women: The Case of the Witchcraze," *Politics of Gender in Early Modern Europe,* Sixteenth Century Essays and Studies 12 (Kirksville, Mo., 1989), p. 61n.3.

62. Hieronymus Rauscher, *Hundert Außerwelte grosse, unverschempte, feiste . . . Papistische Lügen* (1562); this was the first of five books that each recounted a hundred

Rauscher had concentrated his venom largely on discrediting the historical exempla and saintly legends communicated in the late Middle Ages by such works as Jacopo da Voragine's *Golden Legend*. Those who followed him demonized more completely and viciously the contemporary missionary activities of the Catholic Church. In a pamphlet published in 1566, a Lutheran minister explained that the Jesuits were able to work their numerous conversions by smearing magical salves on their pulpits to attract the young and simple. This writer advocated that Jesuits be burned at the stake, rather than merely being expelled from Protestant territories; that, he said, was the only way to end their black magic.[63] In 1576, a pastor in Württemberg fabricated the story of an imaginary Jesuit named Georg Ziegler who allied himself with a witch to conjure up demons. After capturing one of these spirits in a jar, the Jesuit used it to perform his dark works. One day his demon escaped. Flying across the Protestant territories along the Neckar and Main rivers and across Alsace, the spirit had wreaked havoc with the climate and destroyed crops—which, the writer said, explained a bout of very bad weather that afflicted these regions in 1576.[64]

Allegations of diabolic sorcery worked in the Roman Church abounded throughout Protestant Germany in the late sixteenth century. Around 1600, the diarist Enoch Widmann at Regensburg related a legend that he said was then being retold to explain his city's "Fair Mary" pilgrimage. Whether or not the tale was actually being retold can never be determined; but the Protestant clergy would likely have drawn upon it and used it in their efforts to demonize the Roman Church. In Widmann's relating of the Protestant tale, the pilgrimage to the town's shrines becomes a case of priestly black magic. As we have seen, an early Reformation account had attributed the shrine's popularity to Jewish magic; now, however, Regensburg's Protestants focused the charge on the cathedral preacher Balthasar Hubmayer who, after pronouncing in-

"popish" lies. The impact of this remarkable collection is examined in greater detail in Schenda, "Hieronymus Rauscher und die protestantisch-katholische Legendenpolemik"; and idem, "Die protestantisch-katholische Legendenpolemik," *Archiv für Kulturgeschichte* 52 (1970): 28–48.

63. Johannes Janssen describes the work in *History of the German People* 16:457.
64. Ibid., p. 456.

cantations over a human heart, had allegedly enclosed the talisman inside the chapel altar to lure pilgrims to the site.[65]

Such sorceries, Protestant pastors and propagandists warned repeatedly, were not only a historical legacy; they were still occurring in the present. Sometimes, though, their tales triumphantly celebrated the exposure and defeat of some new case of Roman deception. An illustrated broadside published in 1569 told how a Jesuit had costumed himself as a demon to frighten a Protestant girl into relinquishing her religion (fig. 10). "Through the Almighty's intervention," the text stated, a male servant had discovered the deceit and run the Jesuit through with a sword, thus preserving the young girl from the "monkish" devil.[66] Another anonymous broadside printed in the same year mocked a Jesuit's attempt at Vienna to set himself up as a false Messiah; when his efforts to raise a dead man had failed, he had been permanently exiled from the city.[67]

There was almost no crime so hideous or bizarre that it could not be attributed to the counter-reformers. The Jesuits were a favorite target; although on the outside they appeared to be the very model of a well-ordered piety, their private lives were conducted, it was claimed, in luxury and sensuality. In 1570, for example, a broadside circulated recounting the story of a pregnant male Jesuit in Vienna. Apparently, he had carried a picture of a woman under his clothes, whereupon his seething, unrequited lust had produced this magical progeny. To celebrate the miraculous birth, the Jesuits had set up the man's childbed in a public location to which people could make pilgrimages and direct their worship. The account concluded by condemning clerical celibacy for producing both impious devotions and magical progeny.[68]

The charge that the Jesuits could and did sire demonic progeny was common in the late sixteenth century, partly, no doubt, thanks to the widespread contemporary fascination with strange and hor-

65. "Enoch Widmanns Höfische Stadt Chronik," in *Fortgesetzte Sammlung von alten und neuen theologischen Sachen* (Leipzig, 1735), pp. 430–434.

66. *Newe Zeytung unnd warhaffter Bericht eines Jesuiters welcher inn Teuffelsgestalt sich angethan* . . . (Augsburg, 1569), reproduced in Strauss (ed.), *German Single-Leaf Woodcut, 1550–1600* 3:1335.

67. *Von Eynem Jesuwider, wie der zu Wien inn Oesterreich die Todten lebendig zumachen* (1569), reproduced in ibid., p. 1397.

68. *Newezeitung von diesen M.D. Lxx. Jare, welches uns ein recht fruchtbar und Fröhlich Jubel Jahr*, reproduced in ibid., p. 1338.

rific births. And in this vein, no one ever quite matched the efforts of Johann Fischart of Strasbourg. A close associate of Johann Marbach, Fischart in the 1570s presented in single-page illustrated poems a simpler, more immediate condemnation of Catholic sorcery—in the form of a "history" of the Jesuit order—than was to be found in the Strasbourg church president's voluminous polemics. Adopting the pen name Jesuwalt Pickart, he told how Lucifer had grown sick as a result of the Reformation's message. The pope, saddened by his colleague's illness, smeared Satan's buttocks with a magical salve, causing him to give birth to a child through defecation. The pope christened the child "Anti-Christus," but Lucifer, familiar with the German language, made the Holy Father change the name to Jesuwider (literally, Anti-Jesus). It was this child who had founded the hateful Society of Jesus and sent his recruits into the empire to work their diabolic miracles. In other poems, Fischart continued to demonize the Jesuits and other counter-reformers working in contemporary Germany, through use of equally grotesque physical and scatological imagery.[69]

The poet's characterization of the Society of Jesus as the devil's "shit" drew upon imagery that was well established in Reformation-era propaganda. Themes involving the diabolic defecation of monks and the Antichrist had enjoyed a perverse popularity among readers of illustrated broadsides during the early Reformation;[70] but the imagery gained its broadest currency thanks to Luther's own polemical efforts. In 1545, the year before his death, the reformer had published a pamphlet entitled *The Papacy at Rome, Founded by the Devil*, with evocative illustrations by Lucas Cranach the Elder. In one image, the devil is shown squatting to relieve himself of his "devil's shit"—the pope and the Roman curia—while around him these "offspring" are being suckled and reared by demons (fig. 11). The nine additional illustrations in the pamphlet explore the relationship between bodily excrement, Satan, demons, and the Roman Church, with, for example, worshipers defecating in the papal tiara

69. Johann von Fischart, *Von Ursprung und wunderlichen Herkommen des Heyl. Ordens der Jesuiten* (Strasbourg, 1577). For a discussion of the author's anti-Roman poems, see von Haufen, *Johann Fischart* 2:98–135.

70. See Scribner, *For the Sake of Simple Folk*, pp. 84–88.

and German peasants baring their bottoms to fart defiantly at the pope.[71]

Luther took great pride in this work, referring to it as his "testament," and as one of his last publications it was widely distributed.[72] But while this was one of his most extreme attacks on the papacy, it also represented a highly personal statement about his own struggle for salvation. A longtime sufferer from hemorrhoids and urine retention, the reformer may actually have had his salvific breakthrough while in the monastery privy—a fact that the psychoanalyst Erik Erikson, in 1958, stressed in attempting to explain Luther's psychic distresses, noting that the realization of the *sola fide* was connected to a physical catharsis and cleansing.[73]

Although Reformation historians have persistently attacked Erikson's attempts to psychoanalyze the dead Luther, in the years since his work first appeared they have also shed their reticence concerning Reformation-era scatology. Luther's "cloaca crisis" now appears less a sign of his emotional instability than an experience consonant with both the popular culture and the learned traditions of the late Middle Ages. In popular superstition, the privy was a placed haunted by maleficent spirits, and the devil was believed to stink like human feces. Medieval monastic literature, too, warned of the dangers that lurked in the water closet.[74] The fact that Luther's breakthrough and his triumph over Satan occurred in the monastery privy, then, must be placed in the context of a society in which defecation was both a sign of human humiliation and a precarious function exposing men and women to the dangers of evil spirits.

The Protestant reformers' uses of scatological imagery thus had

71. On this extraordinary pamphlet, see R. W. Scribner, "Demons, Defecation, and Monsters: Popular Propaganda for the German Reformation," in *Popular Culture and Popular Movements*, pp. 277–300; Edwards, *Luther's Last Battles*, pp. 182–200; and Oberman, *Luther*, pp. 163–166.

72. Besides Fischart's employment of the imagery, the polemical theologian Martin von Chemnitz also depicted the Roman Church as the "devil's shit"; see Janssen, *History of the German People* 8:239.

73. See Erik Erikson, *Young Man Luther: A Study in Psychoanalysis and History* (New York, 1958), pp. 204–206.

74. On popular superstition, see Scribner, *For the Sake of Simple Folk*, p. 84, citing H. Bächtold-Stäubli (ed.), *Handwörterbuch des deutschen Aberglaubens* 1:93. On monastic traditions concerning the privy, see Oberman, *Luther*, p. 164, esp. n. 8.

numerous meanings. Although throughout sixteenth-century Europe there was in general little reserve about bodily functions, and scatological language was freely used, Germany was apparently characterized by a strongly negative focus on excrement at this time.[75] German cesspool cleaners, for example, were considered members of a "dishonorable profession" (*unehrliche Gewerbe*), a designation that marked them as a marginal caste.[76] When seeking to redress libels and slanders, members of the German nobility often sent "defamatory letters" that included illustrations showing their enemies' seals or coats of arms being plunged into steaming dung.[77] The tendency to associate opposing opinions and enemies with feces was strong in every layer of German society. In the numerous medieval and early modern depictions of the "Jewish sow" (*Judensau*), a popular anti-Jewish denigration, German artists sometimes showed the animal eating feces.[78] But scatological images also served satirical and comic purposes. In the carnival plays that survive from fifteenth-century Nuremberg, references to defecation appeared only slightly less frequently than those to sex. In fact, sexual and scatological metaphors were often blended, forged into new kinds of images that, like Luther's and Fischart's, depicted reproductivity and regeneration as arising from the degenerative act of defecation.[79]

This imagery evokes what Mikhail Bakhtin once termed "the material bodily lower stratum."[80] By referring to feces, defecation, and urination, one could humiliate an enemy by inverting his thoughts, deeds, and actions and associating them with the most primal functions. In his now-classic study of Rabelais's *Gargantua and Pantagruel*, Bakhtin argues that the provenance of this language lay in a "popular culture" that rejoiced in carnival and other ritualized

75. See the following studies of modern German scatology that include discussions of late medieval and early modern usage: Dieter Rollfinke and Jacqueline Rollfinke, *The Call of Human Nature* (Amherst, Mass., 1986); and Alan Dundes, *Life Is Like a Chicken Coop Ladder* (New York, 1984).

76. See Michael Kunze, *Highroad to the Stake: A Tale of Witchcraft* (Chicago, 1987).

77. Scribner, "Demons, Defecation, and Monsters," p. 293.

78. Isaiah Schachar, *The Judensau: A Medieval Anti-Jewish Motif and Its History* (London, 1974).

79. Johannes Müller, *Schwert und Scheide. Der sexuelle und skatologische Wortschatz im Nürnberger Fastnachtspiel des 15. Jahrhunderts* (Bern, 1988), pp. 195–215, esp. p. 212.

80. Mikhail Bakhtin, *Rabelais and His World*, trans. Helene Iswolsky (Cambridge, Mass., 1968), pp. 368–436.

forms of play which reversed normal patterns and conventions.[81] Rabelais's satire, according to Bakhtin, appealed to a simultaneously moral and comic sense that was fast disappearing in the sixteenth-century West. He derided the late medieval Schoolmen for their extremely intellectualized and routinized logic, degrading their efforts by connecting the realm of the intellect with the lower stratum of bodily needs. In place of Scholastic sterility, thus, Rabelais exalted the popular culture of the marketplace, whose rites celebrated the organic functions of degeneration and regeneration.

While the French author's imagery may have found its inspiration in the popular culture of the marketplace, as Bakhtin theorized,[82] German uses of scatology were more universal. Unlike Rabelais, who directed his attacks against what in his view was a sterile intellectual culture, the propagandists of the late sixteenth century employed the material bodily principle to destroy residual Catholic devotion. Indeed, as the religious situation grew ever more tangled, polemicists like Fischart were to heighten the brew of diabolism and scatology to baroque proportions. In the late Reformation offensive against a renewed Catholic priesthood and its miracles, Lutheran theologians and propagandists rarely ventured merely that Catholicism was a merely deluded religion; their jeremiads warned incessantly that it was a diabolic cult.

In tales of sorcerous priests and diabolically produced miracles, late Reformation pastors, poets, and pamphleteers strove to destroy the enduring allures of Catholic thaumaturgy and the saints. That many in the Lutheran leadership believed these charges cannot be doubted, if only because of the then-reigning explanatory malaise in which Satan was playing an ever greater role. Yet these negative attacks could never really inoculate the Protestant laity against the resurgence of clerically promoted miracles then under way in many South German regions, for they carried no "purified" Protestant doctrine of the supernatural as a countermeasure.

On just what such a theology should include, indeed, there was little agreement. Some, like Marbach, argued that the "true" miracles of the present were those that increased the gospel of faith.

81. Ibid., pp. 196–277.
82. For a dissenting evaluation of Bakhtin's work, see Gurevich, *Medieval Popular Culture*, pp. 177–179.

At the same time, however, many Lutherans were promoting the founder of their confession in ways that could have been lifted directly from the late medieval thaumaturgic and prophetic traditions. Revering his image and retelling his prophecies, they celebrated signs that confirmed his divine inspiration and message. Some searched the heavens for clues that would reveal the date for the impending conclusion of world history; others continued the trade in strange, prodigious tales about cases of divine interventions worked in the seas, grain fields, and childbeds of Europe. While we cannot doubt that Protestants feared the onslaughts of Satan, they were nevertheless unwilling to credit him with everything inexplicable that occurred around them.

In the limited confines of cities like Strasbourg, Augsburg, and Regensburg, where Catholicism was as politically, socially, and economically threatening to burghers as it was religiously ominous to the Protestant clergy, the repeated warnings of Lutheran propagandists may have helped prevent a renewal of the traditional Church.[83] Beyond urban gates, however, in rural Alsace, Franconia, Bavaria, and other territories throughout South Germany, Protestants proved incapable of stopping the intense missionary efforts of a resurgent Catholic clergy. As this group increased its efforts, miracles began to reverberate once again from pilgrimage chapels like those at Eberhardsklausen and Altötting. There hundreds, and sometimes even tens of thousands, of reports of healings and intercessions would be assiduously recorded and circulated during the late sixteenth and seventeenth centuries.[84] Clearly, many Germans after a half-century of Protestantism were still inclined to agree with the Catholic reformers: if the miracle's end result was good, it was surely a work of God.

83. See Abray, *People's Reformation*, pp. 83–87, 116–141.
84. Ibid.; Paul Hoffmann and Peter Dohms, eds., *Die Mirakelbücher des Klosters Eberhardsklausen* (Düsseldorf, 1988); Chatellier, *Europe of the Devout*, p. 154; and Hsia, *Social Discipline in the Reformation*, esp. pp. 154–159.

6

"Spiritual Medicine for Heretical Poison"
Pilgrimage and Propaganda in the Early Counter-Reformation

The protracted polemic that Martin Eisengrein's pilgrimage book precipitated assured Bavaria's Catholic reformers that they had hit one of Protestantism's weakest links: its inability to foster widespread devotions that could rival the thaumaturgic and intercessory appeals of traditional religion. For his part in defending the Altötting shrine and in crystallizing the debate over miracles, Martin Eisengrein was celebrated as a Counter-Reformation hero. In Bavaria, he was lauded with carmina; and abroad, knowledge of his skilled defense of the shrine spread even to Rome. In an apostolic letter of 1571, the pope made the theologian and the Altötting provosts who succeeded him extraordinary bishops of the Catholic Church. With this appointment, Eisengrein now gained the prestige he had long desired. Prior to the publication of *Our Lady at Altötting*, he had been offered the Austrian bishopric of Laibach several times, but the Wittelsbach duke had refused him permission to leave Bavaria. To satisfy the theologian's desire for important office, Albrecht instead named him superintendent of the University of Ingolstadt in 1570. Now the duke rejoiced in Eisengrein's triumph and presented him with a jeweled bishop's staff to commemorate his elevation.[1]

The Ingolstadt theologian's propagandistic defense of Altötting probably convinced few truly committed Protestants of the truths of the Roman religion, but it does appear to have prompted Duke Albrecht to dedicate himself to the revival of the Bavarian pilgrimage network. Although during the fifteenth and early sixteenth centuries the Wittelsbach dukes had frequently undertaken imposing

---

1. König, *Weihegaben an U.L. Frau von Altötting* 1:68–71; and Pfleger, *Martin Eisengrein*, pp. 79–80.

processions to their territory's shrines, between 1522 and 1571 they had abandoned these public displays.[2] In the summer of 1571, however, even as Protestants continued to circulate black legends about Catholic shrines and their sorcerous miracles, Albrecht stepped forth to present his own testimony to the power of the saints and local pilgrimages, telling a story about aid he had received after praying to Our Lady at Altötting. Caught in a fierce storm on the Austrian Abersee the previous summer, he had prayed to Our Lady, promising a pilgrimage to Altötting if she rescued him from drowning. He survived, and Albrecht and his court now journeyed to the shrine to present Our Lady with her reward: new, ostentatious regalia for her shrine. The duke styled his visit as a renewal of his family's erstwhile support for the important pilgrimage.[3] Among the many objects included in his "gifts to the Virgin" were a set of altar cloths for the chapel embroidered with silver and gold thread, twenty-one silver statues of the saints, a silver-and-gold communion service, and new festive vestments and hangings for the chapel embroidered with pearls, precious gems, silver, and gold. Albrecht requested that the archbishop of Salzburg come to Altötting to meet his procession and consecrate the regalia with a pontifical mass. As an additional stimulus to Altötting's revival, the Wittelsbach prince stipulated that the new regalia could be used only on the shrine's most important feast days, traditionally the times when most pilgrims flocked to the site to avail themselves of a Church's indulgences.[4]

In his letter of benefaction, the duke expressed a deep concern over the widespread renunciation of the practice of pilgrimage in Bavaria and announced his intention to revive once-popular shrines. In the years following his journey to Altötting, pilgrimage began to emerge as a recognizable element in the Bavarian state's confessional policies. Like the extravagant support he had granted the urban Corpus Christi celebrations, Albrecht's patronage consisted largely of grand gestures. During the reigns of his successors, Wilhelm and Maximilian, the dynasty's exertions on behalf of the shrines steadily mounted. Nowhere in Germany was there a Catholic succession more unfailing in their allegiance to the Roman

2. Ludwig Hüttl, *Marianische Wallfahrten im süddeutsch-österreichischen Raum* (Vienna, 1985), pp. 104–105.
3. König, *Weihegaben an U.L. Frau von Altötting* 2:73–76.
4. Ibid.

Church than these Bavarian princes. The essential congruity of the religious policies each duke pursued now provided the Counter-Reformation program with a long interlude in which traditional religious practices could be nurtured and expanded.

Rather than supporting distant journeys to major international shrines like Rome or Loreto, the Wittelsbach state and its clerical elite concentrated their efforts domestically in order to achieve sacralization of the territory. The extent of their bias may be seen in one telling example. During the jubilee year 1575, the Wittelsbach court preacher Johann Rabus, already famous to the duchy's readers for his part in the polemic over miracles, organized a pilgrimage to Rome. Enlisting representatives of the Munich elite, including court officials, nobles, and even one Wittelsbach family member, the preacher's pilgrimage wended its way through the Tyrol, northern Italy, and on to Loreto before finally reaching the Holy City. En route Rabus kept a journal of every site they visited; returning home he revised and edited his notes into a polished manuscript that extolled the long journey. Presenting the work to Albrecht, he requested a subvention to defray the cost of publication. These funds were never provided, however, and the manuscript was not printed.[5] The duke saw no reason to subsidize publicity about Rabus's international trek when Bavaria had shrines aplenty needing state support.

For the Wittelsbachs, pilgrimage was one means of solidifying ideological and political control over their state. Like the Corpus Christi processions of Munich, journeys to local shrines elicited at least the physical compliance of subjects. It would be mistaken, however, to judge these efforts as calculated "thought control"; after all, Albrecht, Wilhelm, and Maximilian each sincerely believed that the revival of Bavaria's holy places was of paramount importance for the spiritual welfare, prosperity, and protection of the territory. They agreed, in short, with the statement of one Counter-Reformation theologian that pilgrimage was one of the Church's best "spiritual medicines for heretical poison."[6] Each duke therefore required his officials to participate in the Corpus Christi parades,

---

5. See Karl Schottenloher's introduction to the twentieth-century reprint of Rabus's manuscript *Rom*, pp. ix–xix.

6. Daniel Baradin, *Geistlich Artzney Für Ketzergifft und jetziger zeit böse Lufft, auß H. Göttlicher Gschrifft, heyliger Vättern Büchern . . . allen vnd jeden Christen . . . zugericht* . . . (Munich, 1600), pp. 124–139.

annual pilgrimages, and weekly religious processions. In their own religious devotions, Wilhelm and Maximilian in particular shared an abiding affection for rituals that required great physical effort. Wilhelm, for example, spent four hours kneeling in prayer each day, and during the 1575 jubilee he and his wife conducted a two-week public fast. As duke, he made frequent journeys to Bavaria's shrines on foot dressed in rough-spun clothing. His son Maximilian's exertions were similar.[7] Convinced of the protection and benefits that accrued from these physical displays of religious adherence, Wittelsbach state and clerical officials now began to use the pilgrimage as an act of faith—an *auto da fé* in the true sense of the words—for those they forcibly reconverted from Protestantism. In 1584, for example, the entire village of Miesbach, recently brought under the duke's authority and forced to renounce Lutheranism, became one of the first parishes required to make a pilgrimage. In subsequent decades the directive was to be expanded.[8]

Although state and clergy sometimes relied on compulsion to bring people to the territory's shrines, both recognized that it was beyond their power to command every Bavarian to make these journeys. Moreover, the mobility and potential for religious enthusiasm inherent in pilgrimage were dangerous specters. By the late sixteenth century, the need to enforce order on lay religion had become, in the minds of ruling elites at least, more urgent than ever before. This need arose not only because of the continuing proliferation of various and competing religious positions. Like the rest of the empire, Bavaria was beginning to experience profound economic and social changes in this period. The expansions and contractions of a market economy and agrarian commercialism were altering the character of rural society, bringing dislocation, economic stratification, and the multiplication of the landless in their wake. Because of Bavaria's relative isolation, these transformations may have affected the duchy less than other regions. Yet the Wit-

7. Hüttl, *Marianische Wallfahrten*, pp. 104–105.
8. Gierl, *Bauernleben und Bauernwallfahrt*, p. 18. During the seventeenth century, most Bavarian villages became linked in pilgrimage alliances, which obligated a delegation of villagers to make a circuit of pilgrimages each summer. See Hermann Hörger, "Dorfreligion und bäuerliche Mentalité im Wandel ihrer ideologischen Grundlagen," *Zeitschrift für bayerische Landesgeschichte* 40 (1977): 244–316; and idem, *Kirche, Dorfreligion und bäuerliche Gesellschaft. Strukturanalysen zur gesellschaftsgebundenen Religiösität ländlicher Unterschichten des 17. bis 19. Jahrhunderts aufgezeigt an bayerischen Beispielen*, pt. 1 (Munich, 1978).

telsbach princes nevertheless feared the growing ranks of paupers, vagrants, and beggars they observed in their midst. The fear that religious enthusiasm might combine with demands for social reform was justified, bolstered by a lineage of late medieval revolts that combined religious devotion to Mary and the saints with calls for change. Although early modern rural and urban rebellions in fact rarely arose within the poorest strata of society, to a ruling elite anxious to consolidate its power over all sectors of its state and conditioned to distrust sudden outbursts of religious enthusiasm, the relationship among economic change, mobility, dislocation, and revolt was quite clear. As a consequence, the need seemed great for the creation of institutions that could contain the centrifugal tendencies of traditional religious practices.

The most significant of all the developments aimed at revitalizing and shaping the character of piety at Bavaria's shrines, one that wielded an influence well into the eighteenth century, was the confraternity. These new religious associations began to appear in the late 1570s in many of the Catholic regions of Europe. In Bavaria they sprang up in the towns and cities where papal nuncios, legates, and counter-reforming clerics like Peter Canisius worked, and within one short generation spread to almost every corner of the duchy. In contrast to the urban sodalities of the later Middle Ages, these new organizations enjoyed little autonomy from the institutional Church, for counter-reformational orders carefully supervised and controlled their devotional life.

Yet even though the Jesuits, Theatines, Capuchins, and other resurgent orders moved quickly to impose discipline, the wave of confraternal piety was amazingly popular from the outset. In Bavaria, the first of the new sodalities was founded at Ingolstadt in 1577, and the next arose in Munich—where the Wittelsbach duke set himself firmly at the head of the new association—one year later. Inscribing his name in the book of Munich's Confraternity of the Major (or "the Major," as it was known for short), Albrecht compelled members of his family and court to follow his example. By 1584, only six years after its foundation, the Major's rolls numbered 138: 80 students in the city's colleges, 32 clerics, and 26 laymen representing the Wittelsbach court and the town's nobility.[9]

9. Chatellier, *Europe of the Devout*, p. 15.

As members of the various professions and guilds expressed a desire to enter into the religious life of the elite Major, new sodalities proliferated to accommodate them; soon a system of confraternities arranged along occupational lines had begun to emerge, both in Munich and in other Bavarian towns.

As in other parts of Catholic Europe, these congregations often took their patrons from the celestial figures revered at local shrines. The Marian cult in particular benefited most decisively from these associations' devotion. During his reign, Duke Wilhelm became the first to inscribe his name in blood in the membership book of the newly created Archconfraternity of the Altötting Madonna, and after only three decades the association numbered more than 6,200 members in its various branches throughout the duchy. Bound by the obligation to repeat common prayers and perform regular devotions, members of the Bavarian Altötting confraternity also made a pilgrimage on foot to the shrine once every four years.[10] Altötting was not the only place to benefit from this outpouring of confraternal largesse in the late sixteenth and early seventeenth centuries; what occurred there was also happening at Andechs, Bettbrunn, and numerous other sites throughout the territory.[11] The increasing numbers of pilgrimage confraternities and their steadily mounting membership rolls, in fact, were beginning to provide Counter-Reformation shrines with an assured and disciplined constituency.

It was the Jesuits who established themselves as the leaders of this new devotional movement. Together with the Franciscans, Capuchins, Augustinians, and various other orders they now moved to occupy religious houses that had been abandoned or had fallen into decline in the previous generations or, in places where only one or a few priests had formerly functioned, to establish new

10. Georg Schreiber, "Strukturwandel der Wallfahrt," p. 29; and König, *Weihegaben an U.L. Frau von Altötting* 2:90–91.

11. On the relationship between the emerging confraternities, especially the Marian congregations and the shrines, see Chatellier, *Europe of the Devout*, pp. 153–155; L. Paulussen, "Marianische Kongregation" in *Lexikon für Theologie und Kirche*, ed. Michael Buchberger (Freiburg i. B., 1930–1938); Philipp Löffler, *Die marianischen Kongregationen in ihrem Wesen und ihrer Geschichte* (Freiburg i. B., 1911); Josef Miller, "Die marianischen Kongregationen im 16. und 17. Jahrhundert: ihr Wesen und ihr marianischer Charakter," *Zeitschrift für katholische Theologie* 58 (1934): 83–109; Anna Coreth, "Die ersten Sodalitäten der Jesuiten in Österreich: Geistigkeit und Entwicklung," in *Spiritualität aus dem 16. und 17. Jahrhundert: Jahrbuch für mystische Theologie* 9 (1965), pp. 7–65.

religious houses. Assuming the responsibility to minister and provide the sacraments to pilgrims at local shrines, the revived clergy were assiduous preachers, confessors, and promoters of miracles. Where they found no or little residual devotion, they set themselves the task of creating and fostering new cults. By the second half of the seventeenth century, their efforts had yielded results: now few districts in Bavaria could not claim their own wonder-working image or statue, carefully tended, protected, and ensconced, often in a striking baroque edifice.[12]

From the outset, the Counter-Reformation forged clear, often explicit, ties with the medieval religious life of Bavaria. Yet the movement cannot be understood as anything less than a departure, in which older notions about shrines, pilgrimages, and the saints were heightened ritually and rhetorically to dimensions far beyond their foundations. This process of attenuation reflected a rising self-consciousness, one already evident in the writings of the counter-reformers and in the devotional life of the late sixteenth-century Marian and saints' sodalities. Choosing triumphant images like the Madonna of Victories as their standards, these organizations imagined themselves as the vehicles through which a Catholic reconquest of Europe would be accomplished. This victory, however, could be achieved only with the purity of mind, body, and soul of each of the sodalities' members. Like the Wittelsbach dukes, adherents of these at first male-dominated and later exclusively male organizations dedicated themselves to an often physically rigorous campaign to discipline mind and body. Through frequent participation in the sacraments—especially confession and the Eucharist—ascetic regimens like the wearing of hair shirts and flagellation, and disciplined prayer, the new devout hoped to accomplish both a personal and a communal catharsis and purification.

In this emerging devotional climate, journeys to saints' shrines became an act of Catholic dedication, and writers and preachers rushed to define pilgrimage in ways that had not hitherto been made explicit. Their clear arguments certainly did not "trickle down" to inspire and inform the religious life of all Bavarians; but

12. See especially Robert Böck's statement in "Die Wallfahrtsinventarisation der bayerische Landestelle für Volkskunde," *Bayerisches Jahrbuch für Volkskunde,* 1960, p. 7.

for those who participated in the new religious associations, a rationale for pilgrimage was now available.

A high degree of literacy was typical of the first members of Counter-Reformation sodalities. During the late sixteenth century, as a result, Catholic writers began to produce an increasingly varied literature to satisfy this readership, with an eye to refining saintly devotion and the pilgrimage process itself. Preachers and clerical writers alike, for example, attempted to enhance the veneration of the saints by multiplying its meanings. In the early 1570s, Johann Nass, once Bavaria's enthusiastic Corpus Christi promoter, turned his attention to the cause of the saints and their shrines. Speaking to a crowd of pilgrims at the hilltop church of Andechs, he rhapsodized about the role of mountains in God's salvific plan. With frequent references to the Old and New Testament, Nass reminded his audience that the Lord frequently imparted special messages and wisdom to the faithful from atop mountain peaks. Journeys to these numinous sites were thus exercises of humility and submission, rewarded by God with gifts of gnosis, intercession, and grace.[13] In contrast to such nature mysticism, Melchior de Fabris called attention to the strongly didactic purposes of the sacred journey. In his *Guide for All Crusaders, Pilgrims, and Procession-makers*, he stated that by visiting the holy place the faithful could learn to appreciate more fully the transitoriness of human existence. After casting off the cares and pleasures of daily life for a time, they could return to their earthly stations prepared to rid themselves of everything hindering their journey to the eternal fatherland.[14]

Numerous other clerical writers in Catholic Germany joined this effort to define pilgrimage more systematically.[15] For this propagan-

13. Johann Nass, *Ein tröstliche Creutzpredig. Darin von vilerlay H. Bergen . . .* (Ingolstadt, 1574).

14. Melchior de Fabris, *Wegweyser aller Creutzferter, Kirchferter, Wallfarer, oder Pilgram andacht so Christlichen und Catholischen Mainung die heiligen ort besuchen zu befurdern* (Munich, 1584).

15. Martin Eisengrein also published a second sermon seeking to rehabilitate the reputation of the Marian cult entitled *Streittpredig. Darin neben Auszlegung deß Engelischen Gruß und evangelij so auff den tag der verkündigum MARIAE gefaellt . . .* (Ingolstadt, 1575). The following works published in Bavaria and in the other emergent centers of the Counter-Reformation also attempted to elevate the devotional dimensions of pilgrimage: Johann Jakob Rabus, *Christlich Manual oder Handbüchlein von rechtem Nucz und frucht deß walfartens* (Straubing, 1585); Jakob Hornstein, *Catholischer Beweyß und Anzeyg. Das Gott nit durchauß und zugleich an einem Orth wie am andern seine*

distic cadre, the practice had been transformed, to use the terminology of Victor and Mary Turner, from a liminal to a "liminoid" process.[16] That is, it was no longer a practice requiring the faithful to divorce themselves utterly from urban or village surroundings and peers. Rather, what the polemicists imagined was orderly, disciplined ranks of pilgrims, ministered to and supervised by priests, making journeys to places close at hand in the countryside. Pilgrimage, in short, was a sign of penitential devotion firmly located within the structures of a reviving Church and a steadily expanding state. The purpose for these circumambulations, propagandists persistently reiterated, was not to disrupt the believers' lives, but to provide a release. Like the *Spiritual Exercises* of Ignatius Loyola, the peregrinational interval should allow the faithful the opportunity to begin to conquer mind and body, enumerate and expunge sins, and wean life from earthly desires to the embracing of eternal ones.

The world outside Bavaria's sanctuaries, these writers warned, was a harsh, impure place filled with dangers. The depravity of this environment made frequent penance, the Sacrament, prayer, and an introspective spirit all the more imperative. Concern for purity of body, mind, and soul—so evident both in the writing of Catholic reformers and in the piety of the emerging sodalities—was in part a response to pervasive fears. Surrounded by hostile Protestant territories, Bavaria's Catholic reformers often deemed their own laity as morally corrupt, degenerate, and filled with "superstitious," and even "godless," notions. These men also sensed true religion to be under attack from the rising numbers of those willing to practice magic, witchcraft, and blasphemy. All these disorders, they declared, were the result of both moral decay and rising satanic activity in the world.

These fears are reflected in a steadily intensifying discourse on the saints and their processions. In his *Processional Sermons*, for instance, Matthäus Tympe recommended that his readers always

Göttliche Wunder unnd Gutthaten wircke und erzeyge . . . (Ingolstadt, 1596); Jodok Lorichius, *Von Bitt, Bilger, Oder Wallfahrten. Christlicher Catholischer Bericht* (Cologne, 1582); Jakob Gretser, *De sacris et religiosis peregrinationibus* (Ingolstadt, 1606), and in German translation, *Processionsbuch* (Ingolstadt, 1612); and Matthäus Tympe, *Procession Predigen Oder Deutliche anweisung wie die Seelsorgen zur Zeit der H. Bett fahrten* . . . (Munich, 1615). On works outside of Germany, see Chatellier, *Europe of the Devout*.
16. Turner and Turner, *Image and Pilgrimage*, pp. 249–254.

follow the venerable practice of conducting their journeys behind the cross to discourage demons from tormenting them. Still others promoted the *cultus divinorum* as an explicit cure for the ills afflicting contemporary society. The preacher Melchior de Fabris advised his readers that processions to shrines were an ancient way of securing God's grace, that the journeys of the truly pious and their display of submission and devotion before the Lord quelled his anger and garnered his protection from every kind of tribulation: war, famine, pestilence, bad weather, and demonic attack. To abandon so potent a practice was, in Fabris's mind, to ignore the commensal duties that banished evil and, indeed, underpinned society as a whole.[17]

By offering such multiple, enhanced meanings for pilgrimage, propagandists strove to guide the emerging devotional climate of the Counter-Reformation. But even as they advanced ever more explicit reasons for making pilgrimages, they astutely sensed that the physical goals of these journeys—the shrines themselves— needed to be similarly cultivated, framed, and adorned. As a result, Bavaria's clerical propagandists began to create a new literary genre, the pilgrimage book, for those participating in this new Catholic resurgence.

Instead of merely reporting miracles, as most late medieval pilgrimage pamphlets had done, the pilgrimage book of the Counter-Reformation treated a wide range of issues. They were often several hundred pages long, embracing numerous interwoven polemical, apologetic, and didactic strains. In part, pilgrimage books served to defend shrines from Protestant attack. Usually published in a modest octavo format, they were also a kind of "pocketbook" guide to shrines for literate pilgrims; for besides recounting a selection of contemporary miracles reported at these sites, they provided detailed, organized lists of the church's relics, indulgences, and most important pilgrims. Most significantly, however, they combined a persistent theological apology for the practice of pilgrimage with legends about the site. In this way, the Counter-Reformation pilgrimage book attempted to create a context and history for a particular shrine's devotion.

17. Melchior de Fabris, *Wegweyser aller Creutzferter*, p. 18; Matthäus Tympe, *Procession Predigen*, p. 3.

Why did writers of these books labor so intently on this last task? To answer this question, let us consider a fledgling cult imported into Bavaria around 1500 at the height of the late medieval expansion of pilgrimage. At about that time, a group of pious monks in the city of Regensburg brought an Italian painting of the Madonna to their abbey, whereupon they tried to nurture the development of a pilgrimage to the image. Because the painting was unknown to the local population, the monks placed a frame around it that told the legend, history, and miracles in which the Madonna was the principal actor.[18] In short, they inscribed a referential border around the work that allowed literate pilgrims and their illiterate associates alike to revere the Virgin based upon the painting's past intercessory usefulness.

The historian Richard Trexler once observed that the urban religious experience in late medieval and Renaissance Italy was one in which holiness was cordoned off and demarcated with art and architecture. Such architectonic "frames" served two purposes. By capturing and limiting sanctity, they prevented religious reverence from spilling over into more worldly areas of the city. Yet they also insured that the faithful would render proper devotion and observe decorum before the religious image or relic in its own special environment. *Hic est locus,* those "frames" announced: this is the place—that is, where power resides.[19] For the Bavarian counter-reformers, the need to frame the shrine for this purpose—as a way of insuring reverence—had taken on increased importance, since they faced the task of reviving devotions that had fallen into neglect as a result of the Reformation. Like the pious monks at Regensburg who surrounded their miraculous image with a narrative frame, the Catholic propagandists, too, adapted, rewrote, and even created legends for their shrines. These stories forged links between religious sites and the great events of biblical and ecclesiastical history, often bringing shrines to the center of a drama deemed to have a kind of "world historical" significance. Further, the myths the counter-reformers promoted in pilgrimage books provided an explanation for the continuing reports of contemporary miracles asso-

18. The painting is in the museum of the city of Regensburg.
19. Richard Trexler, *Public Life in Renaissance Florence* (New York, 1980), pp. 47–54, 96–110; Peter Brown has also made similar observations about the shrine in late antique Rome in *Cult of the Saints*, pp. 86–88.

ciated with these places. By locating the source of devotions within the distant past and alleging a continual stream of wonders up to the present, or by placing the shrine at the center of events deemed to have implications for all Christianity, Counter-Reformation legends created powerful historical apologies for their cults.

Throughout Bavaria, a revolution in shrine-oriented mythmaking is evident in the years following 1570. Of course, such legends had been common during the Middle Ages as well. Because many medieval Bavarian shrines had lacked relics and images with which to attract the faithful, legends had often served the crucial purpose of explaining why a particular pilgrimage existed. In the absence of a saintly tumulus or wonder-working image, these stories "legitimated the sanctity of holy places" by linking the saint to the site.[20] We possess few clues, however, as to how that overwhelmingly oral culture of myth and legend operated in medieval Bavaria. For it was only with the coming of the Catholic Reformation in the late sixteenth century that the narratives of many places were first codified through the culture of print.

For the counter-reformers, legends assumed a renewed, heightened importance because the stories they labored to place into circulation now possessed a polemical purpose in the ongoing war against Protestantism. These legends, moreover, moved beyond the traditions of medieval storytelling, which had attempted merely to legitimate by linking the saint to the site. In the apologetic pilgrimage book, the shrine's past and its contemporary miraculous *praesentia* were linked into an ongoing narrative testimony to the site's power throughout history. Since the Catholic reformers were attempting to renew the pilgrimage as a ritualized and routinized journey to specific places, these narratives concentrated on the goal of these journeys, rather than on the person of the saintly patron. They labored to explain how the site's holiness had been revealed over time.

The plot lines of the counter-reformers' legends fall generally into three broad categories (though considerable cross-fertilization was evident). They are stories about holiness tried yet triumphant, holiness lost and found, and holiness suddenly revealed. With these

---

20. Bächtold-Stäubli (ed.), *Handwörterbuch des deutschen Aberglaubens*, s.v. "Ort"; quoted in Rothkrug, "German Holiness and Western Sanctity," p. 166n.14.

narratives, Counter-Reformation writers strove to defend saintly
devotion from the attacks of Protestants and to forge pilgrimage
into an expression of militant Roman Catholicism. In the remainder
of this chapter, we will examine how Bavaria's pilgrimage propagandists employed these legends during the early decades of the
Counter-Reformation.

HOLINESS TRIED YET TRIUMPHANT

The notion of a Church Militant, tested and tempered by multiple
ordeals, had marked the Counter-Reformation propagandistic campaign from the start. In rituals like Corpus Christi, state and Church
had imaged Christian history as continually embattled and the
Eucharist as a source of unity that emerged ever victorious from
its skirmishes with the "godless." The preacher Johann Nass, the
hagiographer Laurentius Surius, and the shrine propagandist Martin Eisengrein had each used this tragicomic emplotment to treat
ecclesiastical history, the saints, the sacraments, and the numinous
locus. Each had stressed the visibility and tangibility of Roman
tradition. Emerging from frequent crises, trials, and heresies, *ecclesia militans* offered its unity and miracles as witness to its divine
presence. For the propagandists who dedicated themselves to the
renewal of specific shrines in the late sixteenth and seventeenth
centuries, tales involving cultic crisis and victory were to become
the single most important means of reviving, rehabilitating, and
defending their devotions.

The images of ordeal and triumph from which numerous such
legends were eventually to be forged shared themes with late medieval Bavarian religion. The mid fourteenth and late fifteenth centuries had seen an increase in pilgrimages to places in the countryside that justified and celebrated the persecution of the Jews.
Promoted to give grounds for crusades against this increasingly
marginalized group, myths about Jewish host desecration had dominated as an explanation for these cults. In the numerous late medieval stories of crimes against the host, Jews were charged with
buying consecrated wafers from Christians and torturing them in
ways that recalled the Crucifixion: driving nails through them,
hammering them on an anvil, or trampling them under foot—topoi
that raised the specter of Christ's torture and sacrifice. As a result of

this Jewish crime, these stories noted, the Eucharist would begin to bleed. To conceal what they had done, the Jews would cast the host into a fiery furnace, but it would not be consumed. Finally, in desperation, they might throw the sacred objects into a river or well—which would immediately turn to blood. They could not hide their crime; soon it would be discovered and avenged through a pogrom. In Bavaria, sites of alleged crimes against the host often grew to be enormously successful pilgrimage shrines, and the Eucharist's desecration, its "miracle" of discovery, and the subsequent punishment of the perpetrators became the focus of devotions that memorialized, through reenactment, the crucifixional victory.

Widespread in the decades before the Reformation, Bavaria's Bleeding Host pilgrimages illustrate how clerical and lay perceptions concerning thaumaturgy and miracles diverged. No clerically maintained miracle testimonies survive at these shrines; in other words, the Bleeding Host devotion flourished largely without the lure of clerically promoted miracles. Certainly, the burghers and peasants who came to these sites may have attributed intercessions to these "holy hosts," and evidence suggests that they did. After narrating the tale of Jewish desecration of the Eucharist at Deggendorf, for example, the author of a 1520 poetic ballad about the shrine alleged that this "miracle" had been followed by other wonders of healing in the village. A broadside promoting the Passau host pilgrimage in the late fifteenth century, moreover, concluded by depicting the altar of the new shrine draped with votive images, gifts traditionally presented to the saints to give thanks for a miracle.[21] But at neither place did the clergy maintain records of these testimonies.

Various and complex factors underlay this clerical reluctance to link Bleeding Host pilgrimages to a tradition of contemporary intercession. Unlike wonder-working images or relics, the host was not a mere man-made object that served as a channel between God and human beings. It *was* God and hence could not be seen to intercede on people's behalf in the same ways that the saintly image, the tumulus, or the relic did. To have promoted the Bleeding Host as a source of thaumaturgy and intercession would have threatened the

---

21. See Hsia, *Myth of Ritual Murder,* pp. 50–56.

very uniqueness of the divine presence that resided in the eucharistic wafer.

In attempting to maintain the Bleeding Host cult free from miracles, however attractive they might be, the Bavarian clergy were also reacting to the widespread magical use of the Eucharist in late medieval Europe. Ground up and sprinkled on fields, sewn into childbeds, or placed in charms and amulets, the host had enjoyed a long tradition as a magical agent. Yet even as these necromantic uses of the Eucharist continued unabated, fears about Jewish magic steadily intensified.[22] To promote miracles worked in conjunction with a Bleeding Host shrine threatened not only to make the Eucharist into a mere conduit of grace; it also raised the dangerous possibility that those faithful who visited these sites might associate the host's efficacy with magic, especially the magic of the Jews.

In Bavaria, the pilgrimages to the Bleeding Host shrines at Deggendorf and Passau appear to have endured relatively intact from the later Middle Ages through the Counter-Reformation. Although the clergy at these sites did not record miracles, it is clear that their devotions were nourished on pervasive suspicion and hatred of the Jews and the perception that viewing the tortured Eucharist conveyed a particularly immediate and potent salvific grace.[23] Because these hosts were revered like relics, entering into a site of eucharistic desecration brought the pilgrim directly into the presence of Christ.

The first of these shrines, Deggendorf, had its origins in a wave of pogroms that occurred in South Germany in the mid–fourteenth century. In 1337, the Christians of the town exterminated the Jewish population, after which they followed the common practice of erecting a church on the site of the razed ghetto to commemorate their "victory." Dedicating their new chapel to the "body of Christ," Deggendorfers now set about sanctifying the site. Over the years they acquired various indulgences for their church, but it was not until 1401—more than sixty years later—that one was issued citing

22. Ibid.; Browe, *Die eucharistischen Wunder des Mittelalters*; and idem, "Die Eucharistie als Zaubermittel im Mittelalter," *Archiv für Kulturgeschichte* 20 (1930): 134–154.
23. Bynum, *Holy Feast and Holy Fast*, pp. 53–54, reviews the development of the visual veneration of the host in the Middle Ages.

the crime of host desecration as the cause for the 1337 pogrom. Offered to pilgrims on the memorial of the destruction of the Jewish community (from September 30 to October 4 each year), this indulgence became known in the later Middle Ages as the *Gnad*, or "grace," and the pilgrimage to the church in which it was available acquired the same name.[24]

In the case of Deggendorf, the legend of the desecration of the host was apparently first applied as a justification and explanation for the *Gnad*'s developing devotion only decades after the extirpation of the town's Jews. By the late fifteenth century, however, tales of eucharistic torture had acquired an independent ability to inspire and sustain persecution. At Passau in 1478, for example, accusations of violence enacted on the Eucharist served not as after-the-fact legitimation, but as the very cause for a pogrom. Arrested for theft, Christoph Eisengreishamer, a Christian servant, confessed to having sold hosts to the town's Jews. Passau's magistrates reacted immediately by arresting and questioning a number of Jews and extracting confessions from them. In the wake of the resulting executions, expulsions, and forced conversions, the town's synagogue was demolished and a new church erected, to which a pilgrimage ensued.

Both Deggendorf and Passau remained popular devotions in the early sixteenth century, and a rich lore of oral tales grew up around each, with all the common motifs—as seen in the account of an anonymous poet-chronicler who visited Deggendorf around 1520. He narrated with scrupulous attention to detail the various tortures the Jews had worked on the wafers—sold to them in this instance by a Christian woman. They had scratched it with thorns and punctured it with an awl to make it bleed before throwing it into an oven. There it remained unconsumed by the flames while a vision of the Christ child appeared in the fire. As these tortures were occurring, however, a sentinel standing guard at the town's gates heard the Virgin Mary bemoaning the fate of her son. He alerted the town fathers, and Christian society soon rose up to avenge the murder by exterminating the Jews.[25]

24. Rothkrug, "Holy Shrines, Religious Dissonance, and Satan," pp. 282–283.
25. *Von Tegkendorf das geschicht wie die Iuden das hailig sacrament haben zugericht* [Augsburg: S. Otmar, 1520]; cited in Hsia, *Myth of Ritual Murder*, p. 56.

The adornments of this narrative—including the betrayal of the Christian community and the Eucharist by a woman, the multiple tortures of the Eucharist, the vision of the Christ child, and the discovery of the crime aided by the Virgin and sentinel—linked Deggendorf's *Gnad* to other sites, where the same incidents had been alleged. By the late fifteenth century, a unified discourse had emerged concerning crimes against the host; indeed, many places now shared virtually the identical legend.[26] Yet despite the similar motifs and topoi, their purpose was not to alleviate potential doubt or to erase the reality of the crime. In the late fifteenth and early sixteenth centuries, it was generally believed that these events had actually occurred. In accepting stock details, pilgrims to one site could merge what had happened there to a lineage of other crimes throughout Germany.

In the course of the sixteenth century, however, an increasingly critical—and largely Protestant—scrutiny of Hebraic rites and texts raised serious questions about the allegations of Jewish host desecration, which sometimes found their way into the ongoing Protestant-Catholic polemic over miracles.[27] The widely distributed pamphlets of Hieronymus Rauscher, Lutheran court preacher in the Upper Palatinate, for example, recounted a number of traditional legends about eucharistic crimes, transforming them into cases of clerical black magic. For Rauscher and other Protestant polemicists, Bleeding Host "miracles" became testimonies to the frauds, lies, and "magic" that the Roman clergy and Satan had worked to delude simple people.[28]

Nonetheless, in Bavaria knowledge of the crime against the host remained common at every layer of society. In a show trial held in Munich during 1600, Wittelsbach state officials persecuted the Pappenheimer family, itinerant beggars and cesspool cleaners, for the crime of witchcraft. Under torture, one family member confessed without prompting to having stolen and sold hosts to Straubing's Jews. For the state's officials, the fact that this admission came from a group of marginalized, "dishonorable" persons lent it credibility,

26. Hsia, *Myth of Ritual Murder*, pp. 54–56; Browe, "Die Hostienschändungen der Juden"; and Johannes Heuser, " 'Heilig Blut,' " pp. 10–13.
27. Hsia, *Myth of Ritual Murder*, p. 147.
28. Schenda, "Hieronymus Rauscher."

and ducal emissaries were immediately dispatched to investigate the Straubing Jews. Insufficient evidence, however, was discovered to support the claim.[29] Similar results obtained in subsequent investigations of Jewish host desecration, yet fear and hatred of the Jews persisted, and allegations of eucharistic torture continued to be made sporadically, even into the twentieth century.[30] When the charge appeared in early modern Bavaria, however, it was brought before a state judicial bureaucracy that was more scrupulous about evidence than medieval authorities had been. One result of this skepticism was that because the tale lacked de jure recognition, few new Bleeding Host pilgrimages appeared. Even so, both the Wittelsbach state and the clergy worked to sustain the memory of the state's preexisting medieval host cults by publicizing them systematically. The eucharistic pilgrimage—like the Corpus Christi procession before it—was expanded and its rituals elaborated. The legend of the Bleeding Host was now conflated with the contemporary Protestant abandonment of the orthodox Eucharist, and both were used as a visible testimony to Catholic truth against ongoing attacks by both Jews and Protestants.

It was with a dual purpose—to polemicize against Protestant attacks on eucharistic legends and to proclaim the truth of these tales to the Catholic devout—that the Wittelsbach court preacher Johann Rabus set about treating the origins of the cults of Deggendorf and Passau. In 1583, he preached a sermon before Duke Wilhelm and his court on the Bleeding Host shrine at Deggendorf. Then, at Wilhelm's prompting (and likely with his financial support), Rabus published an expanded version of his remarks entitled *A Short, True, and Essential Report Concerning the Revered, Widely Famous, and Eminent Holy Sacraments at Deggendorf and Passau* (1584).[31] Rabus had participated in the great annual pilgrimage, the Deggendorf *Gnad*, on two occasions, and in his pilgrimage book he reports that the procession was still carried on by the villagers of the region (though alas, no documents exist to allow us to assess the intensity

29. Kunze, *Highroad to the Stake*, pp. 155–160.
30. The last allegation of Jewish host desecration in Bavaria was reported in 1926; see Browe, "Die Hostienschändung der Juden," p. 178.
31. Johann Rabus, *Kurtzer, warhaffter und gründtlicher Bericht von dem hoch und weitberhümbten wundersame H. Sacrament zu Deckendorff und Passaw* (Munich: A. Berg, 1584). The Berg publishing house was supported financially by the Wittelsbach state.

of this traffic at this time). Through his sermons on the subject and his printed defense of Deggendorf and Passau, however, Rabus was clearly attempting to promote these shrines to a broader audience. As he states in the dedication, he intended his pilgrimage book not only to defend these cults, but also to "edify" those who made the pilgrimage. As in the case of other Bavarian Bleeding Host shrines, the Wittelsbach court preacher did not join the Eucharist at either shrine to a contemporary tradition of thaumaturgic and interces- sory miracles; rather, he concentrated on narrating the story of the host's torture at the hands of Jews and the Christian discovery and punishment of the crime. In this way, the publicity he crafted for Deggendorf and Passau departed from the narrative conventions of late medieval accounts of these shrines.

Rabus devotes the majority of his *Short, True, and Essential Report* to the Deggendorf shrine. Instead of beginning with the alleged Jewish crime against the host, however, the preacher lodges his treatment of Deggendorf's origins within a long prologue and the broader context of a crisis in Christian history: the political rivalry between the Wittelsbach emperor Louis the Bavarian and Pope John XXII during the first half of the fourteenth century, which eventually resulted in the pope's deposition of Louis as emperor.[32] Even as this famous dispute was unfolding, Christianity, already divided by political and religious controversies, was weakening and would soon be subjected to renewed Jewish attacks. During the summer of 1327, ten years before the Deggendorf host crime, a fiery comet appeared in the skies over the empire, a sign to Jews of the imminent arrival of their Messiah. Because they believed that their salvific prophet would not arrive without the collapse of Christian society, the Jews began to practice their age-old crimes: they poi- soned wells, committed ritual murders of Christian boys, and tor- tured the host. Thus, in Rabus's account the events at Deggendorf are transposed from the level of a local incident similar to ones experienced in many places, to that of a Pan-European, decade-long offensive waged by Jews against Christianity.

After relating the stories of Jewish crimes against the host and the resultant "miracles" at Deggendorf and Passau, Rabus concen-

32. Ibid., fols. avi ff. He cites as his source for these observations the humanist Johannes Aventinus's popular *Bavarian Chronicle*.

trates his polemical energies on rehabilitating Catholic miracles from the Protestant charge of diabolic magic. Here, anti-Semitism and anti-Protestantism merge into a single discourse. For the court preacher, the reformers become "Pharisees," whose attitude toward true Christianity and its Eucharist is the same as that of the Jews. Citing a number of ancient and medieval theologians, he labors to prove the reality of Christ's continuing power to perform miracles through his presence in the Eucharist. As is typical of Protestant and Catholic polemic alike, he portrays his opponents as deluded by Satan into attributing Christ's wonders to the Archfiend himself. What is interesting about Rabus's argument, however, is the predominance of eating imageries. The devil, for instance, "nourishes" then "spits out" lies and slanders against the honor of the Church's miracles. Certainly the act of eating was central to the Eucharist, and it is not surprising to find the preacher employing its dichotomous opposite of spitting out to treat Protestant attacks on the eucharistic miracle. Through employment of this literary device, he reduces Lutherans and Calvinists to those whose denial of the simple truth of the tortured host is comparable to a lack of mastery over one of the most elemental of human functions: eating. By attacking the veracity of these Bleeding Host miracles, Protestants become "devourers" whose gluttony causes them to eat away at the truth of Christ's miracles, reducing them to demonic slanders.[33]

In 1604, the priest and theologian Johann Sartorius published another pilgrimage book, *Memorial of the Miracles of God*—though here he confines himself to relating just the myth of Deggendorf, in particular its host miracle.[34] The story closely follows the outlines of

33. Johann Rabus, *Kurtzer, warhaffter und gründtlicher Bericht*, esp. p. avi; the observation is especially interesting in light of the recent studies of Caroline Bynum in *Holy Feast and Holy Fast*.

34. Johann Sartorius, *Memoria mirabilium Dei. Das ist, Von dem hochwürdigen Sacrament deß wahren Fronleichnambs Christ so Anno M. CCC. XXXVII. zu Deckendorf in Bayrn von den Juden hochfrävenlicher Weiß centiret, seythero daselbst auffgehalten und sambt andern wurdigen Heiligthumb mit Andacht besuchet und verehret wirdt* (1604: 2 eds.). The first edition was printed at Ingolstadt; see Stalla, *Ingolstädter Buchdruck*, p. 17, no. 31. I quote from the second edition, printed by Simon Haan at Straubing. Biographic details concerning Sartorius, including his dates of birth and death, do not exist. The title page lists the author as "Ioannem Sartorivm, Arenspergensem, H. Schrifft Licentiaten, Dechant und Pfarrherr daselbsten."

Rabus's book, but rather than locating the Deggendorf eucharistic crime within the context of Christian divisiveness and Jewish offensive, Sartorius turns to the entire corpus of host legends retold in the later Middle Ages. In 1592, the Cologne cleric Valentin Leucht had collected and edited these tales into a compendium, *An Illustrated Mirror of the Holy Eucharist*, a sort of comprehensive guide to the Church's most "miraculous" hosts.[35] Drawing upon this source, Sartorius styles what occurred at Deggendorf into an ongoing testimony to a tradition characterized by Jewish hatred and tortures of the Christian God. By multiplying instances of eucharistic desecration in general he labors to verify systematically the reality of the Jewish misdeed that occurred in the Lower Bavarian town.

Focusing on Deggendorf in particular, Sartorius begins by relating the earliest history of the town's major churches and monastic foundations.[36] Like Martin Eisengrein's historical prologue to *Our Lady at Altötting*, this section offers a kind of parallel biblical narrative. Showing how the apostolic succession was established in Deggendorf and its vicinity, Sartorius uses this foundation to explain the town's consequent "miracle" of the Bleeding Host. In successive chapters he treats the appearance of the Jews at Deggendorf and alleges a variety of crimes they worked there before their most heinous one: the eucharistic desecration itself.[37] The priest then turns his attention to the latter crime, granting considerable space to each "horror" the Jews enacted on the Christian God. To enhance the drama of this account, he includes separate short chapters for each of their tortures. One, for instance, describes how the Deggendorf Jews drove holes through the host with a sharp awl, another the host being scratched with thorns, another the host's internment in the fiery baker's oven, and so forth.[38]

Like Rabus's account, Sartorius's pilgrimage book follows the story of the Deggendorf Jews to its gruesome conclusion and draws essentially the same message from the tale. Both rely on latent Jewish hatred, not only to defend their pilgrimages, but also to

35. Valentin Leucht, *Speculum illustrium miraculorum SS. Eucharistiae* (Mainz, 1592, 1598, and 1606).
36. Sartorius, *Memoria mirabilium Dei*, pp. 9–30.
37. Ibid., pp. 31–54.
38. Ibid., pp. 54–98.

make them into a self-conscious affirmation of Roman truth against the "lies and deceits" of Judaism and Protestantism, which are now fused into a single tradition of hate.

To answer the charges of Protestants against cults like those of Deggendorf and Passau, moreover, Rabus and Sartorius wove their tales of eucharistic desecration and triumph into a broader context. For Rabus, the origins of the devotion still visible at Deggendorf lay in a period when Christianity was internally divided owing to the struggles between emperor and pope. As a consequence of the Church's turmoil, the Jews had moved to attack the host. Today in yet another period of strife, his polemic warned, the offensive against the Roman Eucharist was continuing in the guise of the Protestant heresies. His work thus urged its readers to remain faithful to an eternal visible truth that had been and was still being assaulted by various heretical and demonically inspired groups. For Sartorius, the truth of the incident at Deggendorf was demonstrated by a verifiable lineage of similar crimes worked in almost every European country. In citing Valentin Leucht's eucharistic compendium, he hoped to convince his readers through a kind of protohistorical method. Piling incident upon incident, and recounting the Deggendorf crime of eucharistic desecration in particular in minute detail, he hoped to gather a wealth of detail too massive to deny.

Both authors saw the mystery of their shrines residing in the cults' great episodic reenactment of the Crucifixion; by throwing into relief the "enormous" events that led to the shrine's founding, each also attempted to maintain his cult free from the appeal of a tradition of thaumaturgy and intercession. The implicit argument was that such extraordinary eucharistic miracles did not warrant a subsequent legacy. For Rabus and Sartorius, the purpose of pilgrimages to Deggendorf and Passau, among other sites, was rather to memorialize a crucifixional torture and victory and to celebrate Catholicism's prowess in repulsing onslaughts against its truths.

Without a doubt, the two books represent dismal episodes in the Bavarian Counter-Reformation's propagandistic campaign. Yet it is at least comforting to realize that such exertions were now necessary because the myth of eucharistic desecration had begun to be subjected to criticism. By the late sixteenth century, Deggendorf's and Passau's Bleeding Host legends needed to be carefully tended and nurtured by clerical promotion if they were to grant continuing meaning to annual rites like the *Gnad.*

No case so vividly illustrates the Bavarian Counter-Reformation's deliberate fostering of pilgrimages redolent with the imagery of crisis and resolution as that of St. Benno's shrine in Munich. The saint, an eleventh-century bishop of Meissen, had excited controversy from the earliest years of the Reformation. In the late fifteenth century, his cult had blossomed at Meissen, and the episcopal government and the princes of Ducal Saxony had lobbied Rome intensely for his canonization. In 1523, when their efforts finally succeeded, the bishop of Meissen and the Saxon prince planned to use their newly canonized saint to counter the early Reformation movement in their region. Publicity for the rites surrounding Benno's elevation inspired Luther and other early Protestant pamphleteers to issue tracts denouncing the cult. These attacks proved futile, however, and the shrine, still sponsored by its prince and bishop, retained its notoriety during the 1520s and 1530s. Then in 1539, just hours after the death of the last Catholic Saxon prince, a crowd entered Meissen's cathedral, tore down the shrine, and threw its shards into the Elbe. Meissen's cathedral canons, however, having foreseen this attack, had already spirited their saint's relics to a nearby monastery for safekeeping.[39]

Here matters remained for over thirty years. In 1572, several Catholic princes approached the episcopal government at Meissen, requesting to transfer the saint's remains to more congenial locations. After four years of negotiations, the bishop awarded the saint's remains to the Bavarian duke.[40] Dispatching his emissaries to Meissen, the duke had the relics secretly taken to the Bavarian border; they were met by a triumphal procession that carried them on to the duchy's capital, where their arrival was celebrated as a Wittelsbach victory in the ongoing war against heresy. In those same years, of course, Albrecht and his state officials were redou-

---

39. Robert Böck, "Die Verehrung des hl. Benno in München," *Bayerisches Jahrbuch für Volkskunde,* 1958, pp. 53–54; Martin Luther, *Widder den neuwen Abgott und allten Teuffel der zu Meyssen soll erhoben werden* (Wittenberg, 1524), in *Luther Werke,* 1st ser., 15:170 ff. The pompous ceremony of elevation is described in Ozment, *The Reformation in the Cities,* p. 43.
40. Böck, "Die Verehrung des hl. Benno," p. 56.

bling their efforts to expel Protestants from Munich. Hence the arrival of this saintly thaumaturge must have been seen by the city's Protestant burghers as yet another sign of the direction in which both state policy and religious affinities were moving in the capital.

Following the welcoming festivities, Benno's remains were housed in the Wittelsbach family chapel, where they remained for several years like a "Counter-Reformation trophy."[41] In 1580, however, Duke Wilhelm moved the relics to the city's parish, the Church of Our Lady (Frauenkirche). At the time, both the Wittelsbach duke and the canons of this church were working to have the capital of the local diocese moved from Freising to Munich. In so doing, Wilhelm hoped to wrest control from the sometimes obstreperous, aristocratic cathedral canons at Freising. Benno's placement in the city's parish church and his subsequent naming as patron of Munich (fig. 12) were clearly intended to bolster Wittelsbach episcopal ambitions.[42]

From that time well into the eighteenth century, in fact, Benno was to be employed for numerous pious, polemical, and political ends. In 1596, having failed to secure episcopal status for Munich, Wilhelm began a massive building program at the Church of Our Lady. Finally completed in 1623 during the reign of Wilhelm's successor, Maximilian I, this redecoration had as its focal point the so-called Benno Arch, which until its demolition in the mid–nineteenth century dwarfed everything else inside the church.[43]

Symbolizing the triumph of the Christian relic cult over the "lies and deceits" of Protestantism, Wilhelm's artistic program at Our Lady aimed to fulfill a variety of ends for the Wittelsbach state as well. The Benno Arch was to be a national shrine and, much like the medieval French chapel of St. Denis, a kind of dynastic showcase,

41. I have drawn the appropriate phrase *gegenreformatorische Trophäe* from Karin Berg, "Der ehemalige 'Bennobogen' der Münchner Frauenkirche," in *Um Glauben und Reich. Kurfürst Maximilian I,* ed. Hubert Gläser (Munich, 1980), 1:312–317.

42. J. Kirsch, "Beiträge zur Geschichte des hl. Benno Bischofs von Meissen (1066–1106)" (Ph.D. diss., Munich, 1911), pp. 63ff. The canons of the Church of Our Lady were also concerned to protect the status of their own parish against the then-rising position of the Jesuits within the spiritual life of Munich; see Heinz Jürgen Sauermost, "Zur Rolle St. Michaels im Rahmen der Wilhelminisch-Maximilianischen Kunst," in Gläser (ed.), *Um Glauben und Reich* 1:167–174, esp. p. 170.

43. A complete history of the building program is described in Karin Berg's "Der Bennobogen der Münchner Frauenkirche: Geschichte, Rekonstruktion und Analyse der frühbarocken Binnenchoranlage" (Ph.D. diss., University of Munich, 1979).

recalling to visitors some of the ruling family's most important members. Underwritten with funds from the Wittelsbachs, the city of Munich, and other towns and monasteries throughout Bavaria, the structure covered the church's presbytery and, beneath it, a newly remodeled Wittelsbach mausoleum.[44] In placing the dynasty's graves close to Benno's relics, Wilhelm and his successor, Maximilian, adopted the traditional practice of burying their dead with a saint (*ad sanctos*). In the Middle Ages, such burials were believed to place the deceased within the protective "odor of sanctity" that emanated from the corpses of the saints. These Bavarian dukes certainly desired the benediction of their new saint, even in their graves. Perhaps more importantly, however, the new Wittelsbach mausoleum, with its rescued saintly patron, glorified the dynasty's consecrated role as a "defender" of the faith.

Among the graves of ancestors buried in the church, that of the notorious German emperor Louis the Bavarian was granted primacy of place directly beneath the structure. Attended by angels, Louis's huge bronze catafalque far outshone St. Benno's opulent yet life-sized reliquary. Indeed, the edifice surrounding the emperor's resting place created a frame that memorialized him as a kind of "unofficial saint." In presenting Louis to worshippers in this manner, the Counter-Reformation had in fact effected a most creative rewriting of the past, for during his tenure as emperor Louis had waged war against Rome and been deposed by the pope. The "shrine," in short, reflected the increasing determination of the Wittelsbachs to define the counter-reformational program according to their own pious and political needs. By placing their family members within the "odor of sanctity," Wilhelm and Maximilian hoped to appropriate the trappings of sacral kingship and create a visible buttress to their increasingly determined attempts to dominate the religious practices of their territory.[45]

For the Wittelsbach dynasty, Benno was a kind of sanctifying agent; his consecrated life and dramatic rescue from Protestant

44. On the funding for the Munich *Bennobogen* see Böck, "Die Verehrung der hl. Benno," p. 60.

45. Berg, "Der ehemalige 'Bennobogen,'" pp. 313–314; Peter Bernhard Steiner, "Der gottselige Fürst und die Konfessionalisierung Altbayerns," in Gläser (ed.), *Um Glauben und Reich* 1:253, 258; and Wolfgang Braunfels, "Cuius Regio, Eius Ars," in ibid., pp. 133–140.

Meissen reflected and underscored the Munich princes' role as defenders of Catholicism. Yet the saint's "official" life also contained strains and themes uniquely well suited to the spiritual tastes of Munich's clergy and laity. During the eleventh-century Investiture Controversy, for instance, Benno had remained true to the Roman pope over the demands of the German emperor.[46] During the early Reformation, the attacks on his cult lent the saint an even greater notoriety and made the protection of his devotion into a self-conscious affirmation of Catholic truth vis-à-vis Lutheranism and Calvinism. While the imposing monument in Munich's parish church may have glorified the Wittelsbach dynasty more than it did the Meissen bishop, there can be no doubt that the town's faithful yearned after Benno's ecclesiastically sanctioned power. As participation in the young devotion grew, followers' attentions focused on the role of Benno as intercessor, wonder-worker, and pious paragon. Shortly after the saints' translation to the Church of Our Lady, votive offerings began to turn up at the saint's reliquary and processions from villages in Munich's vicinity started to make their way to the nascent shrine. By 1598, Munich's Jesuits also showed their approval of the cult when they staged a Latin School drama of the saint's life and wonders.[47]

In 1601, a new life-sized reliquary bust appeared on the church's high altar as a testimony to the affections Benno had stirred in Munich. Made of silver and decorated with precious gems, the sculpture cost almost 1,700 florins: a princely yet appropriate commemoration to a saint whose distressed life and afterlife suited the devotional needs of Counter-Reformation Catholicism.[48] More than half this sum came from Munich's burghers, a sign that the imported saint had found a considerable following among the town's inhabitants. The male elite of Munich had formed a new St. Benno confraternity, which was now working to promote the greater glory

46. Sauermost, "Zur Rolle St. Michaels," p. 170; and *Lexikon für Theologie und Kirche*, s.v. "Benno." The Investiture Controversy was a mid-eleventh-century dispute between the German emperor and the Roman pope, which centered on the secular prince's rights to appoint bishops and archbishops; see Brian Tierney, *The Crisis of Church and State, 1050–1300* (Englewood Cliffs, N.J., 1964).

47. Kirsch, "Beiträge zur Geschichte des hl. Benno," p. 74.

48. Böck, "Die Verehrung des hl. Benno," p. 60. The *Bennobogen* was demolished in the nineteenth century when the Frauenkirche was returned to its original Gothic appearance; see Berg, "Der ehemalige 'Bennobogen,'" p. 312.

and expansion of the cult. For its pious works, the brotherhood chose to aid the impoverished, providing them with food and shelter and underwriting the expense of placing their children in trade apprenticeships. During the first decade of the seventeenth century, this sodality received a number of indulgences for their devotion.[49]

The Benno cult thus fulfilled a variety of aims for the various constituencies in and around the town. Not only a symbol of Bavarian unity, Benno embodied Catholic confessional truth, a testimony to the province's championship of the Roman resurgence. In the nearby countryside, villagers looked to the saint for intercession and healing, while for members of the Munich male elite he served as a symbol and patron of "brotherly" unity.

Around 1600, the clergy of the Church of Our Lady moved to promote their new devotion in a more systematic manner, recording and publishing the saint's miracles in order to draw the faithful to Munich. In the century that followed, however, only 546 wonders were set down at the shrine, a relatively modest number when compared to other places. These miracles reveal, moreover, that the character of Benno's cult did not differ significantly from that of numerous other popular devotions in early modern Bavaria: for those seeking intercession, Benno served primarily as a healer. These miracle accounts also disclose that the pilgrimage remained relatively geographically circumscribed, with the faithful coming primarily from Upper Bavaria, the southernmost part of the territory. Beyond this region, the reputation of the cult was limited.[50]

Munich's Church of Our Lady may never have gained the same following as the most popular Counter-Reformation cults, but this was not because of lack of promotion. During the seventeenth century, the clergy of the Frauenkirche conducted an extensive printing campaign to develop the reputation of their devotion. The largest portion of books published by the shrine were thin miracle pamphlets similar to those issued in the late Middle Ages.[51] Al-

49. Böck, "Die Verehrung des hl. Benno," p. 60.
50. These findings are summarized in ibid., pp. 62ff.
51. My conclusions are based on a reading of the following miracle books: *Von allerlay Miraclen und Wunderwercken so Gott der Allmächtig durch das Fürbitt und Verdienst deß heiligen Bischoff Bennonis, nach seinem Todt und Erhebung augenscheinlich gewircket* (Munich, 1601); *Gründtliche Verzaichnus Etlich fürnemmer Wunderzaichen zu Endt deß*

though often more polished, possessing a greater degree of explanation, and more complete than late medieval books, they nevertheless remained a truly popular literature, in that by virtue of their
cost and modest vocabulary they addressed the broadest possible
readership. They would, of course, have been read by clerics and
members of the Bavarian elite as well, but by and large these slight
volumes, emblazoned with images of the saint, were meant to
cultivate an awareness of Benno's miracles among the literate and
semiliterate artisans and villagers who visited the site.[52]

Yet miracle pamphlets were only one part of this publicity campaign. Like Altötting and an increasing number of other shrines,
the Frauenkirche also distributed the apologetic pilgrimage book. In
place of the thin, terse style of the miracle pamphlets, these works
were intended for a more elite audience of clergy and laity, and they
sought not only to publicize the wonders of the saint but also to
explain the historical origins of his cult. For these explanations,
however, clerical propagandists turned not to an examination of the
early sixteenth-century controversy over Benno's cult, but to the
saint's life in the eleventh century. In his own times, they argued,
Benno had persistently proven his superhuman capabilities of sur-
mounting enormous difficulties. From then until the present, he
had thus been an important source of aid, a conduit through which
divine power could be garnered. In the first of several pilgrimage
books printed for the site, *A Certain and Approved History of St. Benno*,
an anonymous clerical author adapted the conventions of medieval

---

1601, und im Anfang deß 1602 Jahr in München (Munich, 1602); *Umbstendig: Und
warhaffter Bericht was sich zu end deß 1602. und 1603. gantze Jahr bey s. Benno in München
für Wunderwerck begeben* (Munich, 1603); *Kurtze Verzaichnuß etlicher Miraclen und Wunderwerck so sich Anno Domini 1604 bey S. Bennonis heylthumb in München zugetragen*
(Munich, 1604); *Kurtzer Bericht Etlicher Miracul unnd Wunderwercken so sich in dem
entwichnen 1605 Jar Bey S. Bennonis Hailthum in München zugetragen* (Munich, 1606);
*Warhaffte Beschreibung etlich sonderbarer Wunderzeichen und Genaden so Gott der Allmäch-
tig durch Fürbitt deß H. Bischoffe Bennonis Anno 1606 unds 7. jar . . . gewürcket* (Munich,
1608); *Extract unnd gründtlicher Bericht etlicher Gnaden: und Wunderwercken . . . deß
H. Bischoff Bennonis . . .* (Munich, 1609); *Miracl und Wunderzaichen deß H. Bischoffs
BENNONIS von dem 16. Junij . . . 1609 biß . . . 1615 Jahrs* (Munich, 1615); *Miracl und
Wunderzaichen von . . . 1615 biß . . . Anno 1617* (Munich, 1617); *Miracl und Wunderzaichen . . . Deß H. Bischoffs BENNONIS . . . von dem 8 Junij deß 1615. Jahre biß
auff sein Fest deß 1622 Jahr* (Munich, 1623); *Extract unnd gründtlicher Bericht etlicher
Gnaden und Wunderwercken . . . Deß H. Bischoff Bennonis . . . in den nechst entwichenen
sechzehen Jahren* (Munich, 1643).

52. Chartier draws similar conclusions about the dissemination of miracle literature in early modern France; see *Cultural Uses of Print*, pp. 145–182.

hagiography to the contemporary circumstances of Benno's cult in Munich. Following the treatment given the medieval life of the saint, he divided his book into sections that examined St. Benno's *vita* and his posthumous *miracula* at Meissen and Munich. As a bonus, he provided a translation of the papal bull canonizing the saint. Woven throughout, needless to say, was also the standard anti-Protestant polemic, coupled with a counter-reformational concern for rehabilitating saintly devotion generally.

Like many pilgrimage book authors, the anonymous writer of the *Certain and Approved History* explicitly located Benno and his wonder-working power within the lineage of the apostolic succession, narrating the Christianization of Meissen's surrounding region and the establishment of an apostolic see in the town— two events that explained Benno's subsequent miracles as part of the Church's continued accretion to biblical narrative. As his main source the author drew from Hieronymus Emser's pre-Reformation hagiography of Benno, published in 1512 almost a decade before the saint's canonization.[53] (During the subsequent controversy over Benno's elevation, Emser also wrote a tract attacking Luther for denouncing the cult.)[54] Like Emser, the author of the *Certain and Approved History* stressed the sanctity that the future bishop of Meissen displayed from an early age. Upon entering the Benedictine order, he observed, the saint could not even read mass without breaking into tears.[55]

Emser, however, had concentrated on the saint's ability to balance the competing demands of spiritual and worldly life, and to rise above human frailty. By contrast, although our anonymous author mentioned these traits, they were subsumed to the demands of a new, more militant piety. He focused, for example, on Benno's participation in the eleventh-century *Heidenmissionen*, the savage annual campaigns that forced the conversion of the Slavs and

---

53. *Gewiß und approbirte Historia Von S. Bennonis* (Munich, 1602), "Vorrede," fol. aii. The work is the book *Divi Bennonis misnensis quondam episcopi vita. Miracula et alia quedam non tam misnensibus quam germanis omnibus decora* (Leipzig, 1512). The author translated the work into German as *Das heilig Lebe und Legend des seligen Vatters Bennonis weyland Bischoffen zu Meyssen, gemacht vnd in das tewzsch gebracht durch Jeronymum Emser* (Leipzig, 1517).

54. *Antwurt auff das lesterliche buch wider Bischoff Benno zu Meissen vnd erhebung der heyligen iungst auszgangen* (Dresden, 1524).

55. *Gewiß und approbirte Historia*, p. 2(r).

Wends in the region around Meissen. Yet the brutality of these militaristic crusades found no mention in our writer's account of the saint's life; instead, he portrayed these people as "arch-heretics" who, like the modern Lutherans and Calvinists, had fallen under the devil's spell. In working for these tribes' conversion, Benno therefore became a kind of Christian exorcist, delivering the deluded from damnation. In addition, our author projected on these Eastern European groups the charges of ritual murder and dualism. The most important members of their pantheon were a "god of light," Svanthewitz, and a "god of darkness," Zcernebok. To propitiate their luminous deity, the Slavs annually offered up a Christian man. Although Benno knew this, he refused to fear, even when taken prisoner. Impressed with his heroic demeanor, his captors quickly converted to Christianity.[56]

Benno's success in converting the Slavs and Wends, however, represented the reclamation of a damned and demonically possessed tribe, a fact that certainly did not please the devil. Thus angered, Satan began to plot against the saint—and here our author alleges a series of ordeals the devil produced in his effort to discredit and destroy the bishop.[57] The most important of these was the Investiture Controversy, in which struggle the bishop remained faithful to Rome, even though it meant defying the emperor.[58] In this history, then, this famous panimperial struggle is described as an event contingent on the successful missionary efforts of a consecrated bishop. As in the forty-day trial of Christ in the wilderness described in Luke 4, Mark 1, and Matthew 4, Satan proved capable of producing numerous snares and temptations for the Meissen clergyman. Yet in this case the demonic offensive against a Catholic saint bore with it the power to change the course of history.

With the conclusion of this extravagant hagiography, our author moved on to recount some of the miracles Benno performed during both life and afterlife. These he presented in separate chapters, attempting to demonstrate an unbroken strand of wonders produced by the saint from the days of his earthly ministry until the

56. Ibid., pp. 4–5.
57. Ibid., p. 5.
58. Ibid., pp. 6–7.

present. In the first section, containing miracles the saint worked while still living, the stories recall the wonders of both the Old and New Testaments. Like Moses, the saint turned a stone into a lake to refresh one of his audience, and like Jesus he was also able to transform water into wine.[59] By attributing the wonders of both the ancient Jews and Christ to the saint, the book again sought to establish a convergence between biblical narrative and the continuously unfolding story worked through Catholicism's celestial intercessors, the saints.

In the remaining two sections, Benno's posthumous miracles at Meissen and Munich are examined.[60] The second of these sections—concerning the saint's miracles recorded in the Church of Our Lady—was given an eschatological cast. In the foreword to these accounts, the author called attention to these miracles as "signs" sent by God to confirm Catholic truth against the attacks of Protestants: "God the Almighty has also allowed his great miracles to shine forth clearly in these our last, confused, and unhappy times in order to confirm powerfully the intercession and intervention of his chosen ones." Again recalling Old Testament language and imagery, he applied the concept of a chosen people to the Catholic Church, and rhapsodized that the miraculous nature of sainthood was in essence a special seal to the "God of Israel's" covenant with that institution. "So [it is] not without reason that David writes that God is wondrous in his saints: Wondrous is the Lord in the mighty ones. The God of Israel will give his people power and strength."[61]

The author of the *Certain and Approved History* thus strove to make Benno's wonder-working power contingent on his standing in the apostolic succession, his relationship to the biblical and ecclesiastical narratives, and the colossal struggle he waged against Satan. However, the concern for the saint's actual life, as found in this pilgrimage book intended for a relative elite cadre of clergy and

59. Ibid., pp. 7–8.
60. Ibid., the section treating the Meissen miracles appears on pp. 12–23; the Munich miracles appear on pp. 23–29. These miracles had been separately published as *Gründtlicher Verzaichnus Etlich furnemmer Wunderzaichen so sich bey S. Bennonis Heilthumb zu München zu Endt des 1601. Und im Anfang deß 1602. Jahr in München begeben* (Munich, 1602); and *Eygentliche Relation, Was sich für ein herrlich Miracl, nechst vergangen Monat Novembris, diß lauffent 1601. in unser L. Frawen Kirch zu München begeben* (Munich, 1602).
61. *Gewiß und approbirte Historia*, p. 23.

laity, was not the staple of the thin miracle books being published for the site at the same time. When the clerics in the Church of Our Lady addressed their broad popular audience through the pronouncement of miracles orally and in the miracle books, it was the ongoing, contemporary testimonies to Benno's sanctity that predominated, not the reputation of the cult's saintly source. Certainly, pilgrims to the imposing Benno Arch during the late sixteenth and early seventeenth centuries could not have missed the intensely visual representation of Benno as a triumphant, legendary figure. Nor could they have failed to mistake the connections that this monument underscored between the legendary sanctity of the Meissen bishop and the contemporary efforts of the Wittelsbach dynasty to sanctify its role as Catholicism's protector. In presenting its historicized apology for the cult, the Counter-Reformation program in Munich thus advanced multiple media: one a pilgrimage book addressed to an elite cadre, the other a visible, artistic representation intended for all the faithful. Nonetheless, these artistic and literary campaigns did share a common subtext, for both explained how a saintly thaumaturge, exorcist, and bishop had ultimately triumphed over Catholicism's detractors with the aid of a consecrated dynasty.

The print campaign conducted for this shrine was one of the most diverse waged by any devotion in Bavaria during the seventeenth century. It was, indeed, an essential component of the program to establish and foster a previously unknown cult. In the end, however, the campaign's successes proved modest, and caution us from assuming that printed clerical advocacy alone could create a truly widespread devotion. In the late sixteenth and seventeenth centuries, as in the later Middle Ages, printed texts remained adjuncts to far more important forms of oral and word-of-mouth promotion. Moreover, it was ultimately Bavaria's pilgrims—her villagers, artisans, and burghers—rather than the nobles, clerics, or other elites, who controlled the destiny of the duchy's shrines, showering these sites with varying degrees of attention. Yet even so, it is not insignificant that in the case of St. Benno's devotion, the Wittelsbachs, Munich's clergy, and her burghers had combined forces to create a reasonably prosperous cult where none had previously existed. At the center stood the figure of a saintly thaumaturge and bishop whose canonization had been relatively recent and controversial. His churchly seal of approval was attractive to both Munich's clerics and Bavaria's princes, who used the cult as an instrument for heightening confessional awareness and demonstrating the unstoppable miraculous potency of Catholicism's celestial intercessors.

In assessing changes between canonization practices in the late Middle Ages and the Counter-Reformation, Peter Burke noted that the Roman ecclesiastical hierarchy in the later period drew its saints almost exclusively from the ranks of clerical elites.[62] The resurgence of Benno's cult at Munich is one episode away from the Church's power center at Rome that fits with this general pattern. The author of the *Certain and Approved History* strove—like the Roman curia's investigators in canonization proceedings—to make wonderworking more clearly a preserve of the clerical caste and the product of an enduring biblical narrative. Nevertheless, diversity persisted with regard to the Munich cult. The Wittelsbach princes appropriated the saint in their rites of translation, in their triumphal procession, and in their artistic representations in ways that glorified not only their ancestry but also their hegemonic ambitions over Bavaria's confessional loyalties. The town's elite male burghers, too, celebrated the new saint as a model of piety, placing him at the center of their own efforts to battle poverty. And within and beyond Munich's gates, artisans and villagers looked to Benno for aid in battling illness and unyielding circumstances. If we read the modest miracle books printed for this audience, we find that their clerical promoters relied largely, if not solely, on the claim of contemporary miracles to nurture the cult's popularity. For this readership, composed of modest craftsmen, merchants, and members of the lower clergy, it was not narrative legend, but the visual embodiment of the Benno Arch that testified to the saint's standing within an ancient succession.

Today, the village of Bettbrunn shows few signs that it was once the site of a busy Counter-Reformation pilgrimage. A hamlet of two hundred inhabitants, it lies about a dozen miles northeast of Ingolstadt in the remote and economically depressed Köschinger For-

62. Peter Burke, "How to Be a Counter-Reformation Saint," in *Religion and Society in Early Modern Europe, 1500–1800*, ed. Kaspar von Greyerz (Boston, 1984), pp. 45–55.

est. During the late sixteenth century, however, the place, located as it was within the borders of Bavaria yet close to the Protestant Upper Palatinate, came to assume considerable importance— greater importance than it might otherwise have enjoyed. Self-consciously promoted as part of Bavaria's counter-reformational policies on the part of both Church and state, Bettbrunn proved a source of irritation to Protestant officials. In the visitation records of the Upper Palatinate, it was frequently mentioned as a place sought out by secret Catholics.[63]

Although Bettbrunn was the site of a pilgrimage dedicated to the "Holy Savior," few documents exist to inform us about its history before the Counter-Reformation. An indulgence bull dated 1330 points to the shrine's late medieval origins, and two pre-Reformation votive candles still survive, indicating that pilgrims visited there in this period. Several mass endowments and land donations were also made before the Reformation.[64] Yet little can be said with certainty about the events that precipitated the devotion. The documentary silence was broken in 1584, however, when Johannes Engerd, a professor of poetics at the University of Ingolstadt, published Bettbrunn's first Counter-Reformation pilgrimage book, *Holy Savior at Bettbrunn.*[65]

Like so many of Bavaria's first-generation propagandists, Engerd was a convert; he was also a close associate of Johann Rabus, Martin Eisengrein, and Johann Nass.[66] The circumstances behind his authorship of the work, moreover, probably reflect how the clergy at many South German shrines developed their print campaigns in the wake of the Reformation. In this case, the local parish priest at

63. "Der altbairische Wallfahrtsort Bettbrunn lag an der Grenze zur reformierten Oberpfalz. Trotz der verordneten Einführung der Reformation zeigte sich in der Pfalz katholisches Leben von Dauer, zumal in den Grenzgebieten, in denen regen Wechselverkehr zwischen katholischer und reformierter Bevölkerung stattfinden konnte" (Alois Döring, "St. Salvator in Bettbrunn," p. 81).

64. A charter from 1374 mentions the place, and the village is cited in the account book of Ludwig the Bearded in 1417; these documents retain their silence, however, concerning Bettbrunn's pilgrimage. See ibid., pp. 75–78.

65. Johann Engerd, *Sanct Saluator zu Bettbrunn in Bayrn: Das ist Von der Alten H. Capellen und wirdigem hochberühmten Gotteshauß unsers lieben Herrn Sanct Saluators zu Bettbrunn in Fürstenthumb Bayrn, Regenspurger Bisthumbs: Auch Von den vielen Wunderzeychen, Heylthumb, Gelübden, Walfärten und anderer Christlichen Andacht desselben Orts / zc.* (Ingolstadt, 1584).

66. *ADB,* s.v. "Engerd, Johannes"; and Karl Prantl, *Geschichte der Ludwig-Maximilians-Universität in Ingolstadt, Landshut, München,* vol. 1 (Munich, 1872), pp. 334–335.

Bettbrunn, Georg Prantl, recruited Engerd to write a book of apology and polemic for his church. Gathering together manuscript miracle reports, a rhymed chronicle treating the shrine's origins, and various other documents for the Ingolstadt rhetorician to use, Prantl paid the professor ten gulden. Within twelve days, Engerd had produced a two-hundred-page book modeled on Eisengrein's *Our Lady at Altötting.*[67]

His source on Bettbrunn's history was allegedly the late medieval poetic chronicle he received from Prantl, which he redacted into the conclusion of his book. Yet Engerd was himself a poet; and the manuscript that he supposedly used no longer exists. Moreover, in his conclusion to his pilgrimage book he admits to having "improved" the older chronicle. Perhaps, like many a propagandist in any period, he wrote the poem about the site himself, drawing upon scattered bits of evidence and lore about the pilgrimage. In any event, *Holy Savior at Bettbrunn* can hardly be considered a dispassionate, detached account of the origins of the Bettbrunn devotion. Like all Counter-Reformation pilgrimage books, it is partly a creative reworking of legend and verifiable history and partly a story constructed for purposes of polemics and zealous piety.

Like Eisengrein's earlier work, Engerd's book was published at the Eder Press in Ingolstadt, the printshop from which most late sixteenth-century pilgrimage works issued. The first edition of seven hundred cost sixty-one florins, four kreuzer to print.[68] It is impossible to gauge at what price these books were marketed at the shrine in the 1580s and 1590s, but even if the Bettbrunn clergy had taken a modest profit, the books would certainly have been within the means of more prosperous artisans and merchants, the upper clergy, and state bureaucrats.[69]

Although only 11 percent of the shrine's still-extant early modern

----

67. Döring, "St. Salvator in Bettbrunn," pp. 126–127.
68. Ibid., p. 127.
69. I derive these conclusions by dividing the total price of the press run (61 fl., 4 kr.) plus Engerd's authorial fee (10 fl.) by 700 (the total number of books), to get 6 kreuzer (1 florin = 60 kreuzer). A Bavarian ordinance promulgated in 1622 stipulated that a day laborer must be paid at least 7 kreuzer, if provided with food, and 10–12 kreuzer without food. The cost of the book would consequently have been about what a laborer was paid for one day's work at the time. This was a sizable sum, yet not beyond the reach of more prosperous artisans, professionals, clerics, and state officials. See Wolfgang Behringer, "Scheiternde Hexenprozesse: Volksglaube und Hexenverfolgung um 1600 in München," in *Kultur der einfachen Leute*, ed. Richard van Dülmen (Munich, 1983), p. 51.

miracle records indicate the occupation of pilgrims, we can make some educated guesses. Because Bavaria was still a peasant society in this period, the largest proportion of visitors to the shrine would have been agricultural workers and farmers from the vicinity. It is logical to assume, moreover, that where an occupation was not mentioned, it was probably because the person came from an unexceptional background. Clerical scribes, after all, would have been more anxious to record and promote the pilgrimages of "honorable" members of the elite than those of simple farmers and peasants. Yet according to the Bettbrunn miracle records, the procession to the shrine was not limited to rural society alone. In those cases where occupation is mentioned in the miracle records, 64 percent were artisans and members of the building trades. Another 10 percent were state bureaucrats (4 percent), academics and clerics (4.5 percent), and army officers (1.5 percent)—all occupations that by the end of the sixteenth century required a relatively high degree of literacy. There was clearly a market for the Bettbrunn pilgrimage book, though it was far smaller than the market that would eventually exist for the thin miracle pamphlets produced in the next century.[70]

In his introduction to the work, Engerd acknowledged his indebtedness to Martin Eisengrein.[71] Following the pattern established in *Our Lady at Altötting*, Engerd began by narrating Bettbrunn's history, including the area's pre-Christian past and its conversion by apos-

70. The 11 percent of accounts that include occupational status also specify that 18 percent of pilgrims to the site were peasants, and 8 percent were servants and laborers. It would be logical to assume that the keepers of the manuscript miracle accounts tended to note city dwellers—artisans, burghers, academics, and clergy— more often than peasants because their journeys were more unusual. Nevertheless, this information does point to a sizable minority of visitors to the shrine from the middle and upper ranks of Bavarian society. See Alois Döring, "St. Salvator in Bettbrunn," p. 194. It appears to have taken about fifteen years for the Engerd pilgrimage book to be sold out, since a new edition was reprinted in 1597. Revised and edited histories continued to be reissued until the mid–eighteenth century. Döring's study of Bettbrunn's accounts (pp. 126–127) shows that in the seventeenth century, three hundred to four hundred of the thin miracle pamphlets were sold each year, but only thirty-five to forty of the longer pilgrimage books found purchasers. The market that prevailed at that time for the longer legendary pilgrimage book, then, was roughly one-tenth the size of that of the miracle book.

71. Johann Engerd, *Sanct Saluator zu Bettbrunn: Das ist Von der Alten H. Capellen und wirdigem hoch beruehmten Gotteshauß unsers lieben Herrn Sanct Saluators zu Bettbrunn in Fuerstenthumb Bayrn, Regenspurger Bisthumbs* (Ingolstadt, 1584), "Vorred," fol. aiii(r).

tolic missionaries during both Roman and early medieval times. He noted, for instance, that within years of the Ascension, St. Lucius Cyrensis was preaching the Gospel at Regensburg, Bettbrunn's diocesan capital. Moving on from these earliest missionaries to consider the Christianization of the heathen Bajuwaren invaders, he then turned to St. Rupert, Bavaria's "first apostle." Engerd made a long sojourn through the earliest ecclesiastical history of the territory, telling of Rupert and his apostolic successors' establishment of episcopal governments at Regensburg, Passau, Salzburg, Freising, and Brixen. The purpose of this prologue soon becomes clear: for Engerd, as for other Counter-Reformation authors, the apostolic succession—with its connections to the biblical drama—possessed a tangibility that explained the subsequent plethora of miracles. Bavaria's conversion by apostolic figures conferred a miraculous presence on the subsequent history of the Church in the province.[72]

In his earlier treatment of Altötting, Martin Eisengrein had transformed his tiny chapel into a place of pagan worship converted to better use by its Christian consecration. Engerd, for his part, insisted that the practice of pilgrimage itself was an ancient Germanic rite, purified by its importation into Christianity. In one digression, he betrays his humanist, rhetorical training and provides an etymology for the word *pilgrimage* (*Wallfahrt*). He alleged that the ancient practice of *Wallfahrt* (which he misinterpreted as meaning something like *Waldfahrt*, or, literally, "forest journey") was a propitiatory rite conducted in the primeval woods to secure the protection of the heathen gods before battles and ordeals.[73] Pilgrimages, he asserted, began

in the time of the ancient Bavarians, [who] worshipped their [god] Alman Argle with chants, songs, and poems. Often before they went into battle or [faced] difficult trials they would make *walfart* or journeys into the forest, especially to the great oak forests. From this, we derive the term "pilgrimage." After they became Christians, they

72. Ibid., pp. 1–29.
73. For a discussion of the etymology of the word *Wallfahrt*, including its humanistic treatment as a form of pre-Christian propitiation, see Wolfgang Brückner, "Zur Phänomenologie und Nomenklatur des Wallfahrtswesens und seiner Erforschung," in *Volkskultur und Geschichte. Festgabe für Josef Dünninger*, ed. Dieter Harmening (Berlin, 1970), pp. 384–424. During the 1960s, a dispute also raged over the precise origins of the term among German folklorists; Brückner's article summarizes the relevant printed exchanges.

visited and revered the churches of Christ, the true savior; Mary, Our Lady; and the other dear saints of God with prayers and Christian pilgrimages.[74]

Engerd hoped that early modern Bavarians, like the ancient Germans before them who sought out their god Alman Argle in the forests before going to battle, would journey to shrines like Bettbrunn to enlist the power that reposed there for waging the battle of daily life. The old customs had been purified by their importation into Christianity, he argued, and blessed by a God who showed approval with "striking miracles." Thus in his account, pilgrimage became a visible testimony to Catholicism's power to work conversions not only on human beings, but on their age-old customs and practices as well.

Following this prologue, Engerd moved on to treat the legend of Bettbrunn's foundation. The devotion at Bettbrunn, he wrote, began in 1125, when a "poor, simple, but God-fearing" shepherd went to mass to fulfill his Easter duties. When it came time to take communion, the shepherd, who was a believer in the Real Presence and a fervent venerator of the host, received the wafer, yet removed it from his mouth and placed it in a special box. Since he could not attend mass often because of his flock, he desired to use the host for his private devotion and to have the Savior near him at all times. Returning to his sheep, the shepherd made an altar by fixing his staff in the ground and placing the host on top of it. Once when his animals grew restless and he was distracted, he picked up his staff without thinking and hurled it at his flock; the consecrated wafer flew into the air and landed on the ground. In great distress, the shepherd tried to retrieve it, but it would not allow itself to be moved or touched. Terrified, he ran to his confessor to tell him what had happened, and the priest hurried to the site to rescue the wafer. Each time he tried to approach it, however, it would move farther away from him beyond his grasp. The priest immediately set out for Regensburg to report the incident to his bishop, who was also "eager to see and experience the miracle" and "traveled to the place in a special, splendid procession." Arriving at the spot, the Regensburg bishop was able to retrieve the host, whereupon he vowed to

74. Engerd, *Sanct Saluator zu Bettbrunn*, p. 28.

build a special chapel to honor the Savior at the site. From that date, Engerd alleged, Bettbrunn became a place of refuge and hope for countless Christians.[75]

The austere myth that the pilgrimage book author related is deceptively simple, for it is a story replete with details that served Counter-Reformation purposes. It begins when a pious yet misguided shepherd decides to take the Eucharist away from the parish so that he can have God's presence by him at all times. There is no hint whatsoever in this account that the herder's intentions were evil: they were but misguided. Although shepherds, like prostitutes, millers, Jews, and women, had often appeared in medieval eucharistic legends as members of marginalized groups who harbored maleficent or magical intentions toward the host,[76] here the shepherd is transformed into a paragon of honorable piety, motivated only by pure desires. When he accidentally throws his staff and sends the host toppling to the ground, he knows immediately the consequences of his action. Once he seeks out his priestly confessor for guidance, the legend becomes a vehicle for outlining the proper flow of authority within the Church. When the priest's attempts prove unsuccessful, it is up to the territory's spiritual overlord, the Regensburg bishop, to recover the mistreated wafer. Thus, only an apostolically consecrated figure is in the end able to counteract and make right the shepherd's mistreatment of the Eucharist, and it is the same man who proposed to build a church at the site.

As we have seen, the proliferation of unapproved and undisciplined devotions was a persistent problem for the late medieval ecclesiastical hierarchy. In Bavaria, the construction of numerous unsanctioned churches and altars had threatened to negate the Church's ultimate control over cult.[77] Engerd, however, in commenting on the legend of the shrine's foundation, intoned the importance of ecclesiastical sanction: "Who first discovered and founded this chapel which has been adorned with so many of the wondrous works of God? It was certainly no Lutheran, neither heretic nor master of the sects, but rather a Catholic man, an emi-

75. Ibid., pp. 30–34.
76. Browe, "Die Eucharistie als Zaubermittel"; idem, *Die eucharistischen Wunder des Mittelalters;* and Heuser, "'Heilig Blut,'" pp. 11, 13.
77. Zika, "Hosts, Processions, and Pilgrimages."

nent bishop, an esteemed, highborn prince and lord, Lord Hart-
wich I, the twentieth bishop of Regensburg."[78]

The devotion that developed at Bettbrunn, though given first
approval by the Regensburg bishop, also represented a rededica-
tion of the site to its original purpose. In ancient times, Engerd
stated, the place had been known as Bettbrunn, literally "well of
prayers"; as proof that the site had been revered by the ancient
tribes who lived there, the author called attention to a primordial
spring that still flowed in the town. By 1125, however, the region
had been largely abandoned, and only two modest houses were
left. The site was now known as Vehbrunn, or "cattle spring."
Following the great eucharistic miracle that transpired there, the
place-name was changed back to Bettbrunn—and thus the event
became in Engerd's account a pronouncement that returned the site
to its original purpose as a place of prayer and devotion.

> When the holy chapel was built on the oft-trod site, the original name
> Bettbrunn was once again adopted. Just as the pious, simple shep-
> herd sought to direct his prayers to the living well of holiness and [to
> use] the true heavenly bread of Christ Jesus for the spiritual succor
> and nourishment of his soul in the same way as he refreshed his body
> with earthly food and the spring of the forest, then we, too, should
> do these same things at this holy chapel of Bettbrunn. We should
> pray by the well of life, Christ Jesus, who is always present in the
> holy sacrament. We should pray by the well replete with God's
> gracious works. We should pray there at the well where our prayers
> and vows are rewarded with such power and wondrous grace from
> God.[79]

Bettbrunn's host miracle, then, was a sign that revealed to local
inhabitants the place's true purpose as a reservoir of God's grace
and power. By concentrating on the power of the place, Engerd also
maintained the traditional clerical reluctance to link thaumaturgy
and intercession with the Eucharist itself. After he had related the
story of the establishment of the first Christian chapel at the site, the
host failed to figure in any of the subsequent narrative.[80]

During the first two centuries of its existence the Bettbrunn
church remained a simple place of prayerful reverence, but in 1330

78. Engerd, *Sanct Saluator zu Bettbrunn*, p. 42.
79. Ibid., pp. 37–38.
80. Ibid., pp. 41–45.

the original building burned down, and the shrine's fate dramatically altered. For in the still-smoldering embers, Bettbrunners discovered their chapel's image of the Savior miraculously unharmed.[81] The pious villagers now built a much larger church to house their victorious image. Miracles occurred, and bishops and popes awarded the cult their official sanction: indulgences. A popular thaumaturgic pilgrimage developed, drawing even Bavaria's nobility and clergy to Bettbrunn's great "house of miracles"; indeed, from that time the Wittelsbachs began to harbor a special and long-lasting affection for the site—as evidenced in Engerd's account by a 1575 pilgrimage of the Wittelsbach son Ferdinand upon recovering from a serious illness.[82]

With his story of perpetual reverence and devotion completed, Engerd turned to satisfying the pious curiosity of his literate readership by pointing out the numerous spiritual attractions of the site. He provided, for example, a twenty-page catalogue of the shrine's relic collection that included descriptions of 28 reliquaries and 110 separate saints' remains.[83] Interestingly, a visitation conducted at Bettbrunn twenty-five years earlier, in 1559, had discovered no relics in the church at all. This lack of saintly remains was, however, typical of many medieval Bavarian shrines, and to remedy it relic collecting often became almost a passion among the clerical elites of the Catholic Reformation. To be sure, swelling collections of relics proved most useful for enhancing traditional visual piety. At Bettbrunn by the late sixteenth century, according to Engerd, the shrine's relics were being displayed in an annual ceremony similar to the great "relic shows" customary in many late medieval German cities, where the entire chorus of local saints would be ceremonially displayed before a large audience and the indulgences attached to the viewing and veneration of each announced to the crowd. At rural Bettbrunn, the practice was largely the same. As each relic was held up for view, Engerd tells us, pilgrims spliced a notch on their walking staffs.[84]

81. Ibid., p. 46.
82. Ibid., pp. 49–56. Ferdinand commissioned a series of murals for the exterior church walls that are no longer extant. Engerd quotes a passage from their inscription on pp. 55–56.
83. Ibid., pp. 93–110.
84. The 1559 Bettbrunn visitation is discussed in Döring, "St. Salvator in Bettbrunn," p. 86. Concerning Johannes Engerd's description of the Bettbrunn relic

Besides picturesque details like these, this work, like so many Counter-Reformation pilgrimage books, painted vivid idealized portraits of the pious behavior of those who visited the shrine. When people emerged from the forest surrounding the village and first saw the holy site, they fell immediately to their knees. They made their way to the shrine, saying Our Fathers with raised hands and staffs in ritualized gestures of prayer. They thanked God and Christ for preserving them and prayed that the Lord would expunge their sins so that they might enter into this "Holy of Holies."[85] Such passages demonstrate clearly that ideal mixture of inner contemplation and outward display of devotion so encouraged by the counter-reformers. With them, writers like Engerd may have been attempting to inculcate a standard of propriety and decorum among their readers. Yet for many of those pilgrims who purchased these books or who were participating in the disciplined devotional resurgence of the confraternities, these pious ideals had already converged with reality.

In the final chapter, Engerd turned his attention to relating miracles recorded at the church.[86] Like the Tuntenhausen clerics, he claimed to have selected these from a much larger number of miracles—some 3,500, in fact—recorded at the shrine between 1573 and 1584.[87] Because the original records from this period no longer exist, this number cannot be verified; yet the offering revenues of the shrine in these decades, when the pilgrimage was just beginning to grow after the initial impact of the Reformation, do not support the claim to such a plethora of miracles.[88]

In relating these testimonies, Engerd, like Eisengrein before him, ordered his accounts under various thematic headings, ones that explicitly recalled the miracles worked by Christ. The first sub-

---

show, *Sanct Saluator zu Bettbrunn*, p. 102. On relic veneration in Germany and Bavaria before the Reformation, see Beissel, *Verehrung der Heiligen*. On traditions of salvific display, see Mayer, "Die heilbringende Schau."

85. Engerd, *Sanct Saluator zu Bettbrunn*, pp. 107–108.
86. Ibid., pp. 113–188.
87. Ibid., p. 119.
88. In 1584, offering revenue at the site totaled 394 florins, 6 kreuzer, a sizable sum. When compared to offerings at other Bavarian shrines, however, an amount of this size does not suggest that 3,500 miracles could be left behind in a little more than a decade. See Döring, "St. Salvator in Bettbrunn," p. 89.

division, which recounted seven cases of demonic possession and exorcism, was typical of the approach he took throughout. After presenting each testimony—including the details of the votant's possession, vow, cure, and pilgrimage—he used the evidence of these miracles to attack Protestantism in a blatant polemic.[89] While Engerd's arguments and rhetorical style may have confirmed among his readers the truths of Catholicism's thaumaturgy, his use of the "signs" of the Gospel narrative, in which he related them to contemporary circumstances, was likely an even stronger testimony to the power of miracle. Christ continued, Engerd assured, to cure the faithful who came to Bettbrunn, just as he had cured the faithful of biblical times. By relating these contemporary miracles to those of the living Savior and lodging them within the context of his Catholic shrine, Engerd presented the contemporary Church's thaumaturgy as having a special relation to the scriptural story. In this way he combated Protestant polemical charges regarding the dangerous and "unscriptural" innovations of the traditional Church's divine cult. He did so, moreover, by turning the reformers' own weapon—the razor of Scripture—on themselves.

In truth, despite the biblical subheadings, the tales Engerd recounted were remarkably similar to those in circulation at other shrines around the same time. Yet there was a difference, for his history of Bettbrunn was also a carefully organized and framed account of cultic development. The site, revered and sought out by Bavaria's pre-Christian tribes, had been largely abandoned by the time of the shrine's precipitant host miracle. Centuries ago, the bishop of Regensburg had witnessed that event and approved the development of a devotion at the site. After two centuries of prayer-filled reverence, a second miracle—this time of preservation from fire—had again occurred there.

In point of fact, however, it is likely, given the almost complete lack of medieval documentation on these miracles, that the ecclesiastical hierarchy figured little in the history of the shrine's birth and development. Nor can Engerd's claim of a long and special affection for the place on the part of the Wittelsbachs be verified. If

89. Engerd, *Sanct Saluator zu Bettbrunn*, pp. 113–119.

family members visited Bettbrunn in the late Middle Ages, they left behind no enduring votive gift to testify to their journey—a curious oversight for princely pilgrims.

The myth of Bettbrunn, with its mix of history and legend and its strains of ancient reverence and subsequent diocesan and ducal approval, lived on in Bavaria for almost two centuries.[90] As the year 1600 approached, the first edition of Engerd's *Holy Savior at Bettbrunn* sold out; a second edition revised by David Mörlin went on sale at the shrine in 1597. One year later, the preacher Jacob Hornstein published a shorter pilgrimage book that repeated Engerd's codification of the legend.[91] By excluding contemporary miracles from his work, Hornstein was able to provide readers with a modest, cheaper alternative to Engerd's tome. In tandem, the two works expanded the audience for the carefully crafted Counter-Reformation story. In his expanded edition of *Holy Savior*, moreover, the editor David Mörlin included four miracles reported at the shrine by Lutherans who desired to "test" the site's power before renouncing their Protestant faith. Satisfied, they converted to Catholicism.[92] These cases remind us of how important the Roman clergy considered Bettbrunn as a testimony to the greater thaumaturgic and intercessory power of Catholicism vis-à-vis Protestantism. Their inclusion in the pilgrimage book indicates that this shrine may have been selected for literary invention more because of Bettbrunn's location in a confessional border region than because of any explicit demands of Catholic piety.

90. It appears, for instance, in a pilgrimage song by Oswald Schenhäuser, *Ein newer Geistlicher Catholischer Ruff, Creutz, oder Walfart Gesang. Von dem grossen Mirackel das in dem 1125. Jar zu Bettbrunn in Bayrn* (Ingolstadt, 1585). A revised edition of Engerd's work was published by David Mörlin as *Sanct Salvator zu Bettbrunn in Bayrn* (Ingolstadt, 1597). Two devotional books expanded on Engerd's legend in the seventeenth and eighteenth centuries: Ambrosius Schnaderbeck, *S. Salvator. Ein gnadenreicher Bettbrunnen zu Bettbrunnen* (Ingolstadt, 1687); and Kornmesser, *S. Salvator zu Bettbrunn* (Ingolstadt, 1754).

91. Mörlin, *Sanct Salvator zu Bettbrunn in Bayrn;* and Jacob Hornstein, *S. Saluator Das ist: Warhaffter kurtzer Bericht von der heiligen beruehmbten Wallfahrtskirchen* (Ingolstadt: Eder, 1598).

92. Mörlin, *Sanct Salvator zu Bettbrunn in Bayrn*, pp. 247–251: "Das 24. Capitel. Von etlichen Sect-Ketzer-Lutherischen, welche sich gleicherweiß bey dem lieben heiligen Salvatorn zu Bettbrunn jhrer obligenden Schwach- unnd Kranckheit halber angezeygt und jhrer Verlobdnuß Gesundheit erlangt haben." Mörlin states that besides these four cases, an additional twelve cases of "Protestant" pilgrimage were cited in the original manuscript records he viewed when compiling the printed book.

HOLINESS LOST AND FOUND

In the early decades of the Counter-Reformation, Bavaria's pilgrimage propagandists also revived and adapted a second legendary type—stories about "holiness lost and found"—to the needs of the contemporary situation. In this topos, a shrine's relic collection, image, or saintly grave, neglected or lost for a time, was "miraculously" rediscovered. Such legends had their roots in medieval patterns of storytelling, including the alleged connection to biblical narrative: a legacy of dramatic resurrections. In the early Church, the rediscovery, translation, and elevation of saintly relics had provided an important focus for Christian piety, and through medieval devotional classics like Jacopo da Voragine's *Golden Legend* these stories had been widely disseminated and celebrated in Europe. Certainly the most renowned of these events had been Constantine's mother Helen's rediscovery of the True Cross in fourth-century Palestine. But the drama of "lost and found" saints had been repeated in many places in early medieval Europe as anxious Christians searched for the remains of distinguished martyrs and holy men to satisfy their appetite for sanctity. In subsequent centuries, stories about these rediscoveries and elevations continued to keep alive the notion that holy objects, though subject to neglect, had the power to renew devotion.

In the late Middle Ages, the Bavarian clergy had begun to promote a spurt of dramatic relic discoveries similar to those reported in late antiquity and the early Middle Ages. In this process, the wonder-working power of the relics of long-forgotten saints like St. Rasso at Grafrath or St. Richildis at Hohenwart had been renewed, and their cults had grown to be enormously popular. Rasso, for example, had worked almost 5,200 miracles in the seventy years or so before the onset of the Reformation, and Richildis's cult had reported more than 2,000 in a little more than three decades before 1520. Still, all over Bavaria this floresence of miracle reporting had withered in the wake of Protestant attacks on pilgrimage.

In the Counter-Reformation, the ideas inherent in these incidents—that lost holy objects could be rediscovered and devotions renewed—were to provide propagandists with a vehicle uniquely well suited to the demands of Counter-Reformation piety. Rather than concentrating on reviving the saintly tumulus cults, however, the counter-reformers applied the idea of holiness lost and found to cults dedicated to the Eucharist, saintly images, and relics. In late medieval Bavaria, the most celebrated legends of this type were associated with the Benedictine abbey at Andechs, with its legend of the three holy Eucharists and impressive relic cache and their unearthing by a mouse. In fact, this tale continued to be circulated in the decades before the Reformation in a series of tersely written, cheaply produced chronicles; in 1595, however, the clergy at Andechs decided to repromote the story, and they now adopted the emerging genre of the pilgrimage book to satisfy the needs of a new generation of readers. The history of the site would be repackaged in a bold, apologetic, and devotional format.

By this time, a pilgrimage confraternity similar to those appearing at Altötting and other sites was working for the renewal of Andechs. Counting among its most important supporters the bishop of Augsburg, Cardinal Otto Truchseß von Waldburg, this organization had been from its inception a distinctly elite body of nobles, burghers, and clerics.[93] It was primarily for just such devotees, in fact, that the Benedictine abbot at the shrine composed his *Chronicle of Andechs,* which treated not only the precipitant legend of the church, but a broad range of counter-reformational issues besides.[94] Like the other books we have reviewed, it delved deep into the past, attempting to "prehistoricize" the site's devotion. In addition, it catalogued and presented visual representations of the shrine's most important relics, so that its literate readers could keep track of the many items they viewed there. The book also explained the customs observed on the site's most popular pilgrimage days, and the reasons why these particular feasts had become important.

Even in the late medieval chronicles published for this church, the Benedictine clergy had promoted the cult's connection with the nobility and the Wittelsbach dukes. Now, though, Andechs's aristocratic pretensions were increased, and the reasons for the nobility's special affection for this site made more explicit than ever before.

93. Zoepfl, *Das Bistum Augsburg und seine Bischöfe,* p. 278.
94. Abt David, *CHRONICON ANDECENSE. Von dem Ursprung, Herkommen, auffnemen im Geistlichen so wol als Weltlichen unnd Herrlichen Stifftungen der Graven von Andechs, deren alten Gravenlicher Sitz und Schloß Andechs in Obern Bayrn Augspurger Bisthumbs der Hailig Berg genannt* . . . (Munich, 1595), fol. aii(r).

Finally, the book was also generously filled with apologetic defenses of the Catholic belief in shrines and pilgrimages.

Following a dedication to the Wittelsbach duke Maximilian I, who was a frequent visitor to Andechs in this period,[95] Abbot David outlined the various reasons people had for visiting his shrine. Many, he stated, came in search simply of physical healing; yet he also called upon a powerful biblicism, natural mysticism, and psychologized piety to promote the site.[96]

In the late Middle Ages, Andechs had already been portrayed as Bavaria's "Holy Mountain," and now the abbot fused this traditional nomenclature with imagery drawn from the Bible. In both the Old and New Testaments, he observed, God often imparted special messages to man from atop mountain peaks, and he went on to list the various hills and mountains that figured in the Scriptures. Andechs too, he said, was one of these special sites, a kind of Bavarian Mt. Sinai, a place from which the deity had from time immemorial imparted wisdom and grace and sealed covenants with the region's inhabitants. Unlike that peak in Exodus, however, this Bavarian "holy of holies" was not restricted to priests and charismatic saints alone. Rather, this holy site has served as a well of "visible grace" to "many men," who have testified to the wondrous miracles God has worked on them. The visit there to commune with the deity has "quickened . . . and confirmed [many] in their Catholic faith," making "the love of God to burn in them." Entrance into the divine presence at Andechs touched in all pilgrims an internal chord of humility, submission, and unworthiness.[97]

For anyone who has visited this church, the abbot's praise for the natural features of Andechs will ring true. Situated at the summit of a high knoll in the middle of the Upper Bavarian plain, Andechs is about fifty miles southwest of Munich. The Ammersee stretches westward from the foot of this hill, and directly south of the shrine the Alps jut up majestically. On clear days, several hundred miles of Alpine terrain and large stretches of the Upper Bavarian plateau can be observed from the church; and in turn, Andechs can be seen

95. Maximilian's first pilgrimage to Andechs appears to have occurred in 1588. Between 1597 and 1626, he visited the shrine yearly; see Emmeram Heindl, *Der heilige Berg Andechs* (Munich, 1895), pp. 51–52.
96. *Chronicon Andecense*, pp. 6ff.
97. Ibid., pp. 6–8.

from miles around. It is a spectacular location, and it is not unsurprising to find the abbot delighting in the physical nature of the place. His statements, however, display less affection for the simple beauty of the site than for the marvels that God had worked there. Unlike Petrarch, who upon ascending Mt. Ventoux gloried in the immediate physical surroundings, Abbot David remained detached from these splendors.

Adopting the style of other pilgrimage books, Abbot David began his narrative of the shrine's development long before any pilgrimage existed at the site. Yet whereas in most respects his account of the Andechs legend was faithful to standard late medieval versions, it differed in two important ways. First, his focus fell less on the great "miracle" of Andechs's rediscovered relics than on events preceding this incident. Second, he moved the origins of the saintly line of early medieval Andechs counts back several centuries relative to other medieval accounts. In the late fifteenth-century version of the tale, the counts of Andechs—who built a fortress on the future site of the pilgrimage chapel—were identified as eighth-century figures given control over their territory by deputies of Charlemagne. Abbot David, however, located their origins in the sixth century—the time of Bavaria's Christianization. Like Eisengrein and Engerd, then, the abbot called up the dark days of Bavaria's pre-Christian past. In a subsequent chapter, moreover, he reproduced a detailed genealogy of this lineage and, by recalling its numerous saintly members, labored hard to establish a claim of enormous sanctity for the family.[98]

Of course, the late medieval chronicles of the site had attempted in similar fashion to connect Andechs with saintly, noble figures from the distant past; now, though, Abbot David multiplied the shrine's noble connections and made their association with the site even more antique. As a result, Andechs's development as a pilgrimage site became even more reliant on the ministrations of a saintly and apostolically consecrated line that had lived and worked in the region from the very inception of Catholicism in Bavaria.

As a pilgrimage site, Andechs was beholden particularly to the tenth-century count St. Rasso. An avid pilgrim and relic collector,

98. Ibid., pp. 11–19.

Rasso had amassed a significant number of apostolic remnants while in the Holy Land, which he installed in his mountaintop fortress at Andechs. In succeeding generations other saintly members of the family added to this collection, and the abbot carefully described each new addition to the cache, the most significant of these being the three holy hosts sent by St. Otto, bishop of Bamberg.[99]

Turning to the subsequent history of the shrine's relic collection and its removal for safekeeping, the abbot again subtly altered the medieval legend. With the destruction of the counts' fortress in 1229, the relics lay forgotten in the ruins; yet even though neglected, they continued to provide aid to the faithful—a topos absent from earlier accounts. Fifty years after the devastation, a woman was cured of an eye illness at the site, and a chapel was built to commemorate this event. Here, according to Abbot David, was yet another proof of the power that had reposed in this site and its relics throughout time.

Although it continued to work intercessions, the wondrous collection was not known about until 1388, when a mouse brought a clue to the relics' whereabouts and laid it on the church altar one day during mass.[100] Because of neglect, knowledge of this precious repository had been lost, and Abbot David did not intend to let these objects be forgotten again. The largest portion of his book was therefore given over to a highly detailed *Heiltumverzeichnis*, a catalogue of all the shrine's relics.[101] Such listings had been common in the Middle Ages: printed for the great annual displays of relics held in many cities, they allowed pilgrims to keep track of the myriad items on view; they also served as a kind of souvenir, recalling to pilgrims the important items they had seen. In Bavaria, however, no relic catalogues were printed in the late Middle Ages, and relic displays, so common in the rest of the empire, were apparently held

99. Ibid., pp. 16–19. These saintly individuals include St. Ulrich, bishop of Lausanne; St. Hildegard, Charlemagne's wife; St. Conrad, bishop of Costnitz; St. Rasso, count of Andechs; St. Otto I, emperor; St. Otto II, also emperor; St. Mechthild, abbess; St. Euphemia, abbess; St. Hedwig, an anchorite; St. Elisabeth, queen of Hungary; and Justitia, Count Otto III of Wolfratshausen's wife, who though not officially canonized was revered for her holiness.
100. Ibid., chaps. 11 and 12, pp. 29–41.
101. Ibid., pp. 41–62.

only in the imperial city of Regensburg and the diocesan capital of Passau.[102] In any case, Abbot David embraced the strongly visual traditions of salvific display, and by the late sixteenth century the shrine was holding an annual relic display of its own, which was indexed by the *Chronicle* catalogue. Not only did it aid pilgrims who bought his book in identifying the many items they saw, but it also allowed them better to relive the event when they returned home.

For the believer who had read about and seen the plethora of saints' relics housed in this church, there could have been little doubt about the site's power. Yet in a place so crowded with the physical remains of the saints, the drive to see everything might have led to chaos. For this reason, the abbot attempted to discipline the piety of his faithful readers. In passages similar to those in other pilgrimage books, he stressed the deep interior spirituality, humility, and introspection of those who visited the church. Warning of the dangers of impatience, he cautioned the devout to direct their hearts and wills to God while on the "sacred journey" to Andechs. In prayer, the votant should foster a quiet and contrite spirit, rather than expending effort in outpourings of verbiage, for the Lord did not "desire a lot of chatter," but rather a devout heart "without which he has nothing for which to care."[103]

After discussing proper pilgrimage behavior, Abbot David turned in the final sections of his work to describing—again, in considerable detail—the major indulgences and benefices given to the shrine as well as some of the contemporary miracles recorded there. Again, following the pattern of other pilgrimage books, the abbot grouped similar intercessions under categoric headings, thus highlighting the variety of cases in which the saintly relics at Andechs had provided aid. Like Eisengrein's *Our Lady at Altötting* or Engerd's *Holy Savior at Bettbrunn*, this book presented the miracles

---

102. An unprinted manuscript catalogue survives from the 1496 relic show at Regensburg. The Regensburg relic show was instituted at the instigation of the Wittelsbach dukes of Lower Bavaria during the late fifteenth century when they controlled the city. See Leonhard Theobald, "Die Regensburger Heiltumweisung und das Regensburger Heiltumverzeichnis von 1496," *Zeitschrift für bayerische Kirchengeschichte* 7 (1932): 17–27. On the Passau relic display (initiated in connection with the city's 1478 "host crime"), see Anton Mayer, "Die Gründung von St. Salvator zu Passau: Geschichte und Legende," *Zeitschrift für bayerische Landesgeschichte* 18 (1955): 258.

103. *Chronicon Andecense,* pp. 63–64.

wrought at Andechs as the logical continuations of a narrative of antique devotion and reverence.

In truth, the Andechs devotion, like that at Altötting, was a relatively recent phenomenon, having originated in the dramatic unearthing of the relics at the end of the fourteenth century. In the *Chronicle*, however, the "miraculous" rediscovery was framed as an event prepared by a centuries-long tradition of veneration by a noble lineage that had given the site rich endowments throughout the Middle Ages. As it developed during the Counter-Reformation, the Andechs legend was broadened in scope: its origins were now situated in the sixth century, the era of Bavaria's conversion by apostolically consecrated missionaries. In this subsequent retelling of Andechs's history, the author assured readers that shrine time represented not a discrete chronology, but a collection of kairotic moments. Like its spatial geography, which was demarcated into areas of greater and lesser power by the relics of Catholicism's intercessors, Andechs's history, too, had been characterized by episodes in which divine grace was made evident to the faithful. In the face of questions raised by Reformation attacks on the saints, the Andechs legend, as retold by Abbot David, counseled perpetual diligence. Here the site's relics had been neglected, disregarded, and yet rescued from their obscurity. As an insurance against disaffection, the clergy at Andechs continued to issue versions of Abbot David's pilgrimage book throughout the early seventeenth century.[104]

HOLINESS SUDDENLY REVEALED

In late medieval Bavaria, previously unimportant, even marginal, shrines that suddenly and inexplicably revealed their power through spontaneous wonder-working had been common, often leading to the development of immensely popular devotions. Images, relics, or the numinous site itself might even "show forth" (*zeichnen*) with signs. From the perspective of Bavaria's ecclesiastical hierarchy, such extemporaneous wonder-working was inherently problematic: it riveted the laity's attention on chapels and altars that

104. Abbot David's version of the Andechs legend was reprinted in 1602 and 1625.

were sometimes unconsecrated, made natural features like springs and wells the objects of religious affection, and threatened to usurp clerical control over worship. Thus, although these devotions continued to proliferate, the Bavarian clergy began to labor to make the divine presence contingent on a site's connection with provincial and imperial history, a legacy of aristocratic benefactions, and affiliation with legendary clerical figures.

In the early Counter-Reformation, Bavaria's clerical propagandists redoubled these efforts, striving to "prehistoricize" and shroud in legendary mystery many sites of religious reverence and stressing their organic role in the biblical drama and the apostolic succession. This "traditionalizing" impulse was now more necessary than ever before, as a weapon against Protestant attacks on saints' cults and pilgrimages as recent clerical, even demonic, inventions. But counter-reformers' efforts to locate pilgrimage within a visible Catholic, confessional lineage also arose from the perceived need to discipline lay religion. By identifying their cults with ancient tribal religious practices purified by importation into Christianity, Bavaria's Catholic clergy attempted not only to link pilgrimage with the region's earliest cultural identity, but also to demonstrate that only the Catholic religion had the power to transform age-old devotions. Moreover, by concentrating on the necessity of apostolic sanction, they tried to show that supernatural intercession was available only through routine clerical channels.

For most of the Catholic reformers, the precise locations of Bavaria's *numina* had been revealed long before at specific times, and they assured their audience that the territory's sanctity was by and large a *fait accompli*. The faithful could add to Catholicism's complement of holy places by importing a disregarded and neglected saint like Benno of Meissen, but his wonder-working now hung solely on his standing within an antique apostolic and clerical succession. The Catholic commonwealth imagined by the counter-reformers required the faithful to display submission, humility, and devotion before what they perceived as a long-revealed religious principle, expressed by the full complement of saints' cults, holy places, and religious images with its legacy of power. In this way, the Catholic reformers used the past not just polemically, but also as a disciplinary agent; saintly and divine presences, they insisted, did not normally appear in sudden outbursts of wonder-working that in turn created episodic religious enthusiasm. Rather, the Catholic heritage was marked by moments of special grace performed by apostolically consecrated figures that engendered lasting religious affection.

These attempts to mold pilgrimage into part of a clear legacy were persistent, but not without deviation. At Flochberg, just across Bavaria's eastern border in the county of Oettingen, for instance, a new devotion without ancient origins appeared after 1583 and was enthusiastically promoted by the local parish priest, Abraham Nagel. Nagel's propagandistic campaign illustrates very well how the defense of pilgrimage and the cult of the saints were gradually appropriated outside Bavaria. The county of Oettingen is also of particular interest to us because its ruling family—and hence its physical territory—was confessionally divided. Thus, development of a thaumaturgic pilgrimage there was aimed—as it was in Bavaria—at opposing Protestant ideas and practices, which carried some weight but did not (yet) predominate in the Catholic part of Oettingen.[105] Moreover, the new devotion aroused immediate criticism from the evangelical clergy in the adjoining Protestant half of the county, leading to another polemical exchange between Protestant and Catholic theologians.[106] Flochberg's success in inspiring controversy, therefore, provides us with yet another proof of the fears the resurgence of Catholic pilgrimage aroused among the evangelical clergy.

In 1583, Abraham Nagel published *Our Lady at Flochberg in the Rye Field* at Wolfgang Eder's press in Ingolstadt.[107] The stylistic and visual similarities between this book and Eisengrein's *Our Lady at*

105. On the Reformation in the county of Oettingen, see R. Herold, *Geschichte der Reformation in der Grafschaft Oettingen, 1522–1569*, Schriften des Vereins für Reformationsgeschichte 75 (Halle, 1902); on the development of the shrine of Our Lady of Flochberg as a counter to Protestantism in the region, see Schenda, "Die protestantisch-katholische Legendenpolemik," pp. 28–48.

106. Spindler (ed.), *Handbuch der bayerischen Geschichte* 3(1):315; Schenda, "Die protestantisch-katholische Legendenpolemik," pp. 28–29, 41–43; and idem, "Hieronymus Rauscher," p. 195n.71.

107. Abraham Nagel, *Unser Liebe Fraw zu Flochberg im Roggen Acker: Das ist, Ein Warhafftige Beschreibung deß newen unerhörten Wunderwercks, das sich newlicher Zeit im Junio dieses jetzt abgelauffnen 82. Jars zu Flochberg in der Graffschafft Oeting zugetragen . . .* (Ingolstadt: Wolfgang Eder, 1583). Few biographical details for Nagel exist beyond what he tells in the preface to his work. There he calls himself "Oetingischen Pfarrherrn zu Wallerstein," or parish priest at Wallerstein in the county Oettingen. Johann Engerd states in *Sanct Saluator zu Bettbrunn* that Nagel had left Wallerstein for Würzburg by 1584; he also lists him as a canon of the *Neumünster* and preacher at the *Julier Spital* ("Vorrede," fol. aii[v]).

Altötting or Engerd's slightly later *Holy Savior at Bettbrunn* are immediately apparent. Nagel displays as well his familiarity not only with Eisengrein's pilgrimage book, but also with the recent dispute over miracles and shrines; he even includes large excerpts from Johann Rabus's *Christian Refutation of "On Miracles and Wondrous Signs."*[108]

Unlike Altötting, Bettbrunn, or St. Benno's shrine in Munich, the devotion at Flochberg was a new phenomenon without medieval antecedent. Thus, Nagel could not draw upon ancient legends or historical accounts; yet he did have the excitement of a contemporary miracle—a series of Marian apparitions— to exploit, and this he did with zeal.[109] Promotion of a "new" shrine was problematic, for it laid Nagel and the Catholic clergy open to the charge of working "magic" and fostering "diabolic" innovations to lead the laity astray.

As the sixteenth century was drawing to a close, Catholic and Protestant authorities alike were scrutinizing events such as were claimed to have transpired at Flochberg more carefully than ever before. The Protestant Johann Marbach, for instance, had already used the presence of Marian apparitions in Martin Eisengrein's Altötting exorcistic account to prove that the Jesuit Peter Canisius was a black magician. But beyond their potential for negative polemical exploitation, apparitions were proving increasingly destabilizing for both Protestant and Catholic clerics, because they threatened "official" control over religious experience. Nagel therefore fused to his account of Flochberg's precipitant miracle a wealth of details designed to protect his story from Protestant attack and to underscore the extraordinary character of the events that had shaken this tiny village. What had happened here, he claimed, was a rare yet verifiable case in which the Virgin had directly interceded to change the course of human history.

He began his account of the devotion on May 26, 1582, when Apollonia Wintzer disciplined her ten-year-old son Wilhelm for neglecting his chores. Enraged by his disobedience, the mother beat the child with a sharp birch rod until he fell into a series of convulsive, epileptic fits. Terrified by her actions and powerless to help the

108. Nagel, *Unser Liebe Fraw zu Flochberg im Roggen Acker,* esp. pp. 241ff.
109. Ibid., chap. 1, pp. 1–12.

child, Apollonia sought advice from her neighbors, who could offer no suggestion to stop the convulsions. In desperation, she sent for her husband, the court tailor to the Catholic counts of Oettingen-Wallerstein. The father, Nagel wrote, "took the gripping pain of his own flesh and blood to heart," repeatedly bemoaning the fact that he could not take the child's suffering upon himself. Seeing his grief, one of his neighbors suggested the father vow a pilgrimage, which he immediately did. Invoking the Virgin, he promised a journey to Our Lady of Kochheim with a pound of wax if the child were cured.[110]

Unlike late medieval miracle accounts, in which relief was formulaically described as "immediate," this pilgrimage book transformed the cure of the child into a dramatic weeks-long struggle. On the first day after the vow, the author noted, the child began to perspire but did not regain consciousness. The next day he revived, but a long period of convulsions followed, usually four or five times each day. The situation continued like this for about two weeks until Pentecost, at which time the child began to report experiencing Marian apparitions during the night:

> Then during the night an earnest and beautifully formed woman appeared beside his bedstead in actual visual form with a blue mantle covered from the hem to the top with shining stars and a gleaming halo surrounding her head. She touched him, lifted his head up and took away [from him] the root which the noble woman, Johanna, countess of Oettingen (by birth a countess of Hohenzollern) had placed there out of pity and compassion for him. And she spoke to him. "Wilhelm, each evening, when you go to say your prayers, go into the adjacent long rye field. There is a root buried there that will help you and make you healthy." And after this she hung the root back around his neck and when the child closed his eyes from fear and dread, she disappeared.[111]

The child, however, failed at first to act upon his vision; the second night, the Virgin reappeared with the same message. Wilhelm then told his mother of the apparition and begged her to let him go to the rye field. Fearing what might happen if the convulsive child left the house alone and dismissing the visions as mere fits, however,

110. Ibid., p. 5.
111. Ibid., pp. 6–7.

the mother forbade him to go to the place. Even though her messages were being disregarded, the Virgin continued to appear to the boy each night for more than two weeks.

The parents still procrastinated, doubting the child's visions and the effectiveness of any root buried in a rye field. Yet each day the attacks reappeared, so that by the end of June the parents and the boy had "scarcely had a day's peace." Finally the father agreed to take the boy to the rye field. Upon their arrival there they said an Our Father, a Hail Mary, and the Apostle's Creed, then entered the space. When the child had walked into the field about thirty steps, the Virgin again appeared to him. This time, however, Mary became a thaumaturge, acting to cure her young patient. First she took the miraculous root of which she had told the child, pressed it on his forehead crosswise, and then produced a vial of holy water out of her cloak. Pouring some onto her hand, she placed her two longest fingers into the water and made the sign of the cross on the child's forehead and heart and on both hands and feet. Finally she gave him the following message: "My son, go. Your illness will not reappear again during your entire life. Be pious. Pray. Call upon God. Go diligently to Church. Listen to God's word and complete your pilgrimage." She turned and walked away, "looking like the clear sun," and soon disappeared from the child's sight. But she left him completely healthy.[112]

Nagel's narrative may appear complex and contrived, yet these very complexities defended the cult of the saints from Protestant attack. Clearly, Nagel reasoned, apparitions occurred—rare, exceptional testimony to Catholicism's wonder-working power, testimony that could not be revealed to everyone. Each component of the story—from the father's vow of the pilgrimage through the son's vision and to the Virgin's cure—served Catholic confessional purposes. In his narrative fashioning of the incident, Nagel's approach was in fact similar to Martin Eisengrein's account of the 1571 Altötting exorcism: he first retold the entire miracle and then proceeded to discuss each episode, refuting in advance, so to speak, any possible Protestant criticisms. Thus, his miracle also served as a vehicle—as did Eisengrein's exorcism—for discussing the nature

112. Ibid., pp. 11–12.

and meaning of pilgrimage, vows, the invocation of the saints, and the veneration of relics and images.

In particular, Nagel's account of the Virgin's healing of the afflicted child affirmed the traditional belief in the efficacy of specific places and objects, a precept that the Counter-Reformation program in South Germany had stressed from the start. In both Nagel and Eisengrein's accounts, the resolution of the votant's affliction began with a Marian apparition that called the faithful to a specific site, one that would prove holy and efficacious. In Nagel's story, however, instead of healing being channeled through a charismatic priest like Canisius, the Virgin herself appropriated the functions of both priest and folk healer.

Our Lady of Flochberg's wonder-working resembled Canisius's in *Our Lady at Altötting* in other respects as well. In that earlier account, the Jesuit father had used a plethora of mediating agents to exorcise the woman's demons. At Flochberg, too, Mary employed various antidotes to conquer the convulsions. She revealed to the boy Wilhelm the secret of a root buried in the rye field and pressed it against his forehead, thus appropriating the tools of folk medicine. Yet her healing also relied on holy water and the sign of the cross, and in that way reaffirmed the efficacy of traditional religious practices and the great degree of protection and aid that the Roman Church afforded the faithful.

Finally, the stories of the events at Flochberg and at Altötting were also similar in that both cast the treatment of the afflicted in a fully "religious," interior, and spiritual light. Rather than the immediate or "cheap" cures of late medieval miracle literature, Eisengrein and Nagel painted the Altötting and Flochberg miracles as the climax to a long period of struggle against illness. This struggle, to be sure, enhanced the drama and veracity of both accounts; but it also transformed the miracle into a process that first demanded internal catharsis and purification before the ultimate cure. In other words, it reflected that mixture of inward devotion and outward demonstration of faith that Catholic propagandists had recommended since the inception of the Counter-Reformation.

At Flochberg, Mary reminded the cured boy that the award of a miracle should be followed by ongoing amendment of life. Her last words were "Be pious. Pray. Call upon God. Go diligently to church. Listen to God's word and complete your pilgrimage." At the end of the Altötting drama, too, Canisius had preached a similar message to the afflicted woman and the audience in the chapel. Thus, in both accounts the receiving of a cure was woven together with a change in living and the diligent practice of Catholic cult, features appropriate to Counter-Reformation purposes. Unlike the medieval Mary, who meted out aid to all regardless of the quality of their piety, this Virgin intended those she helped to change and become rigorous practitioners of the Catholic religion. She might comfort and heal the sick, but the purpose of these ministrations was ultimately to increase the level of devotion of her parishioners. Mary now expected more in return—an internal transformation of the heart and faithful attendance at mass and confession—than a pound of wax or a length of cloth.

Epilogue:
Bavaria Sancta and the Living Past

In the seventeenth century, the story types pioneered by writers of the early Counter-Reformation pilgrimage book continued to resonate in Bavaria. Of these, holiness tried yet triumphant remained a dominant topos in the apologetic histories the clergy crafted to explain and defend their cults. Indeed, the persistence of this imagery of conflict and resolution is a striking feature of Bavarian literature in the early modern period. Long after Protestantism had ceased to be a viable threat to the Roman Church in the region, legends about images and relics imperiled were still commonly called upon to defend local devotions. The survival of this topos and its assiduous promotion by Bavaria's clerics cannot, however, be interpreted as a case of collective paranoia or entrenched xenophobia. For religion continued to inspire political, social, and military conflict in the empire during this time, which in turn affected Bavaria's reviving pilgrimage shrines. Indeed, the accusations of desecration that appeared occasionally in chapbooks, in artistic depictions of shrine legends, and in oral culture were sometimes quite justified.

By 1700 Bavaria's clergy were producing a literature of sorts that traded tales not about people, but about sacred sites. For most of the territory's pilgrims—peasants, artisans, and day workers—these books still were inaccessible. When these people bought souvenirs of their journeys to local holy places, they most often purchased single-page prints, much like that reproduced in figure 13 advertising the Altötting pilgrimage. Typical of a style common in seventeenth- and eighteenth-century Bavaria, this broadside shows Mary suspended above the Bavarian countryside, while below, on earth, she reappears together with SS. Philip and James offering aid to the faithful. Prints like these reminded the pious of the very real fruits of intercession available to those willing to make pilgrimages. And unlike the longer and more involved pilgrimage book, which often appealed to a Bavarian cultural identity and relied on distant events or personages from the past, printed broadsides required only that the viewer recognize the physical confines of the sacred site. In the late seventeenth century, despite a slow and steady rise in literacy rates, most Bavarian pilgrims had still not read the pious and sometimes fantastic histories fashioned by several generations of Counter-Reformation apologists. The direct impact of the pilgrimage book, then, was confined, yet its indirect role as a vehicle for the diffusion of legends about major sites still exerted an important influence on the early modern imagination. Widely circulated among literate clergy and devout laity, works like these helped codify the generally accepted explanations for the origins of Bavaria's shrines.

In the histories of many shrines, life often imitated the art of the pilgrimage book narrative. Mirroring St. Benno's imposing translation to Munich, dramatic image and relic rescues continued to occur throughout the seventeenth century. By a kind of ritualized didacticism, these incidents reenacted visually the text of holiness tried yet triumphant for onlookers on the rural highways and streets of Bavarian towns. These images had suffered but then emerged victorious, and clerical promoters advertised them as sources of power that could be used in the present to wage war against unyielding contingency.

At Passau, diocesan officials nurtured the development of a cult that venerated an image of the Virgin painted by Lucas Cranach the Elder. Produced before the Saxon artist's conversion to Lutheranism, the painting was believed to possess miraculous powers, and its "rescue" from obscurity in Protestant territory was advertised in a manner similar to St. Benno's translation from Meissen: as a victory for Catholicism. Arriving in Passau in 1622, the image was installed in a chapel in the bishop's residence, where a cathedral canon had a copy made for his own personal devotion. Soon the canon learned that candlelight processions were being conducted on Saturday evenings to a previously shunned and feared hillside on the outskirts of the city. Interpreting this "miracle" as a sign that his copy of the Virgin's image wished to be revered at this site, the canon had a chapel constructed there to house the painting.[1] In 1627, a larger church was erected on the spot and a small devotion

---

1. Sperber, *Unsere Liebe Frau*, p. 56.

grew, but it was not until 1633 that the pilgrimage swelled dramatically following Passau's siege by Swedish armies. Clergy and lay people alike credited the picture, the subject of which by now was known as the *Mariahilf*, with saving the city from conquest. The following year, the picture's popularity increased yet again when the local population believed that the horrors of a plague epidemic had been quelled owing to its protection.² The success of the painting in making the previously feared hillside safe, in subduing the invading armies, and in overcoming the demons of disease assured it a venerable history. During the devastation of the Thirty Years War, numerous Bavarian towns, villages, and parishes commissioned copies of the *Mariahilfbild*, and installed them in specially constructed chapels where they were believed to render protection against disease and the chaos of the war. In addition, the *Mariahilf* devotion celebrated the image's "miraculous" rescue from Protestant possession and its arrival in Bavaria, a place where its following could flourish.³

Triumph over oppressors provided the counter-reformers innumerable opportunities for advertising the cult of the saints as an antidote to Protestant heresy. A "miraculous" painting of the Virgin was brought to Straubing from a Catholic cloister in Protestant Heilbronn in 1661 and received in a triumphal procession through the city. This image, like the relics of St. Benno, had suffered at the hands of iconoclasts. Although it had repulsed the first challenge to its power during the Peasants' War of 1525, in 1550 Protestants seized the Madonna.⁴ Its Carmelite protectors produced a copy, but this reproduction was itself threatened with destruction during the Thirty Years War before being finally taken to safety. When it arrived in Straubing in the 1660s, the Madonna thus possessed a rich tradition of trial and triumph, which the Carmelites exploited over the next century in both artistic and textual imagery.⁵

2. Hüttl, *Marianische Wallfahrten*, pp. 43–44.
3. The numerous copies of the image are listed in Hans Aurenhammer, *Die Mariengnadenbilder Wiens und Niederösterreichs in der Barockzeit* (Vienna 1956); Sperber, *Unsere Liebe Frau*, pp. 59–60; Gebhard, "Marianische Gnadenbilder"; and Hans Bleibrunner, *Andachtsbilder aus Altbayern* (Munich, 1971), pp. 174–175.
4. Adalbert Decker, *Karmel in Straubing* (Rome, 1968), pp. 209–210, 272.
5. Trithemius [Ferdinand Auer], *History des Miraculos-Bilds U.L. Frawen von der Nessel in der Karmeliten Kirche zu Straubing in Bayern* (Straubing, 1674, 1728, 1737, and 1761).

In the imperial city of Regensburg, where most burghers were
Protestant, the Catholic clergy rejoiced in a similar, if less dramatic,
victory when, in 1675, cathedral clerics purchased a statue of the
Virgin from a Protestant couple whose children had used it as a doll.
Installed in a chapel near the Cathedral, this image bespoke the
"miracle" of the Virgin's preservation and gave rise to a small, local
pilgrimage.[6]
The triumph of relics and images such as those at Munich, Passau, Straubing, and Regensburg provided the Catholic reformers
with imposing events to exploit in print and art and to transmit into
oral culture as well. The sheer numbers of "tried yet triumphant"
cults that appeared during the Counter-Reformation, and their
wide geographical diffusion throughout Bavaria, are convincing
evidence of the popularity that this explanation for shrines assumed. In the diocese of Regensburg alone, one unsystematic study
has identified twelve cults that developed around images and relics
believed to have been the victims of Protestant torture.[7]
Although tales of holiness tried yet triumphant became com-
monplace, their original polemical purpose was gradually elevated
to a principle of piety in Bavaria. As the Roman Church regained an
unchallenged position in the territory during the late 1600s, moreover, the pilgrimage book gradually came to reflect more the literary
tastes of the Bavarian elite than confessional disagreements over the
cult of saints and their shrines. A work like Balthasar Regler's
Azwinischer Bogen, published in 1679, is typical of this change.[8]
Replete with classical imagery, Regler's account of the legend and
miracles of Our Lady of Bogenberg is full of humanist pretensions.
He arranged his miracle stories according to the four elements—
earth, water, fire, and air—and he clothed the Madonna in rich
literary allusions. In this sense his work, with its elemental physics,

6. *Die Kunstdenkmäler von Bayern*, 2d ser., 22(2):192–193.
7. St. Jobst bei Tännersberg, Fahrenberg, Stadlern, St. Quirin, Beidl, St. Peter in
Tirschenreuth, Ottengrün, Maria Kulm in Egerland, Vierzehnheiligen in Tachau,
Weißenregen, Niederleyerndorf, and Kötzting. See Lehner, "Wallfahrten im Bistum
Regensburg," pp. 216–222.
8. Balthasar Regler, *Azwinischer Bogen. In Ritter-Streit und Frewden-Spil bewehrt. In
dem Fewer Maisterlich gestahlt. Auff der Erden Triumpherlich auffgericht. In dem Lufft
zierlich mit seinen Farben scheinent. In dem Wasser Natürlich nachgebildet. Von dem Hochwürdigen in GOTT Vatter Edl und Hochgelehrten Herrn Herrn DOMINOCO, der Löbl:
Stüfft und Clöster Obern Altaych und Michelsfelden, Respective Abbt und Administratore
&cc.* (Straubing, 1679).

classical motifs, and pompous language, had departed far from the polemical and confessional roots of Martin Eisengrein's *Our Lady of Altötting*. Nevertheless, the canons of content first established in the early decades of the Counter-Reformation still inform the book. Its organization, including the outline of its chapters, mimicked works like Eisengrein's, recounting an intricate legend about the foundation of the shrine and describing the development of the pilgrimage to the site. The story told in *Azwinischer Bogen* was quite fantastic. During a period of iconoclasm in Constantinople, a group of heretics threw an image of the Virgin into the Bosphorus. Swimming against the tide, the statue made its way up the Danube to rest at the foot of the Bogenberg. There Count Aswin, scion of a pious noble line, rescued the image, installed it in his family chapel, and nurtured the growth of the Madonna's devotion.

Regler's account of the torture of a sacred object recalls events the Counter-Reformers had promoted since the earliest days of the Catholic resurgence. Elsewhere in Bavaria, other authors were working to raise the celebration of cultic victories to something approaching "high art." The case of Neukirchen bei Heilig Blut in particular demonstrates how this legendary type—originally born of the medieval tales of *Hostienfrevel*—was used to reanimate Counter-Reformation piety. In the later Middle Ages, Neukirchen had been a site of a Bleeding Host devotion. Sometime around 1600, however, the clerical overseers of this shrine transformed their pilgrimage into a Marian cult.

By 1671, with the publication of the Franciscan priest Fortunatus Huber's *Ripe Pomegranate* (fig. 14), Neukirchen's legend achieved its final codification. Huber drew upon a manuscript about Neukirchen's origins written in 1611 and a brief pilgrimage book published in 1640 to create a work filled with baroque symbolism and sexuality, prayers to the Virgin, and a detailed account of all the "historical" facts known about the site.[9] In carefully sculpted language, Huber's book explains the circumstances surrounding the

---

9. Fortunatus Huber, *Zeitiger Granatapfel. Der allerscheinbaristen Wunderzierden in den Wunderthaetigen allerheiligisten Jungfraewlichen Mutter Gottes MARIA bey zweyen hoch-ansehentlichen Voelckern der Bayrn und Boehamen* (Munich, 1671). The Neukirchen legend had been first printed in a short version by Roman Sigl, *Unser liebe Fraw zum H. Bluet bey Neukirchen vor dem Ober Boehemer Waldt* (Straubing, 1640). On the fascinating development of the Neukirchen pilgrimage and its legend, see Walter Hartinger, "Die Wallfahrt Neukirchen," pp. 40ff.

Madonna's victory over Hussitism. After relating the history of the surrounding region, he proceeds to tell the shrine's legend. Originally a place where a "rediscovered" holy host was revered, Neukirchen had seen its devotion expand dramatically in the mid–fifteenth century when the church was visited by a group of Hussites, one of whom had worked a series of tortures on the statue of the Virgin. As in the tales of crimes against the host, the "godless" Hussite attacked the image with fire and water. Each time, however, the Virgin returned intact to her place of honor on the altar of the church. In a final desperate attempt, the Hussite stabbed the Virgin's brow, sending forth a stream of "holy blood." Terrified by the consequences of his deed, the offender attempted to flee the site, but his horse's hooves would not rise from the ground. In the end, he could not leave the Virgin's presence until he had confessed and begged her forgiveness. Throughout the text, Huber extols the "garnetlike" drops of the Virgin's blood, which the Hussite had caused to be spilled on the earth of Bavaria. She was, he says, like a ripe pomegranate, which reveals its precious seeds only when placed under the blade of a knife. This great miracle had caused continued intercessions to flow from the "well" of Mary's mercy at Neukirchen.

Our Lady of Neukirchen might have responded with forgiveness in exchange for submission, but elsewhere Mary was not so beneficent. At Weissenregen, purchasers of the shrine's history read a similar legend involving an iconoclastic Calvinist. When he attempted to consign the church's image of the Virgin to a watery grave in a well, the Madonna sprang from the depths and slew the heretic with his own sword.[10]

While tales of tortured images continued to appear, an increasing fancifulness is detectable in both the oral and written legends of this type. At Maria-Ort near Regensburg, for instance, pilgrims viewed an image of what was perhaps Christianity's only "surfing" Madonna. By the mid–seventeenth century, the legend of this shrine had become filled with elements of whimsy. Like Our Lady of Bogenberg, Maria-Ort's Madonna had traveled up the Danube after

10. Anon., *Wundervolles Regenperlein. Oder Wunder- und Gnadenreiches Maria Bild zu Weissenregen* (Straubing, 1748).

Byzantine iconoclasts threw her into the Bosphorus. Yet she had made her journey untouched by the currents, hydroplaning across the waters on a juniper branch.[11]

Within this category of holiness tried yet triumphant must also be included the numerous Bavarian shrines that celebrated the legend of the holy house at Loreto. In that Italian tale, angels had whisked the holy family's house away from impending doom at the hands of infidels in Palestine and brought the structure to Loreto. Popular throughout Europe, this legend became a staple of Bavarian piety thanks to the exertions of the Fuggers in the late sixteenth and seventeenth centuries. Fresh from their successful 1570 pilgrimage to the shrine, the Fugger family sent their architect to take measurements of the Holy House.[12] In the succeeding decades they erected numerous copies of the *santa casa* throughout Bavaria. But the Loreto cult did not bloom solely because of contact with Italy or the enthusiastic support of the elite Fuggers. In Sossau in Lower Bavaria, for example, a "homegrown" Loreto developed that made use of the ideas inherent in the Italian legend. There peasants revered their own *santa casa*, but this one had stood not in Italy, but in a Protestant territory in Germany. Threatened with destruction, the house had been saved by angels who dropped it at Sossau, a place where it could be truly revered by people who realized its immense power.[13]

Alongside the numerous stories of victorious images and statues, legends of dramatic rediscoveries, or of "holiness lost and found," continued to reappear as well in the seventeenth and eighteenth centuries. Not surprisingly, crossover occurred between

11. Although no pilgrimage books survive from Maria-Ort, nevertheless this fantastic legend appears to have been actively promoted. In 1654, Emperor Ferdinand III asked to be taken to Maria-Ort to view the juniper bush on which the Virgin had arrived in Bavaria, a fact that suggests that the legend was enthusiastically promoted. See *Sulzbach Kalendar für katholische Christen* 1869: 76–84.

12. Protestants had mocked the Fuggers' pilgrimage to Loreto, but with the exorcism successfully completed the family was eager to use their victory over the devil both polemically and propagandistically. See Pötzl, "Loreto in Bayern"; Brodrick, *St. Peter Canisius*, pp. 695–697; and S. Beissel, *Geschichte der Verehrung Marias*, pp. 451 ff.

13. Christof Halwax, *Gnadenreiches Rennschiff. Unser liebe Fraw zu Sossau* (Straubing, 1680); idem, *Navigatio Mariana* (Straubing, 1671); and "Sossau" in *Sulzbach Kalendar für katholische Christen*, 1849.

these two plot types, for "rediscovered" images, relics, and statues were often claimed to have been tried by iconoclasts and heretics.[14] Tales of both types also attempted to connect the history of specific local shrines to the great dramas of Christian history.

Although somewhat less common than the "tried yet triumphant" type, legends of holiness lost and found were similarly enduring.[15] As late as 1700, stories similar to that of Andechs were still being reported in Bavaria. In that year, for instance, three drops of Christ's blood were "miraculously" rediscovered enclosed in a vial within the altar of a church in the Bavarian village of Niederachdorf.[16]

In this category should also be included the many legends of "wandering images," or *verschleppte Gnadenbilder*, in which an older, usually medieval, image is "miraculously" rediscovered in an improbable location, such as a tree or brook. Installed at the local parish church, the image continues to wander back to its place of discovery, until finally local villagers construct a pilgrimage chapel at that site. Stories of wandering images appear to have been the popular oral counterpart of the grander, clerically promoted legends of shrines like Andechs, since none appears in the printed pilgrimage literature that the clergy produced. At Dautersdorf in the diocese of Regensburg, for example, a clay copy of the Madonna of Altötting was found in the hollow of a birch tree about half a mile from the village. The villagers were always fetching the sacred image from the tree, where it would go each night, back to their parish church. In the end, a small chapel was built to house the figure and a pilgrimage developed at the site.[17] The story outlines are much the same at Heilbrünnl, where a shepherd discovered an ancient image of the Madonna in a stream. Water would not flow around the image, nor would the picture allow itself to be retrieved

14. The overlap between these two types was evident already in Martin Eisengrein's miracle book, *Unser liebe Fraw zu alten Oetting*, pp. 127–156. In recounting a legend of "trial and triumph," Eisengrein also noted that the shrine's relic collection had been hidden from invaders and forgotten for a time before being rediscovered.

15. Kriss, *Die religiöse Volkskunde Altbayerns*, pp. 32–35, 60–61; Beissel, *Wallfahrten zu Unserer Lieben Frau*, pp. 8–39. Josef Dünninger also finds this legend to have been a popular apology for pilgrimage in the Diocese of Würzburg in Franconia; see his *Die Marianische Wallfahrten der Diözese Würzburg* (Würzburg, 1960).

16. Anon., *Inventa Drachma: oder der gefundene Groschen* (Regensburg, 1703).

17. *Die Kunstdenkmäler von Bayern*, 2d ser., 2:10–11.

until the local inhabitants promised to build a chapel to house it.[18] Stories like these were common during the Counter-Reformation, both in Bavaria and in other European regions.[19] In Bavaria in particular, the statues and images discovered were always either copies of other venerable pilgrimage icons, like the Passau *Maria-hilfbild* or the Altötting Madonna, or very old medieval images. This dimension of the legend appears at least in part to bear the imprint of clerical influence. In the diocese of Regensburg, Bishop Warten-burg, who served during the 1660s and 1670s, decreed that all images revered in churches should be of a venerable age, and he actively encouraged the development of a number of devotions to older images that had been "rediscovered" after neglect.[20]

Meanwhile, the third story type, "holiness suddenly revealed," remained relatively rare. During the 1600s the clergy exploited only one such legend in print, and the controversy that it created reveals a great deal about how the Bavarian clergy was attempting to mold Counter-Reformation pilgrimage. Soon after 1619, a devotion de-veloped at Taxa, a village outside Munich, when a chicken pro-duced a miraculous egg on which was inscribed a star and, within that, an image of the crowned Heavenly Queen. At first, the new pilgrimage was favorably received by the local bishop, the Wit-telsbachs, and members of the Bavarian nobility. When it rotted, Taxa's miraculous egg was replaced with an image of the Virgin that became the focus of pilgrims' devotion. When a group of Augustin-ians assumed control of the pilgrimage around 1650, it flourished even more. In the 1680s, however, a furor arose when the famous Augustinian preacher Abraham à Sancta Clara wrote a pilgrimage book for the shrine entitled *Cluck, Cluck, Cluck: A Miraculous Hen in the Duchy of Bavaria.*[21] When Sancta Clara first submitted his work to the local bishop at Freising for approval, he was forced to remove some of his miracle accounts and in general to "tone down" his

18. Ibid., 1:51–52.
19. Rudolf Kriss, *Volkskundliches aus altbayerischen Gnadenstätte* (Baden b. Wien, 1931), 1:278–279. See esp. Christian, *Apparitions in Late Medieval and Renaissance Spain*, pp. 19–22; idem, *Local Religion in Sixteenth-Century Spain*, pp. 75–91; and Nolan and Nolan, *Christian Pilgrimage*, pp. 257–266.
20. *Die Kunstdenkmäler von Bayern*, 2d ser., 22:192.
21. *Gack Gack Gack Gack a Ga. Einer wunderseltsamen Hennen in dem Hertzogtum Bayern* (Munich, 1687; Vienna, 1732).

rhetoric.[22] We will never know what Freising's bishop found offensive, because the first version no longer survives; Sancta Clara's edited work, however, remains a model of Counter-Reformation rectitude that still ranks as a "classic" of German Catholic literature. Nonetheless, even after Sancta Clara had significantly altered his book, the Freising bishop, who was initially a cult supporter, remained suspicious. And once the shrine's past was exploited in print—that is, broadcast to the reading public—he disavowed the cult.[23]

Why did the bishop of Freising react thus to Taxa, which was a good revenue raiser and from all accounts a focus for popular devotion? The answer is simple. The dominant strains of mythmaking tapped by the clergy to revive Bavaria's shrines were grounded primarily in history and tradition. Such traditionalizing had been necessary to surmount the Protestant charge that contemporary shrines were "diabolic" innovations designed to lead people astray or to raise money for a grasping ecclesiastical hierarchy. By connecting local cults with the great dramas of biblical and ecclesiastical history, Catholic clerics placed these shrines—together with their precipitant contemporary miracles—at the very center of the Christian tradition. Spontaneously pronounced shrines like Taxa, however, had no contact with the great past of which they should have been a product; thus they were to be avoided. Further, such shrines left the Church open to the charge of encouraging idolatry by seeming to make objects like Taxa's short-lived miraculous egg as important as the saints, their relics, or, generally, the long history that gave rise to and nurtured "legitimate" local pilgrimages.

Theatricality and precedent were the primary foundations of the counter-reformers' pilgrimage propaganda; it is not surprising, then, that the early modern pilgrimage book can be mined to reveal Bavarians' perceptions of sacred time and space. Many historians have observed the dearth of great literature in the Catholic regions of early modern Germany.[24] Although these shrine chapbooks can

22. Karl Bertsche, "Die Werke Abrahams à Sancta Clara in den Frühdrucken," *Freiburger Diözesansarchiv* 50 (1922): 50–81.

23. Robert Böck, "Ein Mirakelbuch der Wallfahrt Maria Stern in Taxa (1654–1754)," *Bayerisches Jahrbuch für Volkskunde*, 1954, pp. 62–80.

24. See Eisenstein, *Printing Press as an Agent of Change*, 1:334, 355, and passim; Lionel Rothkrug, *Religious Practices and Collective Perceptions*, p. 122; Melton, "From

make no case for inclusion within what until so recently was confidently referred to as the "universal canon," they were nevertheless literary entertainment for large numbers of people throughout the early modern era. This literature and the revolution in myth-making that it helped to generate has been little noticed beyond the boundaries of Bavaria. Even in Germany, systematic study of these genres has been undertaken by folklorists, not historians, a lack of attention that derives from the very peculiarity of this tradition.

When we open the works of the "universal canon"—from the grobian tales of Rabelais to the epic of Cervantes and the fanciful world of Molière—we enter an imagined society in which the foibles, perils, and delights of earthly existence are satirized, criticized, and extolled. The raw materials of this literature are the problems of life in a civil society. In Bavaria, clerical influence on all literary forms was too far-reaching and persistent to allow this kind of secular literature to flourish. Religious works therefore had to satisfy the appetites of the Bavarian reader, and pilgrimage books were one of the most enduring, pervasive parts of this literature.

In comparing the pilgrimage book with the "universal canon," we at once confront essential differences. Unlike fiction, the pilgrimage book was believed to be true, both empirically and spiritually. And rather than treating life in imagined societies, the work had a subject—the pilgrimage shrine—that lay beyond the social sphere. Both the "universal canon" and the Bavarian pilgrimage book dealt with timeless issues, but in the latter it was man's relationship to the holy and to biblical and ecclesiastical tradition that predominated, not the pleasures and pains of life in society. Indeed, the primary function of the pilgrimage book was to encourage people to depart from society and experience a higher reality at the shrine. Upon arriving at the holy site, the votant entered a new world that projected the fears and concerns of daily existence onto the holy place itself. As represented in Bavaria's pilgrimage books, the shrine was a protagonist, and its relics, images, and intercessions represented the battery of armaments with which the saint waged war against unbelief, sickness, accidents, and the devil.

Image to Word," p. 97; Strauss, *Luther's House of Learning*, p. 128; Schöne, *Säkularisation als sprachbildende Kraft*; and Hsia, *Society and Religion*, pp. 1–2.

The pilgrimage book thus reinforced the notion of geography as a "sacred landscape" divided into places of "hot" and "cold" spiritual power.[25] Text might extol the glories of a particular landscape, but in turn the landscape was itself a text on which Bavarians wrote stories that linked their rivers, mountains, and towns to the great events of the Bible and the history of the Church. In the process, topography often became submerged in service to the greater demands of the *locus sanctus*.

In 1678, for instance, the Bavarian Jesuit Benigno Kyhler published a book called *Miraculous Mirror of Divine Miracles from the Old and New Testament,* a collection of miracle stories intended for edification.[26] Before telling the biblical tales, however, Kyhler discussed the geography of Bavaria. It was not the duchy's mountains, towns, or streams that he summoned up to describe the Bavarian realm, however; rather, Kyhler focused on her shrines, specifically the most important places of Marian pilgrimage, to demarcate the duchy's space. Instead of natural boundaries, castles, and walls, these were the territory's most important defenses, for here Mary ruled as a celestial "duchess," protecting the land from every kind of evil. For Kyhler, Bavaria was the "Holy Land" of Europe, a place where the march of time was suspended and the biblical story was being continually reenacted. That he should associate Bavaria with the Holy Land was not mere poetic license or rhetoric, for thanks to the enthusiastic promotion by Counter-Reformation propagandists of legends about shrines, the territory had been made more holy than it had ever been before.

Although pilgrimage book authors often offered ingenuous, imposing, and even fanciful defenses for their cults, their bravado could not mask the lasting impact of the Reformation. The Protestant challenge appeared in these works as a breach and had to be explained to the Counter-Reformation audience. Pilgrimage thus emerges, to use their own terminology, as a medicine to be applied to heal this fracture. To support the renewal of shrines and to cure a

25. For a more complete discussion of this theme, see the perceptive study on the *Sakrallandschaft* of Bavaria by Hans Bleibrunner, "Der Einfluß der Kirche auf die niederbairische Kulturlandschaft," *Verhandlungen des Historischen Vereins für Niederbayern* 77 (1951).

26. *Wunder Spiegl. Göttliche Wunderwerck Auß dem Alt- und Neuen Testment* (Munich, 1678), "Vorred."

landscape that had been badly battered by the "disease" of Protestantism, they created salving legends drawn from their own religious universe. These legends, moreover, were consciously packed with images of religion as crusade and of the saints and their shrines engaged in an ongoing struggle against indifference and "godlessness." The propagandists then applied these stories to an ever-increasing number and variety of sites. For counter-reformers, the contemporary crisis was but the continuation of battles that had been waged since the days of the early Church, and Bavaria's shrines were the "silent preacher" or testimony to this tradition. This polemical defense of shrines and pilgrimage thus involved both a dissolution of the present and the denial of apocalyptic hope for the future. For it was largely a past that always repeated itself in episodic images, rediscoveries, and saintly intercessions that served to justify the enduring lure of the *locus sanctus*.

These attempts to create and inhabit a mythical past were clearly an important factor in the amazing refloresence of pilgrimage that occurred in early modern Bavaria. In this process of renewal, the pilgrimage cults of the seventeenth and eighteenth centuries often grew to limits far beyond those of their medieval antecedents, as the voluminous manuscript miracle books of many local shrines testify. In these documents, wonders continued to be recorded in terms of the relationship of exchange between saintly patron and the faithful common to the medieval world. Indeed, these perceptions survive in the late twentieth century, not as some kind of residual carryover, but as a dynamic part of Bavarians' daily religion. Pilgrimage, in short, has been far more a modern than a medieval phenomenon.

The creativity of the counter-reformers—especially their ability to adapt and conflate older cultural forms and practices—reveals, too, the manifold ways in which they granted shrines and peregrination a new preeminence within the Catholic faith. Their success in controlling Bavaria's resurgent pilgrimages, however, was not complete. Despite the disavowals of ecclesiastical leaders like the bishop of Freising, spontaneously produced cults such as that at Taxa continued to spring up. The bishop, as we saw, had attacked that shrine's legend even in the packaging given it by the pious and unquestionably orthodox preacher Sancta Clara. But still the pilgrimage to Taxa persisted, even into modern times. Bavaria's ecclesiastical officials and counter-reforming propagandists continued to face the same paradox that had existed in medieval times: they might labor to nurture some cults and to discredit, even prohibit, others, but Bavaria's pilgrims retained the ultimate rights of ownership over the peregrinational network.

However, like the celebrations of Corpus Christi, which grew to be amazingly popular in seventeenth- and eighteenth-century Bavaria, the rituals of pilgrimage in fact demonstrated a general appropriation of ideas first articulated by the Bavarian clergy. At many shrines, for example, the ancient practice of the *Umritt*, a ritualized horse procession, came to dominate the pious displays of the laity. The Ottonian emperors had first used these equine journeys to collect pledges of obedience from their subjects.[27] In the later Middle Ages, Lionel Rothkrug suggests, these processions became linked in Bavaria and South Germany generally with the idea of crusade, and *Umritte* were undertaken to shrines of the Bleeding Host. In addition, equine processions appear to have been mounted to insure the fertility and protection of the land.[28] During the Counter-Reformation all of these strains came together, and Bavarians joined *Umritte* to relic and Marian cults as well. The region now became, as certain Austrian folklorists have picturesquely quipped, "a land exceedingly rejoicing in *Umritte*."[29]

That the association of these processions with crusade and purification rites lingered can hardly be doubted, for it was in the *Innviertel*—that triangular parcel of land in southeastern Bavaria where the shrine of Altötting was the most imposing cultural monument and where Protestantism had gained a strong foothold in the sixteenth century—that *Umritte* multiplied most profusely.[30] The relationship between Protestantism and the proliferation of *Umritte* is clear, for in these ceremonies men on horseback celebrated the triumph over heresy and unbelief and sought protection from pollution, just as Catholic propagandists advocated people do in their

27. R. Schmid, "Königsumritt und Huldigung in ottonisch-salischer Zeit," *Vorträge und Forschungen* 6 (1961): 114ff.

28. Rothkrug, "Holy Shrines, Religious Dissonance, and Satan," pp. 230–231 n.279. In this long footnote, Rothkrug outlines the history of the *Umritt* and answers criticisms of his discussion of the phenomenon in his earlier *Religious Practices and Collective Perceptions*.

29. Ernst Burgstaller and Adolf Helbok, eds., *Österreichischer Volkskundeatlas* (Linz, 1959), map of *Umritte*.

30. Andreas Kraus, *Geschichte Bayerns* (Munich, 1968), pp. 215ff.

pilgrimage books. In addition, *Umritte*, like the numerous legends celebrated in early modern Bavaria that linked particular shrines to great events in biblical and Church history, joined these journeys' destinations to an imposing historical incident: the Crusades. Thus these processions brought specific shrines into the mainstream of Christian history and, in turn, sacralized the landscape by linking the present-day situation with verifiable episodes of Christian triumph.

Umritte grew to incredible heights of popularity in Bavaria during the seventeenth and eighteenth centuries. In 1756, for instance, over seven thousand horsemen took part in the *Umritt* to the shrine at Scheyern.[31] While these events were both festive and pious, they taught that Bavaria and her shrines were in need of constant protection and purification. Like twelfth-century Crusaders who rescued the Holy Sepulcher from the infidels or sixteenth-century Catholic burghers who wrested sacred images from the hands of Protestants, participants in the *Umritte* were also a cavalry that aimed to guard the holy landscape from the onslaughts of heretics and Satan.

The numerous *Umritte*, holy places, and saints' cults that appeared in Bavaria from the late sixteenth century through the eighteenth seized on an imagery redolent with appeals to ordeal and crusade, propitiation and purification. At the *locus sanctus*, heaven and earth joined and time was compressed into a present that was the embodied past. For the thousands of pilgrims who visited these sites, miracles rather than legends remained the enduring testimony to these truths of geographical specificity and suspended time. Records of wonders provide us a glimpse of the mounting popularity of local shrines in early modern Bavaria. Between 1650 and 1680, scribes at Bettbrunn recorded an average of fourteen miracles each year; a century later, the totals had swelled to almost a thousand intercessions annually. This was not an isolated incident,[32] and by the eighteenth century the Bavarian clergy was often unable to cope with the peregrinational flood they had unleashed. At Neukirchen bei Heilig Blut, the Franciscan protectors struggled to keep up with all the pilgrims to the site, who in some years

31. Rudolf Kriss, *Die Wallfahrtsorte Europas* (Munich, 1950), pp. 55–56; cited in Rothkrug *Religious Practices and Collective Perceptions*, p. 66.
32. See, for example, Döring, "St. Salvator in Bettbrunn," p. 175; Hartinger, "Die Wallfahrt Neukirchen," p. 157; and Gierl, *Bauernleben und Bauernwallfahrt*.

numbered as many as eighty thousand.[33] Around 1700, officials of the dioceses of Regensburg and Passau, in an attempt to deal with the very success of the revival of pilgrimage, forbade a number of parishes from conducting processions to local shrines. As one official explained, "So many pilgrimages are held annually that in many places worship and preaching can be conducted [in parishes] during the summer on only a few Sundays."[34] Bavaria, it would seem, had finally assumed the identity first crafted for it by clerical propagandists: it was now mobilized around those sacred sites that perpetuated the traditions of salvific history.

33. Hartinger, "Die Wallfahrt Neukirchen," p. 96.
34. Quoted in ibid., p. 141.

Index